FARNHAM

BUILDINGS AND PEOPLE

By the same author

Farnham Inheritance (Farnham, Herald Press, 1956.
2nd Ed. 1965).
Looking At Things (London, Visual Publications, 1968).
Seen and Not Heard (London, Hutchinson; New York,
Dial Press, 1970).

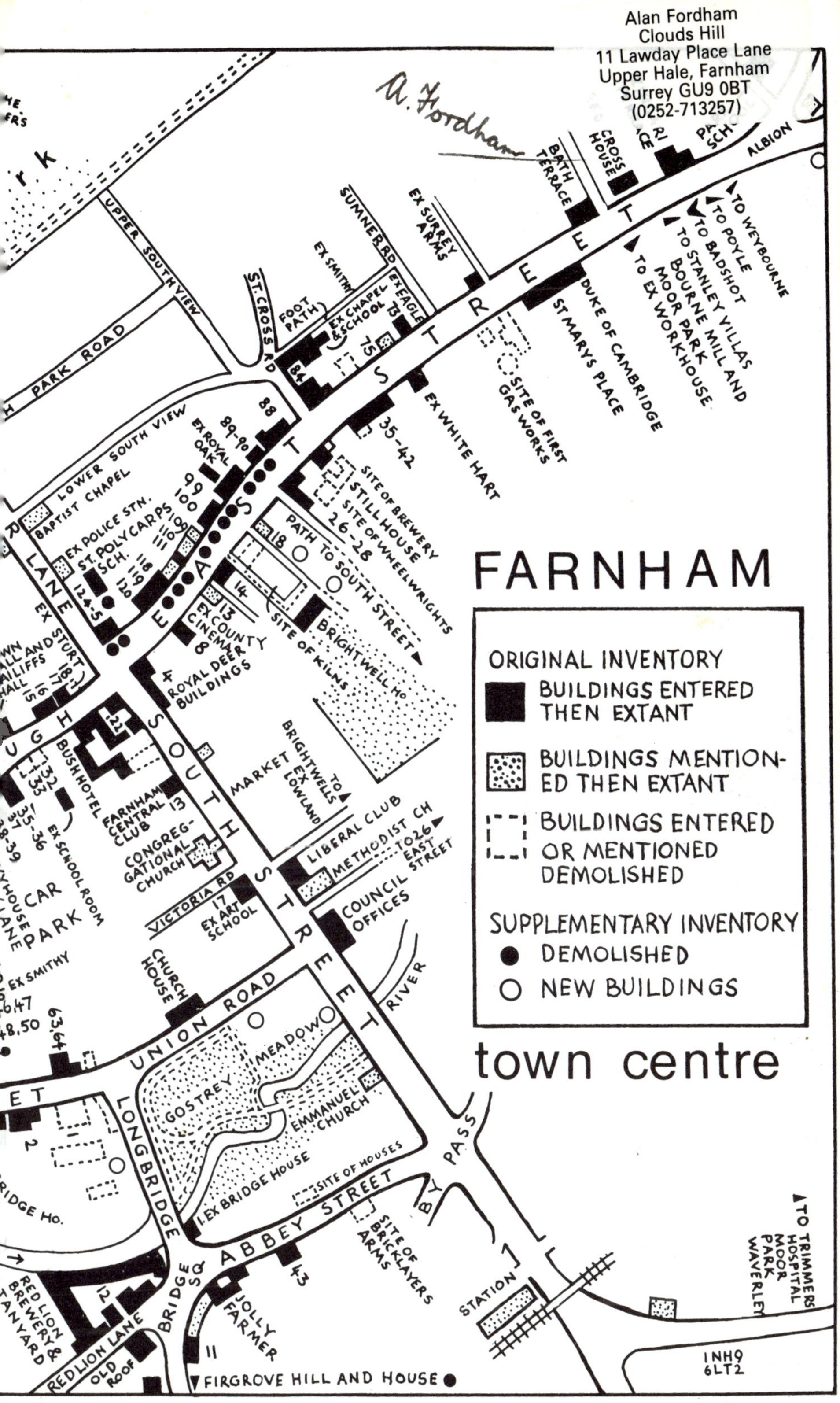

Alan Fordham
Clouds Hill
11 Lawday Place Lane
Upper Hale, Farnham
Surrey GU9 0BT
(0252-713257)
A. Fordham
FARNHAM
town centre
PARK
PARK ROAD
UPPER SOUTH VIEW
LOWER SOUTH VIEW
Baptist Chapel
EX POLICE STN.
ST. POLYCARPS SCH.
EX ROYAL OAK
ST. CROSS RD.
FOOT PATH
EX SMITH
EX CHAPEL & SCHOOL
EX EAGLE
SUMNER RD
EX SURREY ARMS
BATH TERRACE
CROSS HOUSE
OR RD
PARK SCH.
ALBION
STREET
TO WEYBOURNE
TO POYLE
TO BADSHOT
TO STANLEY VILLAS
BOURNE MILL AND MOOR PARK
TO EX WORKHOUSE
DUKE OF CAMBRIDGE
ST MARYS PLACE
SITE OF FIRST GAS WORKS
EX WHITE HART
SITE OF BREWERY
STILL HOUSE
SITE OF WHEELWRIGHTS
PATH TO SOUTH STREET
BRIGHTWELL HO.
SITE OF KILNS
EX COUNTY CINEMA
ROYAL DEER BUILDINGS
LANE
EX STURT HALL
TOWN HALL AND BAILIFFS
BUSH HOTEL
FARNHAM CENTRAL CLUB
CONGREGATIONAL CHURCH
SCHOOL ROOM
VICTORIA RD
EX ART SCHOOL
MARKET
BRIGHTWELLS EX LOWLAND
TO LOWLAND
LIBERAL CLUB
METHODIST CH
TO EAST STREET
COUNCIL OFFICES
SOUTH STREET
CHURCH HOUSE
CAR PARK
EX SCHOOL ROOM
EX SMITHY
UNION ROAD
GOSTREY MEADOW
EMMANUEL CHURCH
RIVER
BY PASS
LONGBRIDGE
EX BRIDGE HOUSE
SITE OF HOUSES
ABBEY STREET
SITE OF BRICKLAYERS ARMS
STATION
TO TRIMMERS HOSPITAL
MOOR PARK
WAVERLEY
BRIDGE HO.
RED LION BREWERY & TANYARD
OLD ROOF
REDLION LANE
BRIDGE SQ.
JOLLY FARMER
FIRGROVE HILL AND HOUSE
ORIGINAL INVENTORY
BUILDINGS ENTERED THEN EXTANT
BUILDINGS MENTIONED THEN EXTANT
BUILDINGS ENTERED OR MENTIONED DEMOLISHED
SUPPLEMENTARY INVENTORY
DEMOLISHED
NEW BUILDINGS
1NH9 6LT2

Numbers 34 to 39 West Street, including examples of Farnham grand manner and speculative buildings built over a century and more from 1718. Sandford House (right) and Willmer House Museum are the architectural climax of a notable street. Also visible are 19th century annexes to the big houses and the entrance to Bishop's Mead — until recently called Brewhouse Yard, and so-named by the 1830s.

FARNHAM
BUILDINGS & PEOPLE

NIGEL TEMPLE

with a foreword by

SIR NIKOLAUS PEVSNER
C.B.E., M.A., PH.D., F.S.A., F.R.S.A.

*Professor of History of Art,
Birkbeck College, University of London.*

PHILLIMORE
London and Chichester

First published in 1963 by
THE HERALD PRESS
Farnham, Surrey
in a limited edition of 500 copies
Second edition published by
PHILLIMORE & CO. LTD.
Shopwyke Hall, Chichester, Sussex

1973

Printed in Great Britain by
Fletcher and Son Ltd., Norwich.

Contents

DATES IN TEXT

* denotes dates arrived at indirectly by calculation. These may be inexact for two main reasons, e.g. a person aged 70 in 1800 need not have been born in 1730, although such a date, marked by an asterisk, would appear in this guide in that case. It has also been found that many people did not know their age or deliberately mis-stated it on occasions.

b, born; d, died; m. married.

List of Plates

The foregoing material has been selected mainly to illustrate some subjects of this book. It includes reproductions of early 19th century topographical artists' work and some photographs of later Victorian days. An attempt has been made further to extend published photographic records of the present or recent states of buildings — many of them lesser ones not known to have been permanently recorded elsewhere.

SOURCES OF PHOTOGRAPHS AND REPRODUCED MATERIAL

THE ASHMOLEAN MUSEUM, OXFORD: 22, 24.

THE BRITISH MUSEUM, LONDON: 3, 9, 13, 23, 25, 32, 34, 41, 44, 46, 47, 51.

BIL JORDAN, FARNHAM: 21.

LANGHAMS LTD., FARNHAM: Frontispiece, 7, 20, 26.

ANONYMOUS PHOTOGRAPHERS: 1, 2, 4, 5, 6, 11, 28, 38, 49, 50, 52.

AUTHOR: 8, 10, 12, 14, 15, 16, 17, 18, 19, 27, 29, 30, 31, 33, 35, 36, 39, 40, 45.

Acknowledgements are made to the institutions and people above who have given permission to reproduce their material.

Foreword

By Sir Nikolaus Pevsner

Being myself inextricably involved with the inventorization of buildings, I can probably appreciate more fully than most what Mr. Temple has done here. Users of his book will find in it excellent descriptions, neither skimpy nor dull, and presented in an attractive layout, with sympathetic illustrations and a carefully considered typeface. They will find lots of information not previously presented, many details found by Mr. Temple in archives and newspapers and plenty of entertaining bits and pieces on Farnham people. They will also learn how often Georgian façades can be deceptive as regards the real age of a house, and they will even be introduced to a pretty well unknown early building by Lutyens—1894, and yet already in a revived Queen Anne. Mr. Temple discovered this in 1961 and in a letter to the Editor advised *Country Life* of it. But the most valuable thing they will find is a tender appreciation of the character of Farnham which comes out more or less on every page, implicitly where not explicitly. Yet Mr. Temple's is not simply a preservationist book. He believes in today and wants to guide developments not to prevent them. This does in fact pose a problem greater than he can hope to solve in a book of this kind. The architectural enthusiast must, to solve it, get together with the visual planner to determine the right mixture of respect for the past and boldness for the future. Of the pair, Mr. Temple will always be the one who knows Farnham best, but a sensitive visual planner may yet have something to contribute.

Meanwhile, those who read Mr. Temple's book—and may there be many of them, for the sake of Mr. Temple and of his enterprising and public-spirited publisher—will be Farnham experts, too, and the more such experts exist, the safer must be the future of the town.

N.B.L.P.

Introduction to First Edition

This book has been written because I hope that wider general interest in Farnham might increase the town's chances of future healthy development — which, to me, does not mean mass-preservation and imitation of the herebefore, any more than it did to those who built so much of Farnham in the 18th century. Three years ago it became obvious that the town was about to experience a spate of large-scale development and that something should be done to make a record of a large number of its smaller buildings. The record has been made. Development has begun.

Most town guides seem to forget that they are dealing with a complex of buildings regenerated and expanded by people to live and work in. Usually, some supposed facts about the principal buildings suffice. Scholarly works by local historians are seldom suitable for on-the-spot reference because of their format, content, size or price. More general works, such as county architectural histories, seldom have much space for smaller towns and cannot concern themselves with the many vernacular buildings or the families and tradesmen or artisans who built and lived in them.

A book on Farnham, with its remarkable accumulation of smaller houses, seemed to need a new approach if it was to serve the purpose in mind. The presentation used for this guide is based on separate sections or chapters for each of the principal streets, the buildings in them being ordered numerically. Most entries are of three parts: first there is a concise, objective report of the building's present appearance. Unless otherwise indicated, this concerns the main (usually street) front. The second part includes some facts and opinions concerning the building itself. The third part records some associations of the building. These often include people as well as events and uses. Topics of a more general nature are also frequently included within this section when appropriate.

Farnham Castle and principal churches have been omitted, whereas some Non-Conformist chapels and Church schools are included. The omissions have been made as the buildings have been the subjects of considerable research already and writings on them are already available in compact form. Of the town's other buildings (about 260 are covered by this guide) only a handful have previously been the subjects of any known research. After the street guide is a section dealing with some outlying houses. This includes entries on some now demolished, to which literary or documentary references may be encountered elsewhere.

Many buildings previously undated by evidence have now been placed — with varying degrees of exactness — some to within a few months of building or reconstruction. Their builders may be named. Those who had them built may also have been identified and their trades and family relationships been noted. An attempt has been made especially to record families in building and allied trades.

There have been surprises, particularly in the dating of some accepted 'Georgian' houses, which are in fact products of about the mid-19th century. As investigations recorded here are concentrated in the two hundred years from the late 17th century little original material appears about the development of timber-framed houses. A great deal of local work needs still to be done to establish dating criteria and the evolution of plans, types and styles. This work is made difficult by many examples having been refaced or encased with later brick; it is made urgent by the demolition imminent of some examples — perhaps seldom recognised — and by the continuous alteration and repair of others.

Illustrations are of three kinds. They include drawings, reproductions of drawings by topographers, and photographs. My own drawings intend to reconstruct the appearance of houses demolished, show how existing buildings looked earlier, or heighten details extant but often unnoticed. The reproductions of earlier drawings help to complete publication of works normally rather inaccessible. With those which appeared in *Farnham Inheritance* and the *Topographers' Farnham* series of articles (published in the '*Farnham Herald*' from April to December, 1959) all the important Hassell drawings at the British Museum have now been reproduced. The photographic plates partly illustrate this guide and help to widen the range of printed graphic material by including a large proportion of lesser buildings in their present or recent state.

Several references will be found to *The Buildings of England—Surrey*, by Ian Nairn and Nikolaus Pevsner (Penguin 1962). This excellent county guide is referred to in the text as Pevsner and Nairn, for brevity. Farnham was in Mr. Nairn's territory.

It is hoped that *Farnham Buildings and People* will provide townspeople and visitors with a compact and functional guide to buildings, people and their occupations, and future researchers with a worthwhile collection of new material and a useful tool for their own work.

Churchdown,   NIGEL TEMPLE
Gloucestershire.
August, 1962

Acknowledgments to First Edition

First I wish to thank Professor Nikolaus Pevsner for the honour he has done my work by contributing his Foreword to it.

Completion of this book was taken on with fresh heart when The Farnham Society, under the Chairmanship of Sir John Verney, Bt., showed confidence in the manuscript by making a generous and unsolicited grant towards the cost of publication. This had been undertaken by E. W. Langham Ltd. with little hope of commercial reward. I am most grateful to The Farnham Society for their remarkable gesture and to the Publishers for their confidence and patience.

Without the help of a great many householders and business people who made premises and papers accessible relatively little new material could have been gathered. Long correspondence and short visits have alternated over two years. These have been suffered by them with unusual understanding. I thank them all.

Mr. H. G. A. Booth, A.T.D., A.M.A., Curator, sent measurements of the façade of Willmer House Museum, Mr. Francis Dallett (now of the American Museum in Britain, near Bath) provided valuable notes on Smiths, the painters. Miss E. M. Dance, M.A., PH.D., Curator, Guildford Muniments Room, gave generously her time and advice and I am grateful to Mr. B. Ewbank Smith for some notes on deeds of College Gardens and on some Nelsonian relationships. He also actually located Lutyens' plan of the Liberal Club, for which I had been looking for years. Miss Williams, of The Minet Library, helped with material in the Collections, while Miss M. Gollancz, M.A., of The Surrey Record Office, advised on material in her care.

For help in making material available from their Collections (reproduced graphic work is acknowledged elsewhere) I wish to thank officials of The Ashmolean Museum, The Bodleian Library, The British Museum, The Farnham Public Library, Ministry of Housing and Local Government, The National Buildings Record, The National Maritime Museum, The National Register of Archives, The Public Record Office, The Royal Academy, The Royal Institute of British Architects, Somerset House Principal Probate Registry, The Tithes Redemption Office and The Victoria and Albert Museum.

N.H.L.T.

Author's note to the New Edition

This edition of *Farnham Buildings and People* is unlikely to have materialised but for intermittent goading by Mr. Dennis Collett and the untiring encouragement of Sir John Verney, Bt. Continual complaints about the unavailability of the book were reassuring evidence that their optimism might be well founded.

The original edition of this book was published by the Herald Press, reorganisation of which followed the death in 1967 of its founder-proprietor, E. W. Langham. The vigilance and editorial policy of vigorous support by his newspaper of campaigns in the interest of Farnham amenities have been outstanding. Despite change of ownership, editorial concern for the future of the town continues. I am most appreciative of the enthusiasm and editorial generosity with which Mr. Oliver Meddows Taylor guided the original edition of this book.

Another of Farnham's many blessings is Phillimore's interest in writers about Farnham. As the traditional publisher has passed a new one has appeared in the hour of need.

Sir Hugh Casson addressed members of the Farnham Society in 1960. I am grateful to him for his permission to quote from *Town Sense*—the booklet which appeared as a result. I am also grateful to Mr. A. J. A. Mason, Clerk to the Council, and to Officers of the Council, for their help in connection with facts about recent buildings.

This revised edition appears 13 years after work on *Farnham Buildings and People* began. The economics of publishing are such that it is not a viable proposition to re-set completely a substantial body of print, when the sales potential of a work is necessarily limited to a relatively small public. Modern techniques, however, do offer facsimile photo-copying and this process—which does not readily allow for corrections or additions to the original text—has been used for the present edition.

The additional Introduction following this Note attempts an appraisal of Farnham in 1971 and comments on major developments since 1963. The Supplementary Inventory notes some buildings which have appeared, disappeared, or been substantially altered since the first edition was prepared.

These new sections keep within the original brief—to record buildings and places in or near the town centre. Selection is subjective. Concern is largely for the exterior appearance of the built environment and related townscape qualities. Internal alterations are not recorded, neither are many continuously changing details such as shopfronts, occupancies and uses of buildings. It is, though, hoped that all important developments are included and that a generally acceptable priority has been given to those minutiae which have been seized upon in the general appraisal.

Finally, I would like to thank Sir Nikolaus Pevsner for allowing his Foreword to stand also for this edition, and Miss Dorothea St. Hill Bourne for locating and correcting an error concerning the Vernon family.

Introduction

THE CONTEXT OF URBAN CHANGE IN FARNHAM

It is outside the scope of this introduction to consider regional and sub-regional matters in planning and their possible influence on the future of Farnham. The purpose is to emphasise some extant townscape qualities and to comment on them: the more intimate scale parochial problems, whose successful solutions are likely to be, to some extent, within the power of local bodies and individuals to influence if not to control.

Before consideration is given to recent transplants, face-lifts and self-inflicted wounds, it appears fit to summarise and enlarge upon some points scattered throughout the original text of this book.

Running east and west is the main axis of Farnham. Important arteries of communication—roads, bypass, railway—and the river—are all parallel to and are contained within a chalky incline to the north and gravelly terraces to the south. The two heights are separated by the Wey. It threads a meandering course along the green flood plain virtually to divide the old town centre from the southerly residential area.

Older buildings concentrate about the one northern limb —Castle Street—and its junction with the Borough. The latter forms a link in the mile-long continuum of West Street and East Street, which is built up, mainly one deep. Downing Street drops south across the meadows to link the Bridge Square—Abbey Street suburb, south of the Wey.

Northwards, fields and parkland enclose a diversity of properties running back from street facades: water meadows, similarly, seal the south. Longish, narrow plots, with gardens, brewhouses, barns and stable-yards are at right-angles to street lines. Side access is usual. But additionally, at about 100 yard intervals, are public corridors which connect streets with fields beyond, both north and south.

Passages, yards, alleys or lanes: all are different in width, light, gloom, pitch or paving. Some are arched; others, narrow, penetrate cliff-like walls. They all have their quirks but share qualities of intimacy and act as paths from fields, as well as to them. They read both ways.

The transition from built to unbuilt Farnham has been clear-cut and direct. The contained space of buildings and

streets has been sharply defined. Containing parks and fields
are fresh, open and varied.

These keenly contrasting spaces all have visual qualities
as distinct and different as their respective functions. Their
pattern is related to the fundamental geography and organic
growth of the place. Main routes into and out of the town
reveal their own dramas. Some are sudden: others slowly
unfold natural, fortuitous, or contrived sequences of visual
events.

It would be ironical, as well as tragic, if such precious
assets—immensely expensive to build into a soulless place—
were to be built out of a town which already has them.
They are scarce enough anywhere. Allied to a strong local
vernacular style and high quality of building, they are rare.

While there is a risk that kindness could kill Farnham
at mock bow window level, there is real danger that its
underlying structure will be lost by default, without emergence of another with equal potential to develop.

LARGE-SCALE CHANGE

A typical pattern of change following central depopu-
lation is well known and is frequently related to outward
spread of residential provision. Centres die. Fringes neutralise.
Country disappears. The difference between contained
urban development and undisciplined expansion has been
likened to the difference between pouring tea into a cup,
and splashing it on a table top. Farnham has few natural
constraints upon expansion or absorption of its edge. Control must result from decision. If the decision is to contain,
it will be necessary to infill some sites and re-develop others.
The Chantrys estate has been built and large internal sites
have been redeveloped. By and large the town has not suffered ravages to the extent common elsewhere. If it has
so far been spared the worst this is largely because of local
concern *and action:* not good luck alone.

Building has begun in the Hart. Here, perhaps more
than anywhere vulnerable, balance is fine. The horizon is
vital enough, but on more delicate scale protection and sensitive development of the capillaries is of immense importance, too. Quite apart from entry, direction, enclosure and
flooring, there is the ultimate vista on emergence.

What is the reward for exploring Lion and Lamb yard?
Concrete posts, pigwire and a banal warehouse. What of
College Gardens—a lost chance if ever there was one—and
Timber Close? Or try Babbs Mead and Bear Lane. Have
they fared well? But overcare and selfconscious treatment
bring their own brand of ruin too.

Regeneration of large central sites usually becomes possible today on the fusion of properties into a single block. Woolmead is an example. Alternatively, long-established businesses may be wound up. This happened at Waggon Yard, Mills' and the Maltings.

Theoretically, both vehicles of change allow for positive progress and integrated redevelopment. Pressures can be great, and public concern, particularly in connection with East Street, Longbridge and the Maltings, has not been the least of them.

If the charge against plans for the Police Station was for their being 'an unbelievably reactionary design', the same could not be said for Woolmead. That the rebuilding on Mills' Yard 'was the dire tragedy of Longbridge', or 'the real beginning of the end for Farnham' are other arguments put forward through the local press. Neighbouring Maltings are not in the hands of either the Council or of speculative developers. The enthusiasts who bought the site will need abundant faith, energy and resourcefulness to realise their admirable and public spirited vision for its re-use.

DETAILS THAT COUNT

While Farnham has not recently lost a house of first architectural importance, significant lesser buildings have gone. Firgrove House, impressive for its siting and some interior detail, was a memorable eminence, if rather aloof. Speculative redevelopments of such sites rarely retain or reinstate venerable qualities, but may bring many new lives to town centres and simultaneously curb expansion. Calamities of a high order are not unknown and decisions can be hard to take in the face of economic advantage.

Small changes, too, can desolate. Incidents of little importance in themselves can be indispensable to the success of a group or vista. They might be eccentric or even downright plain constructions, but because of their placing, scale, linking value, or less tangible attributes, have an influence totally disproportionate to their power in a different context.

A happy peculiarity of Farnham streets is in features which close, punctuate, turn an angle or hold back a view. Some components are probably fortuitous. Others may be of calculated effect. The Royal Deer is one: the Town Hall another. If given to fantasy, the cynic might suppose that a campaign is afoot systematically to eliminate such focal elements.

Take the Albion—now emasculated, but once a forthright, poised and authoritative closure at the point of Farnham's adieu.

Take Spencers (at the junction of the Borough, West Street and Downing Street). Big, dull, yet commanding, it was demolished in 1964. With it went more than a point of demarcation and a pivot which simultaneously secured the West Street view. The opportunity to replace the building with one of equal impact yet also really interesting in itself was also lost. To say that the actual result is underwhelming is an overstatement.

Take Send House (demolished in 1968)—exact equivalent to the Albion in visual purpose—and at the other axial extremity.

But the scale can be reduced. For example, the Castle Street north-south axis was punctuated at skyline by a Victorian Tudoresque chimney on Fox's tower and by Italianate chimneys on Westminster Bank to the south. They were of minute bulk in terms of bricks and mortar, but a monumental forfeiture of dramatic effect has resulted from their removal.

While continuity of street line survives in the centre, extremities, east and west, have been exploded or broken. Early development was less intense. Now it is simple to remove walls and hedges which enclosed gardens and yards to make provision for the parking, passage and sale of cars.

With more imaginative forethought and sensitive aftercare these important approaches could have been made promising and the exits memorable. Real care, even now, might remedy erosion at its worst and prevent alien redevelopments from killing what's left.

TOWN AND PEOPLE

It has been said that in terms of where they live, people get what they deserve. What does Farnham deserve? By the action of a small group the Farnham Trust soon proved it possible to rehabilitate condemned dwellings of character and quality both more quickly and more cheaply than by building anew. Formed in October 1968, the Trust had acquired a lease of Cemetery Lodge from the Council by March 1969. Three months later the Lodge had been restored, improved and re-occupied. Church Cottages were finished six months later. Then attention moved to Bridge Square. A coal distribution plant, and its attendant dirt, noise and heavy trucking, was averted in 1967 by protest. East Street has long been a battle ground. The results will satisfy few, but without continuous action by the Council, groups and individuals, the outcome might have been very much less successful than it was. Then, without the support of public funds, £30,000 was raised in six weeks to keep the Maltings. Alternative solutions to official plans for the South Street intersection were drawn up, and at the Redgrave Theatre site building has begun. The Farnham Society has done much to promote public awareness of issues and to advise on crucial developments. There is a long history of concern, but on the part of relatively few.

In the context of Farnham's progressive development, it is sad to reflect that no really distinguished modern building has appeared in the town. There have been chances. The West Surrey College of Art and Design is promising but as yet incomplete. Is courage lacking? Would the equivalent of St. Andrew's Tower have gained planning permission to-day if it had not already been there? How can the town both progress and retain its identity?

There was a memorable occasion in December 1960 when Sir Hugh Casson spoke to the Farnham Society on *Town Sense*. He said:

'You here in Farnham are living in a beautiful town which has kept its identity and character. That is not due entirely to luck. A great deal of it is due to much hard work and forethought and very often to a few eccentrics—creative nuisances, they might be called. Most towns have them. I hope there are some here. They won't leave things alone. They are an absolute curse to the local authority, but they get their way.' He continued by quoting Sansovino, who said, in 1492, that 'A town should be for the convenience and satisfaction of its inhabitants and a great surprise to strangers.'

Convenience, satisfaction and surprise: Farnham will need its full share of creative nuisances in the future. But they cannot be relied upon to appear in a continuous succession, at the crucial moment, for ever. They will need backing and complementing by ever more inhabitants as pressures inevitably grow.

Supplementary Inventory

Below is an additional inventory of buildings. These were listed in the First Edition as individual entries and have since been demolished or extensively redeveloped.

*Buildings listed individually, but now demolished, are marked * in the margin against the original text.*

There follow short notes on some buildings constructed since completion of the original text.

1 DOWNING STREET (Police Station)   Page 69.

The house and builder's yard, with timbersheds and workshops in a pretty state of disrepair, gave way to the new Police Station, which was formally opened by Earl Jellicoe, Minister of State, Home Office, in July 1963. Here is the first new police station to be built in the Surrey Constabulary for 25 years. Cost was stated as £148,000. Farnham's first police station is said to have cost £881. A larger one was provided in 1888.

The buildings, plans for which were heavily attacked when published in June 1961, appear soon to have become accepted as part of the Farnham scene. Three months after their opening Alec Clifton-Taylor, writing about Farnham in *Country Life*, commented on the building's neighbourliness and probable ability to settle quickly into the surroundings.

John Harrison, A.R.I.B.A., Chief Architect to Surrey County Council, was responsible. The north end wall bears relief carving in stone depicting aspects of history and life in Farnham done by students of Farnham School of Art.

28-30 (Between) LOWER CHURCH LANE   Page 88.

The builder's premises, known as Waggon Yard (Plate 26), were bought with Nos. 25 to 28 and 30 and 31 Lower Church Lane, by Farnham Council in 1965.

The maltings and light industrial buildings were subsequently cleared to make a public car park. Premises on the Church Lane side are now occupied by The Old House Bookshop and the Ashgate Gallery, which has brought to Farnham the work of many distinguished living artists.

The bookshop was previously at 86-87, East Street, which was reconstructed in 1970, simultaneously performing a *volte face*.

FIRGROVE HILL. Trafalgar Court (ex Firgrove House)

Pages 100-102.

Phase I of this residential development was granted planning permission in June 1961.

A proposal to demolish Firgrove House (Plate 45) was considered by Farnham Council in September 1963 and in February 1964 Farnham Town Planning and Development Committee referred to the County Council an application by Laurence Knight Settlement Ltd., for demolition and redevelopment with more flats.

Permission to demolish the house was granted in mid-1964 and plans for building 20 flats and 17 garages were approved in December. A year later, building was nearing completion.

Vandals destroyed the fine carved staircase and interior fittings while the house stood empty and the two magnificent 17th century carved stone pineapple gate-pier finials have gone. Harold Falkner, not long before their final dismounting, fought for their reinstatement and succeeded. Their new-found security was short-lived.

Both phase I and II of Trafalgar Court were by Osterley Tudor Estates Ltd., with Messrs. Maxwell Aylwin consultant architects.

E A S T   S T R E E T Woolmead

Pages 125-131

By the '60s the wisdom of gutting unselectively older towns in the name of progress was being more widely questioned. Individual crusaders, forward and backward-looking groups and the specialist press intensified their protest.

Central government has now taken action. Local authorities are encouraging public participation in the decisions which will influence the quality of their surroundings and lives. And on the day of writing these comments the Daily Mail has printed an opening article by the first Environmental Reporter to be appointed to a popular national daily.

Farnham's first sweeping redevelopment plans came relatively late. It was exactly ten years ago that rumours of a major property deal in East Street were confirmed. 'About £50,000' was being mentioned. The transaction concerned 89-97 East Street (Plate 11) and plans for their redevelopment had been deposited by February 1962 by Cooper Properties Ltd. Drum Development also had plans for 110-119 East Street and 2-12 Bear Lane.

On the publication in March 1963 of drawings showing

proposals of the Land and House Property Corporation Ltd., there was outraged public protest. Characteristically, Harold Falkner rose to and above the occasion. Within a fortnight his counter-drawing was in print. Predictably reactionary, his vision was positive: a colonnaded neo-Georgian Blomfield-ish crescent of no fewer than 37 bays with flanking 3 bay pavilions was the answer. Existing buildings could be re-erected—some in the Park. Even Falkner admitted that the impression given was a little grandiose. Demolition went ahead. The first phase of Woolmead was opened in 1966.

What has East Street lost? Some neo-Georgian shops (three by Falkner himself and one—Patrick's—he judged his best in the town); a well-placed picturesque group with massive tiled roof and first floor supported magically by plate glass (demolished February 1966); a dozen or so shops mostly built as dwellings; a public lavatory, bus shelter, undertaker's and some cottages. (Plates 11 and 35).

They were a motley, but largely homogeneous group, gradually unfolding that quality which distinguishes so many old (but so few new) streets; a quality of infinite variety of detail and incident with an intuitive handling of proportion, scale and materials, enriched by natural and human agencies of erosion and change.

What has Farnham gained? A new road which helps traffic-flow and allows off-street unloading of heavy vehicles. This makes East Street less frustrating and safer generally, although other problems arise instead. Pedestrians have a new public space and may view or enter purpose-built shops from the protective colonnade. There is a miniature arcade with access to a higher level and a subway for crossing safely the new road separating residential areas from Woolmead.

The rebuilding is no longer than that it replaces, but it is deeper, higher and of much greater bulk. It sets a new and larger scale, but includes town-centre residential accommodation as well as shops and offices and has variety in rhythm, material, skyline and incident within its overall unity. The backs, though by calculation more widely visible, appear like those they replace, less carefully considered than the fronts: a criticism which might equally well be levelled at Willmer House and most Regency town housing too.

Woolmead is probably Farnham's largest central redevelopment since the Victorians built their Town Hall. That really was alien to local tradition and to its architectural context as well. But even so it would be judged differently today from even 15 years ago. Perhaps, as a Woolmead developer suggested, in some 300 years time there will be protests against the vandalism of demolishing his historic building. It could well last that long.

Attention has now turned to the opposite side of this street. Protests have been made. Counter drawings have been published. Again, complete demolition is going ahead.

What have we learned? One definition of intelligence mentions the ability to benefit from experience.

There is a path between total levelling and all-out unselective preservation, if the indigenous nature and organic articulation of the familiar can be allied to commercial viability, genuine contemporanity and the unified reconsideration that large scale redevelopment allows. Where there could be little gain from compromise, a synthesis might offer the best of both.

The greater part of Woolmead was finally developed by the Land and House Property Corporation Ltd., and east of the arcade was by the Bristol and West Building Society. The architects respectively were W. H. Robbins & Associates and Alec F. French & Partners of Bristol.

A 14ft. high mural sculpture, 'Farnham Flame', a maquette of which is in Farnham Museum, is by Allan Collins. It symbolises the flames of Farnham pottery kilns.

WEST STREET (Crosby Doors)   Pages 180-181.

The Fox and Hounds was closed in August 1967 and pulled down 13 months later, while the street frontage of Lion Brewery buildings (excluding Lion Brewery Stores—which still stands), was demolished in June 1969.

The new frontage is strong, if severe. The large and exposed expanse of plastic coated corrugated aluminium cladding contrasts strongly its pale green finish with the warm and textured dark brick. The new building appeared virtually finished, except for proposed planting in the bays, in November 1970. It has not received popular acclaim, but its potential contribution to the street scene should perhaps be judged in relation to possible development of the corner site in Babbs Mead, which might partly screen the obtrusive light green flank. There is an opportunity to improve, if not to rectify, and at the same time to contribute an integrating element to the desolate scene thereabouts. See 59 West Street. Luker Moore and Partners, architects, for Crosby & Co. Ltd.

59 WEST STREET (ex Send House)   Pages 183-185

Despite protests, Send House was demolished by the Council in 1968.

Comments on the resulting townscape minor tragedy are made in the Introduction to this edition.

Farnham Museum has acquired a drawing of the house as when it was Longhurst's High Class Grocery; an unbelievably eclectic essay in turrets, finials, parapets and porches. This possibly accounts for the tradition of a tea merchant's 'pagoda' here.

As a result of demolition and neighbouring erosions to the street line, this quarter cries out for sensitive treatment if it is to regain any quality of place.

WEST STREET (College Gardens)   Pages 192-193

If in the main streets of Farnham an important visual element and a general amenity is conspicuously absent, this is grass and trees. Apart from the recent appearance of alien stone planting troughs, there is virtually nothing for the length of the town.

Yet, there was a place: it was College Gardens.

The little plot was deliberately planned about 100 years ago to relate to Sandford House, opposite. It was interestingly planted, mature, intimate: an essentially pretty, but unfussy, sumptuous and conspicuously inconspicuous green refuge. To echo the opinion of the late Harold Falkner, it was incredible that the Council could be wise enough to buy the garden and then set about destroying it.

Removal of the arbour resulted in mutual exposure of Beaver's Yard and Sandford House. Redevelopment of one cold-shouldered the other. Railings were rent by a motor crash prior to national wartime extractions. With the demolition and non-replacement of buildings on the west side of Beaver's Yard the delicately, if fortuitously, articulated sequence once Potter's Gate was simultaneously breached.

The new dwellings provided by the Ewart Bequest undoubtedly provide superior accommodation. A social need has been provided for.

One can only speculate on how different might have been the result had this all happened after the Farnham Trust's rehabilitations of Cemetery Lodge, Church Cottages, Bridge Square and Red Lion Lane.

Gilbert & Hobson, architects for Ewart Bequest buildings.

96-97 WEST STREET (Craven House)   Pages 206-207

Applications for redevelopment were being considered in 1960. For years these uneasy neighbours (Plate 21) stood empty. Alongside ran Timber Close—a narrow path from the street to the Hart, heavily endowed with qualities that no instant pavement can offer. It was worth a ricked ankle every five years just to know it was still there.

The two buildings were being demolished in January 1967 and within a year Craven House was built. It is in neo-Georgian style, parapetted and with much mortar.

This was the last building designed by G. Maxwell Aylwin (1880-1968), who did not see its completion. Farnham owes much to this architect who, for very many years, really cared for the qualities of its buildings and the town as a place. A plaque on the new building commemorates its designer.

107 WEST STREET (General Post Office)   Pages 214-215

The old buildings were demolished in 1969. Designs were being discussed by early 1968 and revised plans were approved by the Council late that year. What had been described as white painted concrete and plastic-coated corrugated iron had been replaced in the interim by bush hammered concrete and hand-made bricks. The rebuilding includes a public office, sorting office and expanded telephone exchange.

Approved by the Royal Fine Art Commission, Surrey County Council, Farnham Council and The Farnham Society, the new drawings were published in January 1969. The supervising architect was D. C. Wye of the Ministry's Southern Regional H.Q. With all that, and a cost of £200,000, it should be good.

Michael Fairclough won a competition to design an external mural panel for the street front.

121 WEST STREET (International Stores)   Pages 225-227

Early in 1964 plans for total demolition of 121 and the rear of 122 were considered. Ultimately outbuildings behind 121 were cleared and the shop floor was expanded to include what had been carriage access in the westernmost bay. A once-pilaster had become a column with the shop front recessed some feet behind it.

A report of January 1968 stated that the new front had been approved despite the omission of a second column. Nothing has fallen down. But the visual need for a vertical at the intended point remains.

The following buildings have been constructed since the writing of the original edition of *Farnham Buildings & People*.

EAST STREET, Brightwell. The Gostrey Club. In January 1964 the building was nearing completion and about half the £8,000 appeal had been raised. The premises were opened in October. A. J. & R. L. Stedman, architects. Farnham Urban District Council.
The Health Centre, opened 1968. Raymond Ash, architect. Surrey County Council.

GUILDFORD ROAD. Fire Station. Stated to have been opened in February 1967 and to have cost £85,000. J. Harrison, A.R.I.B.A., architect. Surrey County Council.

THE HART. Cobgates. Home for the Elderly. It was stated that £17,500 was to be paid for the site of 1.3 acres. Five years later, in June 1969, the homes were opened, having cost £122,000. Raymond Ash, architect. Surrey County Council.

THE HART. West Surrey College of Art and Design. Use of the 10½ acre site was approved by Farnham Town Planning and Development Committee in the later part of 1963. By May 1969 Phase I was in operation as a school. It cost £250,000. Amalgamation of the Farnham and Guildford Schools of Art, combined with recognition for Dip.A.D. courses, has resulted in situations which should bring advantages to the town: one not unnoteworthy is a Design Award of the Guildford Branch of the South East Society of Architects for this part of the new building. Raymond Ash, architect. Surrey County Council.

MORLEY ROAD. Farnham Grammar School. Extension. Opened in July 1963. J. Harrison, architect. Surrey County Council.

SOUTH STREET. Bridge House. Property, including shop front by H. Falkner, was demolished for this redevelopment which was occupied in January 1969. A. G. Anderson & Partners of Bournemouth, architects, for Simo Properties Ltd.

UNION ROAD. Expedier House. Garage premises were cleared for this redevelopment for Heath & Wiltshire. It came into use in June 1962. Osborn & Hollis, of Woking, architects.

THE BOROUGH

The Borough is central, runs east and west, and is the short, narrowing shop-lined link which connects all the main streets. With its dominating Town Hall Buildings and busy, congested, commercial character, it is a climax of the progression along Farnham's major axis.

Visual serenity is enhanced because all views are blocked: east, by the Royal Deer; west, by a curve of shop fronts; north, by the Castle and down the little alleys by lesser buildings. The courtyards and alleys are of great importance as contrast to the main street in their direction, light, intimacy, quietness, scale, texture and stillness. Most are entered by archways, which help seal in their differences and close the scale.

THE BAILIFFS' HALL, The Borough, as it appeared before (left) and after alterations made about mid-nineteenth century.

1   THE   BOROUGH   (Lionel H. Smith, Ltd.)

Shop premises of three asymmetrical bays on three floors under a slate roof, with gateroom above bay three. The first floor is of exposed timber construction with tiled weathering above. The second floor façade is cement cased.

Fenestration: Ground floor, a double shopfront; First floor, three wood-transomed windows with rectangular leaded lights; Second floor, bays one and three, three-pane wide recessed three-quarter sashes, in bay two a blind window, all three architraved in cement.

Alongside, leading from the gateway, is a yard penetrating deeply from the street.

The front, now a Tudor sandwich. This was the last building in the group of four to receive its Victorian cement front, and the first to shake some of it off. Before cementing and the addition of its top floor (both late 19th century) the house had been converted to a shop, but even in mid-Victorian times the functional timber frame was unexposed. Windows then were three-pane wide sashes, the boxes of which projected slightly from the wall surface; a device which sometimes indicates hidden timber framing. An eaved tiled roof with a flat-topped dormer window and casements capped the building.

A clue to the fact that 1 The Borough was built up after 122 was refaced was in the latter building's peculiarity of having an irregular coign (seventh above the shopfront). At this level was 1 The Borough's eaves. The first floor was jettied, probably with plaster filled coving under.

Opinion as to the wisdom, architecturally, of exposing (mid 1954) this framework varies. 'Noddyland', condemns Architectural Review. The alteration certainly does not have the effect of unifying the already pimply and lacerated faces hereabout. Neither does it draw together the elements of its own façade. There are other interesting details to be seen from the yard.

Here, at a time pre-mid-18th century, was The Bear Inn. In 1754 (a press report states) it was leased by Robert Piper from Messrs. Church and Searle.

One hundred and twenty-three years ago the house was owned by Thomas Fraser, and the kilns, outbuildings and garden (built over *c* mid-19th century) which surrounded the yard were owned and used by James Darvill (*qv*). Later The Surrey and Hants News and The Aldershot Gazette were published here (subsequently under a joint title, and more recently The Surrey and Hants News). A. L. Lucy was proprietor and printer.

Thomas Fraser appears in Farnham in 1823 as a bookbinder, but, in opposition to Nichols (*q.v.*) had also set up, in The Borough, as printer and newspaper agent three years later. Fraser fades from the scene about mid-century. As Lucy followed on, it is possible that these premises saw publication of Farnham's first printed newspaper.

There was, however, another printer in Farnham at about this time for an undated pamphlet bears his name. It was Joseph Bucknell. The pamphlet was advertising for subscribers to Cobbett's projected book on 'The Hidden but Important Customs of Farnham'. It had gained 41 subscribers by the time of the advertisement's publication. A guide to its date is that it mentions The Bank of Bristow & Stevens. At about 1 The Borough, mid-century (possibly at number 1) was a printer, bookbinder and music seller of Russian origin named John Naster(?).

Lionel Smith, earlier at 103 West Street (*qv*), bought 1 The Borough in 1920. The business was started in 1911.

4 THE BOROUGH (John Farmer Ltd.)

A symmetrical and parapeted brick and timber built double-fronted shop, with a Venetian window and rosette and flute cornice above.

The present occupiers have been here for most of the century. In 1960 the shopfront was remodelled and Venetian window repaired. This had previously a sham semicircular head to it. Brick obscures partly a timber framed construction, once jettied.

In 1839 this was a property of Henry Nichols (*qv*) of Castle Street, and by the 1870s Samuel Newman (*b* 1816*) and later Frederick Newman, basket makers, were here. In 1841 at about this place was John Cook, also a basket maker.

5 THE BOROUGH (Sweet Shop)

A two-floor shop with asymmetrical parapeted brick façade decorated by panels, recessed and in relief, above ground-floor level. The parapet has a curved step-up to its centre.

Fenestration: A shopfront bay window of 2-3-2 panes, glazing bars breaking towards their heads into simple interlacing Gothick tracery; First floor, a bay window, sashed, and of 3-5-3 panes width. Its deep cornice is decorated with alternating flutings and oval pateriform medallions.

Door: Set asymmetrically, W of the shopfront, it leads to a side passage and the shop. The doorcase has narrow panelled pilasters, slight foliated brackets and is unpedimented. An urn, in relief, decorates the head.

A sympathetic reconstruction of a once banal building. It has for very many years interlocked with number 6, and at times has been in common occupation with it. The pre-restoration front was of simple brick, and level parapeted.

The upper floor had a 1-3-1 sash, topped by a cast headstone. The window was a variant on the basic type (for example at 6 and 7 The Borough) in that although the window surface was recessed, a series of mouldings brought the outer edges of its box flush with the wall surface. Below was a typical basic Victorian shopfront. The building is timber framed.

For practically the whole of the 19th century this was one of three adjoining properties owned by the Page family. See 6 and 7 The Borough. The properties mid-century were probably occupied by Jane Edwards (*b* 1798*) milliner, Henry Smither (*b* 1818*) cabinet maker, and his wife Charlotte (*b* 1824*), and John Bevan (*b* 1802 in Bristol) tea dealer.

6 AND 7 THE BOROUGH (Flair and
    The Brown Owl)

An asymmetrical building interlocking on the ground floor with number 5. It contains two shops, is on two main floors, with dormer windows above. The building is brick fronted, parapeted, and corniced, with paired modillions. Above the shopfronts the building is symmetrical.

Fenestration: Ground floor, three seven-pane-wide bow windows, panelled or of brick beneath, and connected by a continuous cornice; First floor, bays one and three contain 1-3-1 recessed sashes, and bay two a blind window.

Doors: Two shop doors separate the three shop windows. Above each door is a panel with low relief decoration.

Interior: The construction is largely of timber and floor level is well below the pavement.

A timber building largely reconstructed late in the Georgian period to give its present character. After 1850, numbers 5, 6 and 7 rapidly deteriorated. Four undistinguished shop windows vilified the surviving delicate doorheads and curvaceous cornice. The façade of number 8 was heavily veiled with gross lettering from the parapet downwards. Paintwork was drab and woodwork down-at-heel. Fascia boards, fixed above shop fronts, and a dozen enamelled posters advertising Veritas mantles, Nugget polishes, wicks, baths, pails, Peatonite coal savers, sponges, lampglasses, varnishes and enamels were among many other household necessities. The premises were fully ripe for a Civic Trust gala day.

The fact that this group looks as it does, speaks well for those who brought about privately what was, in fact, a venture on the lines of recent Civic Trust schemes: but forty years before Norwich and Windsor. Through Lloyds Bank, Horace Field, architect, and C. E. Borelli (*qv*) this thoroughgoing transformation was brought about without over-indulgence in what might be called faking. There was practically none at 6 and 7 although the whole front at 5 was rebuilt owing to its earlier dilapidated condition and poor quality.

In 1839, numbers 5, 6, 7 and 8 The Borough were owned by Michael Page. Numbers 5 and 8 were cottages; 6 and 7 formed one house and shop combined. The Pages (*qv*) were closely and long connected with this part of The Borough. Michael Pages are encountered frequently in the 18th and early 19th centuries. One, plumber and glazier, had property dealings at The Goat's Head (*qv*). He was probably the elder, as Michael Page, senior, died in 1811 and in that same year a Michael Page, plumber, relinquished his lease on property in the town centre. There are connections, too, with Red Lion Brewery (*qv*). In the 18th century Michael Page, senior, advertised as plumber, glazier and brazier. Michael Page, junior (*b* 1791*) was glazier, plumber and hop planter. He occupied 6 and 7 The Borough, where he dwelt and carried on his business until near his death in 1846. A connection is suggested with Robert (*d* 1711) and Robert (*d* 1718) — both Farnham glaziers.

In 1846 numbers 5, 6, 7 and 8 passed to Mary Anne Page, of Guildford, daughter of Michael, junior. She married Francis Lloyd (*d* 1865 at Gloucester), of Handsworth, three years later, was rich, and went to Selkirk House, Cheltenham, where she was in 1891, shortly before her death. Another Mary Page (widow of Michael, senior), died in 1828.

Mary Page & Son advertised as ironmongers early in the 19th century. A hop sampler bearing their name is in Farnham Museum. It is probable that Michael Varndell was here in the 1730s.

It was after 1915, when Lloyds Bank bought the property, that the modern reconstruction was begun.

9   THE   BOROUGH   (The Queen's Head)

A symmetrical brick façade of three bays and three floors under a slate roof. Upper floors are separated by a brick string course. The eaves, which lie close above key bricks, are supported by widely spaced single brackets.

Fenestration: Windows are all recessed; Ground floor, large three-paned, with gilt-under-glass brewer's fascias above; First floor, bays one and three, 1-3-1 sashes, and in bay two a smaller three-pane-wide sash; Second floor, three-pane-wide threequarter sashes.

Door: The doorcase is central, with pediment, and its entablature broken over panelled pilasters.

A bold front of earlier Victorian character. It has been little altered this century apart from changes to ground floor windows. They were once as those immediately above.

There are at least two clues outside that the building isn't exactly what it appears to be at first glance. There is the junction of façade and west wall above the roof of number 8, and the junction of numbers 9 and 10. Here, at ground level, can be seen what was before, namely a jettied timber frame infilled with brick. More can be seen in the small gap between the two buildings. Inside, but largely obscured, are considerable remains on two floors of a rugged timber house or houses, with extensions northwards. The existing top floor and roof are perhaps later Victorian additions. A print of mid-century, quite accurate generally, shows this as a two-floor building with a dentilled or modillioned cornice, shallow parapet and two low-set flat-topped dormer windows. The cornice was on the same level as the existing string course. In short this is hardly the 'typical untouched Farnham Georgian' claimed in 'Old Towns Revisited'.

As a type, the building is worth comparing with 5 Castle Street (*qv*). Probably locally unique, but visually disturbing, is the dropped centre window.

The Queen's Head was at one time known as The Queen's Head and Coffee House and (according to the owners) before that as The Coffee House. In 1736 a property on the north side of The Borough described as The Coffee House, was the subject of a transaction between Robert Mainwaring (*qv*) and William Bransden, of Hackney. It was referred to in the 1820s as The Queen's Head, at which time Jane and William Page were in occupation. John and Jane Page were victuallers in Farnham in 1785, and Thomas in 1814. The Pages (*qv*) owned considerable property hereabout, including 6 and 7 The Borough. In 1782 a William Page of Farnham married Sarah Bone, and Mary Page married Joseph Patrick in 1790. For at least fifty years before 1888, The Queen's Head was owned by the Knights, from whom it was conveyed to Gale and Co. in that year.

Victuallers, like hopgrowers, often played a double part combining a trade with a capricious, seasonal, or part-time business. In the same decade — 1790s — that we find James

Page a victualler and postmaker, Henry Martin and Richard Knight were both victuallers and hop-planters; also John Swann, victualler and dogbreaker, John Humpries, victualler and horse-dealer, Thomas Cooper, victualler and carpenter, and John Chuter, victualler and sawyer. Or were their wives the working victuallers?

In 1736 The Coffee House, Farnham, (late in the occupation of John Smith, now of George Assiborne) and the shop adjoining (number 8?), occupied by Samuel Ford, hatter, were subject of an indenture with four parcels of land at Wrecclesham. Thomas Hillier, of The Queen's Head, received a portion of the King's Bounty (*qv*) in 1757.

On the gable of an inn in The Borough was once the rhyme:

> 'If I'm alive, I'm up at five,
> And if you do but call,
> I've got a pot, with coffee hot,
> I know will suit you all.'

The inn, according to one report, was known as The Post Boy, the Post Boy being (one imagines) a spritely youth. Farnham's Billy Tilbury was 70, at least. There were others — Thomas Wright and William Mathews — at the same time. During the 1850s the landlord here was Artaxeres Daniels (*b* 1813*).

10 TIIE BOROUGH (Mrs. Browne)

Corner premises constructed of timber under a tiled roof. Timbers above ground floor obscured by plaster. There are three floors, the first of which is jettied and supported by scrolled brackets.

Fenestration: Ground floor, two bow windows facing S, two more facing E; First floor, two 1-3-1 sashes facing S, one more facing E; Second floor, a large dormer window facing S, another E.

A robust timber-framed building (possibly 1610-ish) which seems really to belong more to Castle Street than to The Borough, as its history is closely connected with what is now The Coach and Horses (*qv*). A drawing of 1761 shows it to have been then much as now, except for it then having a projecting shop window on either front under a continuous tiled deep weathering. These windows soon went, and for most of the 19th century jetty and brackets were exposed although the ground floor had stuccoed walls and small windows. Later it was given the full Victorian commercial treatment. A cap was fitted to the (previously flat) south dormer window, and the whole upper floor was clapped into a jacket of floorboards and pebbledash. The process was much as that carried out on the house opposite, even to its reconstruction by the Borelli-Falkner partnership in this century. As a result of their work brick underpinning was removed, the bow windows fitted, and upper parts plastered.

It is probable that Thomas Bunch and Dennis Cook were here in 1736. In the summer of 1782 the house was conveyed to James Lamport and John Cook, mercers and drapers. George Lamport (*b* 1791*), corndealer, was here in the early 1840s with Mary (*b* 1801*) and five children, including another George Lamport (*b* 1833*). A George Lamport was a carrier with his wagon yard in Lower Church Lane (*qv*). George and William were Farnham corndealers in the 1820s, James (*b* 1785*) being here as a corndealer thirty years later. Mary (*b* 1831*) and Elinor (*b* 1838*) were his daughters. Lamports in Farnham were legion. Many will be found in the Parish Registers.

Bunch was a common name in Farnham trade circles in the 18th century. There were many Thomas Bunch's, and a number of Bunch's were drapers or in allied occupations. None, though, seems to have been in the old clothmaking trade, at least not in the later 16th century. Many other 18th century names were associated with clothmaking earlier, for example, Thomas Mabank (the town's biggest producer for ulnage in 1574-5), Henry Braborne, John and Richard Bristow (of Frensham), and George Avenell. Other leading producers and sellers were John Over, Thomas Chaper, Arnold Champion and William Grene in 1574; Richard Hardinge, John Bookham, Robert White and Thomas Warner, fourteen years later. William Mabank died in 1695 and Mary, wife of William, in 1687.

Francis, eldest son of Thomas Bunch, was a draper in the 1790s and two Thomas' (*qv*), mercers, mid-century. A Thomas Bunch bought The Bush Inn, another was a tailor, one died in 1777, another in 1807. Yet another Thomas Bunch, blacksmith, of Odiham, had his son William apprenticed to John Bunch, carpenter, of Farnham. When Thomas and Mary came to 10 The Borough is not yet known, but a Thomas Bunch was married in Farnham to Mary Derby, of Waverley, in 1758. Three successive Thomas', with others living at the same time, make relationships difficult to establish. They were here in 1782. Bunch's brother, an ironmonger, was once at The Nelson Arms (*qv*). Edward probably lived at 88 West Street (*qv*). Elizabeth Bunch married John Jarrett in 1783.

The premises passed in 1852 to James Darvill (*qv*) and from his trustees to his sister Elizabeth Lockerbie (*qv*) in 1855. Two years before that Mangles Brothers had taken a lease and opened the West Surrey Bank here, which had merged with the London Joint Stock Bank long before their 21 years expired. J. H. Knight wrote that they 'came to grief after the Gurney Overend failure in, I think, 1867.'

Another early banking association is through **Cock and Lamport** whose bank was open in Farnham in the late 18th century. As was customary, banking was a second business and they kept up their drapery too, although by 1817 we find 'John Cock, Banker' without the draper. No evidence has been found to prove that his bank was here. It has been wrongly stated in several places elsewhere that here was once The Goat's Head.

FARNHAM TOWN HALL BUILDINGS

The Castle Street frontage is of seven bays on two floors and combines with the first twelve bays of The Borough frontage to form the principal block. To its E is a smaller, attached block of three bays, the upper floor recessed behind a balustrading. Attached to the E of this is a third member on two floors with its main axis running N - S.

This building was completed by stages beginning with the five western bays in August 1932. The architects were Falkner, Aylwin and Benslyn, Harold Falkner being the only partner engaged in the project by the time of rebuilding the extreme east end. The result, though obviously not 'old', affects two predominating idioms — English Renaissance and Jacobean Renaissance transitional.

The building is of suitable scale for its supposed purpose and has more than just a touch of the country town traditional English town hall about it. Considering that it was not built in the 18th century, but at a time when the revived style was usually moribund, this is a relatively lively essay.

At the east end are considerable remains of an earlier building, and the large brick chimney is one of two salvaged from Norman Shaw's bank, formerly at 75 Castle Street (*qv*). But the façade is entirely modern. The shop in this section has a notable fanlight with lantern. It was made in the 1930s by Brown of Hammersmith. The Golden Hind weather-vane was by Thomas Elsley, and the clock is from the former building. It was given by Nicholson of Waverley Abbey.

The history and development of this site is complex, and is here dealt with under the following headings:

    i. The Goat's Head and Stables, which included
   ii. The Bailiffs' Hall.
  iii. The Conduit.
  iv. The Victorian Corn Exchange, which the present building replaced.
   v. The Old Market House which stood in Castle Street.

i.   The Goat's Head Inn and Stables

Entered by a large arch at 76 Castle Street, which gave access to a courtyard, the inn, situated as it was at the heart of the town, was in a fine position. The Old Market House stood at its gate, fairs were held in Castle Street and literally thousands of hop pickers invaded the town annually, paraded in the streets, and slept on the pavement outside the inn. In addition, the London-Portsmouth Turnpike ran alongside. From the brief references which have come to light it appears the inn was not necessarily long established, although it was a particularly popular resort late in the 18th century. Despite its importance then, it was not listed with some larger inns in 1604. They were The George, The Swan, The White Hart and The Antelope (*qqv*).

The Goat's Head passed from Samuel Griffin, pastrycook, to an Odiham victualler, James Marshall, in 1758. Matthew Paine, George Coldham Knight, Michael Page, George Othen and John Stevens were all associated with the inn by the end of the century. In 1790 The Cumberland Friendly Society was instituted here, and at about the same time Michael Page (*qv*) erected two new buildings. They may have been those now in lower Castle Street. The Gosport Diligence left for either London or Gosport eight times a week, and The Goat's Head was referred to as 'a leading inn of Farnham'. But by 1823 no coaches were advertised in a list which gave arrivals and departures from the town and the former 'principal coaching house' was regarded as a 'tavern'. Perhaps decline began after a great fire which devastated most of the premises in 1796: ironical, as part of the buildings had just been acquired for building a fire station (see Conduit).

Hassell's drawings of the 1820s give an impression of neglect and patchwork repair, and the fact that the tavern is not even mentioned in a detailed account of Farnham's entertainment high spots suggests a continued decline into the 'fifties although 1858 did see the inauguration here of

Farnham Freehold Land and Building Society. In the later
1820s concerts were given in a spacious room by J. and E.
Merriott (*qqv*) who were organists at Basingstoke and
Farnham churches. Itinerant lecturers also performed.

The inn's history really ends in 1864 when James Knight
(*qv*) conveyed it to Farnham Market and Town Hall Company. They soon set about tidying things up and provided
Farnham with a new landmark. But The Goat's Head was to
survive as a pub-name for another 40 years as its licence was
transferred. The sign last hung at 40 The Borough (*qv*). But
in the 1890s the house which sported it could have reflected
little of the earlier days. By the last year of its existence
The Goat's Head — once a leading inn of Farnham — had
become 'a common beer house'.

ii.   The Bailiffs' Hall

The name seems to be an assumed one. Although there is
some evidence to support its use, it is of recent adoption.
In the 1820s it was known as The Goat's Head Inn Stables,
and since then the same building has been The Mechanics'
Institute, The Art School, a Non-Conformist meeting-house,
china store, bazaar, hairdressing saloon and a warehouse. It
has served temporarily as the fire station, too.

A DRAWING of the Bailiffs' Hall as it appeared to F. W.
Fairholt (1814-1866) about mid-century. Reproduced with
acknowledgements to the Victoria and Albert Museum.

The building is difficult to date accurately. Hassell's drawing includes an ambiguous inscription on a brick capital: 1537? 1637? Or 1557? More likely, judging by the building, it should be 1657. Nathaniel Lloyd suggests 1670 for the remaining fragments. To add a touch of confusion the restored front is embellished with a cartouche inscribed 1566. Pevsner and Nairn do not hestitate to state that it was built in 1674. And so one can go on. For example, a plaque in the centre of the old front bore a cryptic '16W1'. Anyway, the existing façade is entirely mid nineteen thirties, although there are considerable remains of the 1657(?) building to be seen on either side, mainly above eye level. The front is of some historical significance though, as its design captured, unwittingly, characteristics of the original north end. That had been the important front, with a similar flamboyant gable-ending to the one now on the south. But it, like the street front, was demolished in the 19th century.

What remains of the early building is of considerable interest, as it shows in its rugged-textured brickwork a fore-taste of the 18th century: in two ways, although not of texture. First, the renaissance style — half formed and ill-conceived — makes its appearance in the voluted cut brick capitals. This is the only local secular example illustrating this phase of architectural development. Second, in its promise of magnificent displays of the brick-workers' craft which is demonstrated in some of Farnham's earlier 18th century buildings.

The Bailiffs' Hall had, like the rest of The Goat's Head, fallen into rather a bad state by 1830. By mid-century, as the Mechanics' Institute, it had been refronted and greatly improved. It was, according to one critic, as if to keep up the balance between the physical and the intellectual: a rather dreary affair in which the darkness of the lecture hall was little lighted by either lights or learning. Rejuvenation was short-lived. Ruthlessly, the Town Hall Company cut the building back several feet to its present depth in about 1870 and converted a quaint, richly ornamented front to one of the bleakest brick façades imaginable. It lasted 60 years. Harold Falkner's rebuilding is a spirited composition of undulations in brick.

iii. The Conduit

This was a rather odd building on one floor, having a massive brick arch, with pediment above, centred on either front — one in Castle Street, the other in The Borough. It occupied the corner. A shallow parapet, the coping of which was broken by the pediments, partly obscured a low-pitch roof.

Before it was demolished in the 1860s The Conduit had been built up against and on top of. It was not a very pretty place although the Castle Street arch and the Conduit itself were perhaps to influence the design of the 1866 Corn Exchange. On the same site a pump was retained behind a grilled archway. A similar opening is still there in the new building. It is the west entrance to the Colonnade.

Early in the 1790s the pattern of Farnham streets was not conducive to the healthy expansion of coaching systems. Two considerable alterations were made to accommodate the rush. The Round House (qv) was demolished and The Borough (this part then still known as Dogflud Street) was widened along its north side. Tenements were demolished, and between 1791 and 1793 the Conduit was built, fronting the new street alignment. Soon afterwards it was bought on behalf of the parishioners and used as the fire station. Ladders (too long for the Conduit) were slung under the Old Market House (qv). See also 15 and 16 The Borough.

Before 1793 the Conduit had been in Castle Street, probably in the roadway, and near number 10. An account of Farnham, probably written not long before the new Conduit was built, states that in '1678 [the Bishop] brought water in leaden pipes out of the middle of the Park to the Castle, and also to the Conduit here in the town, by which the Inhabitants are supplied by good soft, water, which otherwise they would have been destitute of . . .'

Other local landmarks cleared at about this time were the Fish Cross and The Butchers' Shambles (qqv).

In the early 19th century George Cottee leased The Conduit from its owners, Samuel Andrews and Thomas Eyre (qqv). Sturt tells us of his memories (of Cottee?) in 'A Small Boy in the Sixties'. Writing of the Conduit he continues: '. . . There was a shoe shop in the same building with the bank, and I can still picture the owner — a heavy man, with a limp when he moved — standing at the doorway to look out into The Borough. But what leading shop keeper in these days would wear, as he did, a white apron and bib, declaring himself, too, a habitual working man?' His wife (Mary?), kind-eyed, had a large fattish face, thickly pitted with smallpox.

Mary Cottee kept the Conduit key when, in 1858, an agreement was drawn **up** for Edward Bromley (*qv*) of The Goat's Head to have free water for the subscription of one guinea. Mary (*b* 1806*) and her husband George Cottee (*b* 1801*) were bootmakers, and were late in the line of many Farnham Cottees who included John (*d* 1798), peruke maker. Samuel and Richard, sons of George, died in 1784 and 1791, James, son of William and Mary, died in 1802, and Ann in 1805, a spinster.

Farnham's main alternative water supply was by wells, private pumps, or by water-carrier. In Sturt's boyhood (1860s), water was 1d. or ½d. a bucket. J. H. Knight (of the motor-car) wrote in 1909 that he recalled it being 4d. a barrel. By the '70s Farnham Water Company had been formed. The secretary, appropriately Wells, ran the office at 112 West Street (*qv*) until it moved to the Corn Exchange. A paving slab in the Colonnade is said to cover the well on which the Conduit depended.

iv.   The Corn Exchange

This was built to replace The Goat's Head Stables, Conduit, cottages and shops, to the design of E. Wyndham Tarn, of London; not Scott as has been stated elsewhere. James Knight sold the property (except the Conduit which belonged to parishioners until the council sold it in 1931) to Farnham Market and Town Hall Company in 1864. They were rebuilding by 1865. There was a grand opening dinner on March 16th, 1866, when, apart from the banquet, guests were entertained by seven songs, sixteen toasts, and a brass band playing Rule Britannia. Mr. Hazell (*qv*) proposed the architect's health. It was this erection that the present buildings replaced in the earlier 1930s.

The new building was not elegant, nor could it claim a highly functional exterior. The materials used were hardly sympathetic to existing surroundings yet their contrast was not of the kind which proved beneficial to both. It was, however, large, pseudo-Gothic (11th *c* and 12th *c* Italian), towered, turreted, parapeted, buttressed and punctuated with blind trefoils against white brick, with blue brick, terracotta and stone in addition. A modest amount of Norman detail helped to set off various forms of Mediaeval column and capital — totalling over 60 in number. The composition, which was crowned by a slate roofed turret of alpine flavour, might be described as a little fanciful.

F. C. Birch (*qv*) was the builder. He used white Huntingdon bricks, gauged red brick heads, Bath stone, red and buff terra cotta made at Blashfield's Stamford works. The building itself cost £3,500.

The new building combined with The Conduit (*qv*) in the form of a Town Pump) to provide the Corn Exchange offices, Town Hall, and a row of shops facing on to The Borough. At the Castle Street Corner, over the pump, was the Clock Tower.

v.   The Old Market House

It stood until 1866 at the foot of Castle Street, on its east side. The Local Board demolished it and the Town Hall Company built the Corn Exchange (*qv*) exactly three hundred years after John Clarke of Farnham is said to have built it at his own expense. He was senior bailiff of Farnham Corporation. In December 1865, when auctioned, the materials raised £55. Fuller considered Clarke a Worthy. He wrote, 'I have been credibly informed that one Mr. Clarke, some seven score years since, built at his charges the Market House at Farnham. Once, reproving his workmen for going so slowly they excused themselves that they were hindered much with people pressing upon them, some liking, some disliking, the model of the Fabric. Hereupon, Mr. Clarke, caused this distich (hardly extant at this day) to be written in that house:

> "You, who don't like me, give money to mend me,
>   You, who do like me, give money to end me!"

I wish this advice practised all over the country by those who vent their various verdicts on praising or reproving structures gratis for the general good.'

THE OLD MARKET HOUSE. A drawing by F. W. Fairholt (1814-1866) reproduced with acknowledgements to the Victoria and Albert Museum. The building stood for 300 years at the foot of Castle Street.

In the 19th century, shortly before demolition, one wrote, '. . . but one owes mention also of the old Market-house, holding enframed the only clock that can be depended on in Farnham. . . . Mr. Clarke's Market-house is now like a supplement to The Times — a mere vehicle for advertisement, and is referred to, we fancy, in a manner similar to that with which the Parisians consult their mural literature, when in search of entertainment. The affiches of Paris, however, have the advantage of being daily renewed in red, blue, green, and yellow dresses; but at Farnham no sooner has one set one's heart upon a lecture, a concert, or a monkey-show, than it appears to have come off six weeks before, or possibly not at all for lack of audience.'

The Old Market House was of timber construction built on oak posts, roofed in tile and turreted. It is well recorded by at least two models, one of which is in Farnham Museum. A century after the reputed date of building, a hearth was charged tax at 'The Markett Howse', Farnham.

15 AND 16 THE BOROUGH
(The Gift Shop and Dewhurst's)

Two shops under a single tiled mansard roof: of brick, six bays and two main floors. Over bays one to four a regularly spaced modillion cornice. Over bays five and six, modillions spaced in pairs and trios.

Fenestration: Ground floor, bays two to four a double shopfront, bays five and six a shopfront; First floors, bays one, three and five blind recesses, bays two and four three-pane-wide recessed sashes, bay six a 1-3-1 recessed sash. Above, three flat topped sashed dormer windows.

Doors: Bay one, a side passage door with brick arch head. Shop doors in bays three and five.

Probably 16 is a little later than 15, and both may date within a few years of 1800. See 112 West Street.

The pair is of interest for behind was the forge owned in the 19th century by Richard Smith (*qv*) and his wife Ann. George Smith (*b* 1821*) was a farrier living hereabout, and Charlotte Smith, ironmonger, had her shop at what is probably now 14. William Jeffrey (*b* 1815*), gunmaker, and Mary Jeffrey (*b* 1816*), neither natives of Farnham, were here by 1841. Perhaps he used the forge in connection with his trade. Later in the 19th and earlier 20th century Samuel and Walter Jeffrey, watchmakers, were at number 15.

Other Farnham gunsmiths include William Woods (*d* 1724), Charles Draper of Downing Street, and William Baker, earlier 19th century, the latter being also an iron-monger. Andrew Dawes (*d* 1779), William Barnes, later 16th century, Charles Elkins (*d* 1793) and Thomas Boxall (who was working later in the 18th century) were others in the same trade. In the early part of the 19th century a Thomas Boxall (*b* 1776*) lived at 3 Downing Street (*qv*).

Farnham's best known clock makers were the Avenells. Philip (*d* 1807) and William, were both working late in the 18th century. Their longcase clocks, some with painted dials, are still in use. Philip Avenell, senior, clockmaker, died in 1783. There is possibly a link with the early 18th century through Henry, son of Elizabeth Avenell, who was appren-ticed to William Russell, a Crondall blacksmith. John Avenell married Sarah Russell in 1784, and a Philip Avenell, black-smith, died exactly a century before another Philip married Elizabeth Stapley in 1788. Yet another Philip married another Elizabeth (Allen) in 1765. But the name, if one includes Avenill, is very common in Farnham throughout the 18th century. One Mr. Avenell was paid 10/6 in 1751 for altering ironwork and fitting a new dial to the church clock.

In the mid 18th century Philip Avenell and Francis Newland were paid £2 each per annum for attending all the fires, for keeping engines in good repair, and for trying the engines at 'the proper seasons in the year'. Two new engines with accessories had been bought by subscription in 1754. They cost £128 18s. 6d. See The Conduit.

Earlier 19th century clockmakers were Edward James (*b* 1801*) of West Street, James Roe (*b* 1776*) of West Street and Downing Street, Joseph and William Ridgway Newland, William Knight (*qv*) and James Wade, Robert Harrington of The Borough, and John Clark (*b* 1796*) of West Street.

17 T H E   B O R O U G H   (S. Bide and Sons)

A three-floor, four-bay, grey brick and slated double-fronted shop.

Here was The Ship Hotel, earlier The Ship Inn, which existed in another building from at least the 1750s when Samuel Spreadborough was holder. This was a timber framed building, burned down shortly after Robert Barrett (*qv*), the brewer, bought it in 1858. A pub hereabouts was owned by Richard Smith (*b* 1811*) towards mid-century. He sold his property to Robert Barrett.

The new building is dull enough to be 1870-ish. In it The Ship carried on. Its shopfront was similar to one lately at 122

West Street. Although the fascia has been replaced and lower parts removed, remains of the earlier front are there. Barretts sold to Farnham United Breweries in 1897. They offered it for sale in 1928. Thomas Steer (*b* 1816*) licensed victualler, and John Rumble, or Rumbell (*b* 1785*) publican, were living hereabout in the early 1850s.

2 2   T H E   B O R O U G H   (Barclays Bank Ltd.)

In 1931 Barclays Bank opened these premises. Here had been George Ransom's (*qv*) bakery and confectionery, established long before the end of the 19th century. The upper part of the building was probably to the design of William Wells (*qv*), who was a pupil of Wonnacott's. Thomas Wonnacott will be remembered for the Congregational Church in South Street, after designing which it is said he moved to the Isle of Wight. He did Riverdale and other South Street properties. Being a dissenter he built chapels rather than pubs in an age when either was rewarding to architects and builders. He favoured a rustic eclectic Gothic style.

26—27   T H E   B O R O U G H   (The Bush Hotel)

A yellow brick block of shops of seven bays and three floors. An archway from The Borough leads to a courtyard. Around this, buildings mainly of brick and tile are arranged.

The Bush is said to have existed in the 14th century, but little documentary evidence has come to light dating from long before the beginning of the 17th century. In 1618 The Crown brought a case against Harding, the innkeeper, and early records also relate to the Venison Feast there. The old estate has been much broken up since those days. In the later 17th century there went with the inn other properties fronting The Borough, practically all of what is now the west side of South Street, two meadow grounds 'commonly known as Gostreeds' (from which, presumably, Gostrey Meadow) and land south of West Street. The whole, about eleven acres, was inherited from his aunt, Joan Smith, by James Hayes (*qv*) about the 1680s, but the Bush itself was occupied, probably tenanted, by Francis Mabberly (*qv*) in 1684. At that same time there was a house 'backsides the inn' which was occupied by Thomas Michiner. It is recorded that in 1660 Mrs. Hayes gave 20/- for bread to be distributed to the poor at The Bush Inn on St. Mathew's Day. Richard Chance, of The Bush, received the King's Bounty (*qv*) in 1757.

Mabberlys are quite frequently encountered in the 17th-18th centuries, but become few by the 1850s. One of the last appears to have been Sarah (*b* 1786*) who was at an address in The Borough in the early 1840s. 1688 saw the death of John Mabberly, another Farnham inn-holder, also the Christening of Edward, son of John. William, son of John Mabberley, died in 1714; his daughter, Mary, in 1709.

The property passed in 1773 from Richard Williams to John Ardley, for £2,300, and fifteen years later it was sold on his death to Thomas Bunch (*qv*). Bunch sold to Benjamin Nichols, William Crump (*qqv*), woolstapler, putting up the money, in 1790. The loan was redeemed in 1808 and in 1839 the hotel and land to the south was owned by Ann Nichols and occupied by Charlotte Smith (*b* 1786*). Another Charlotte Smith (*b* 1816*), probably her daughter, was also at The Bush in the 1840s.

The mid 19th century saw a rapidly developing military camp at Aldershot. With the nearest trains stopping at Farnham one might have expected the rush to have stimulated enterprise at The Bush. It seems, however, that full advantage was not taken of this opportunity. That is, according to one writer. The railway not only brought queens, princes and generals. 'The Bush Hotel, which once disdained the entrance of that very unpleasant item of society, a commercial traveller, had yielded its aristocratic fastidiousness to the practical character of the times . . . but the threshold of the said hostel is the great gossiping point of the town, round which the wearers of tunics do assemble by the score, to hear tell of some new thing. The Bush boasts an Assembly Room — the very dreariest place of its kind that exists, we opine, in the three kingdoms.'

The Assembly Rooms was the name of a building of rather later Victorian character which once stood at the top of South Street, on its east side, just opposite The Bush Tap. The latter was described as newly built in the late 1870s. There was, though, a pub there by the early '60s. It must have been at about this time that the Bromleys (*qv*) arrived as tenants of The Bush. They left in 1888, the new tenant being Charles Hart, of Deal.

The Bush and its extensive lands were put up for auction on the dissolution of John and James Knight's partnership, in 1887. But The Bush was not sold, £5,000 being the highest bid. Trimmer (*qv*) with his offer of £6,000 (still £1,000 below the reserve, according to one record), secured the property in the following year, and in 1928 the Farnham United Brewery offered it for sale again.

In the 1930s major changes were made. Much of the east part was reconstructed, one of Norman Shaw's (*qv*) Castle Street chimneys being rebuilt there. The east yard was cleared and in 1931 the new shops in The Borough were finished, redecking the yellow brick fronts probably built about 1840.

35 AND 36 THE BOROUGH (Borelli's)

Shop premises on two main floors built largely of timber and brick under a tiled roof. There are two main bays with gateroom adjoining the E. The roof has deep-moulded eaves. Upper parts of the façade are plastered and painted.

Fenestration: Ground floor, two shop windows contained between doors, all under a modillioned cornice; First floor, two 2-5-2 aproned bay windows, flat topped and corniced.

Other features: Beyond the gateroom is a stone-set yard containing cottages, stables and stores. Upper house-lights have leaded rectangular panes. Several walls are tile hung.

The S.C.C. 'List of Antiquities' (1939) dates the building 1615, with 18th century additions. It is one of Farnham's many buildings of which it is difficult to say that any one thing is of outstanding merit, yet which, as a whole, makes something of considerable value to the townscape. The yard contributes to that invaluable characteristic of the town centre: the sudden opening up of restricted quiet places into busy jostling streets and bigger scale. The Old Kiln Yard, late next to Woolworth's, could have done the same, even with new buildings. The Lion and Lamb Yard still does, but in a rather pseudo sort of way. This had another great advantage — its leading direct to open countryside. But that advantage, too, has been lost. There are other places with great potentiality still to be realized, for example at 104 and 121 West Street. A recent success was at The Spinning Wheel, in the link between the car park and The Borough. At 35 and 36 The Borough, success is largely due to a happy coincidence of necessity and intuition rather than to a plan.

Hassell's 1822 drawing of The Borough shows 35 and 36 as having three or four upper windows, a shopfront and jetty.

The two premises fronting the street were backed in the 19th century by cottages. At least two of these three dwell-

ings (35, 36 and other cottages) were probably part of
'. . . . the capital messuage then long since in three tenements
in the occupation of John Coutrapp Esquire Richard Watts
Gent and John Warner and then late in tenure of Abraham
Lee James Wroth William Mabank and John Mabberly'
(*qqv*). That was in 1684. All once belonged to Joan Smith,
widow, aunt of James Hayes, of Bray, who was an owner
here late in the 17th century. Francis Mabberly, charged tax
on nine hearths in 1664, occupied The Bush (*qv*) at that time
and this property was once of the same estate.

In 1773 part of the estate (including 35 and 36, with land)
passed from Richard Williams to John Ardley and from him
to Thomas Bunch (*qv*) fourteen years later. He sold to Benjamin Nichols (*qv*).

The Borellis (*qv*) have been jewellers and silversmiths
in Farnham from the late 18th century. Donato (*b* 1806*) and
Clement (*b* 1813*) were in West Street as jewellers in 1839
and at 1-11 West Street (*qv*), advertising as silversmiths, by
1845. Charlotte Borelli (*b* 1816*) was also at that address.
Donato married Charlotte (*b* 1806*) and had daughters,
Madelina (*b* 1841*) and Angelina (*b* 1842*). The firm had
moved to 36 The Borough a little after mid-century.

The late Charles Borelli (*qv*) was responsible for sympathetic restoration of many of his town properties during an
age when fewer people than now cared what was happening
around them architecturally. He also exerted a considerable
influence on buildings belonging to others, and it may be
safely said that much that makes the town centre what it
is today is largely due to the efforts of this one man.

An outbuilding, to the lower east part of the yard of
30-31 was once known as The School Room.

37   THE   BOROUGH   (Cafe)

Shop premises with a symmetrical and jettied timber-framed
façade of three floors and two bays under a tiled roof.

Fenestration: Ground floor, a double shopfront; First
floor, two casements; Above, contained in a pair of north-
facing gables, are two small casement windows.

One hundred and forty years ago the building was much
as now from outside. Hassell shows it with small-paned
double shopfront and rather different upper-window arrangement. The gateroom once on the west is not indicated. It
was there soon afterwards, if not at the time, and gave
access to a rambling yard, and ten-oast kiln. Some of this
yard was absorbed when the bank was built. The main

building is dated 17th century in the 'List of Buildings of Architectural Interest'.

Thomas Eyre (*qv*) grocer, had a shop here in the later nineteenth century and probably long before. He owned neighbouring property and bought 4 Downing Street (*qv*) in 1889. His business was long-established. A Thomas Eyre, grocer, appeared as freeholder in Farnham in 1767. One Thomas Eyre died in 1811, another in 1864, and there were at least three more of the same name. Thomas Eyre (*b* 1828*) was a pupil at Cyrus Blandford's school at 69 West Street (*qv*). Thomas (*b* 1786*) grocer, and Mary (*b* 1791*) his sister, were in The Borough in the 1840s, and Thomas (*b* 1743* *d* 1811) married Elizabeth Piper (*b* 1746*, *d* 1817) in 1780. Daniel Eyre Esquire died in 1786.

In 1896 Eyre sold to Charles Rogers (*d* 1913) who established here the bakery which still remains, under a different name, although there was already a bakehouse in Eyre's time.

38 AND 39 THE BOROUGH
(Westminster Bank)

A five-bay symmetrical parapeted façade on three floors, built of brick under a complex slate roof. The façade employs a wide range of ornaments of classical derivation, is corniced and painted.

Fenestration: Ground floor, windows with segmental heads in bays two to four, divided by plain pilasters; First floor, semicircular heads, pedimented alternately segmental and triangular; Second floor, segmental heads, architraved, with keyblocks. All windows are recessed, plate glass sashes.

Door: one in bay one, another in bay five.

The building, designed as a bank, was built in two stages; in 1865 and in 1904. The three eastern bays are of the first build. Originally, the door was in what is now bay three. The 1904 additions did not modify the style; they multiplied what was already there.

This will probably remain a controversial building. Georgian purists find it coarse, heavy-handed, malproportioned, ill-conceived, outrageous. However, it tilts the scales a little on other points, being big, vigorous and unhesitant — which do not necessarily make it good, but in relation to Castle Street make it a commanding focal point and a positive view-closer when seen from Castle Street.

Its appearance coincided with the demolition of the Old Market House (*qv*), which had done a similar visual job for exactly three hundred years. It did it in a less ostentatious manner, perhaps; but then, the surroundings, too, were not quite so grandiose.

If, as an individual building, it is gross, its virility makes it valuable in this context. And devotees of Victorian architecture may even enthuse. Extravagant, robust, solid, secure, dignified, Pall Mall-like, even respectable. What more could a mid-Victorian bank customer want? Pseudo perhaps, but at least this 19th century model has vigour, which is more than can be said of many 20th century plagiarisms.

As in 1866 this and the old Corn Exchange (*qv*) were Farnham's biggest new central buildings, it is amusing to think of the two as neighbours. Here was the local battleground of revivalist giants: Gothicism versus Classicism. The pseudo-mediaeval contender was soon reinforced by Shaw's Elizabethan Leviathan in Castle Street, but they were both demolished later and replaced by the more complaisant.

There is comparable work at 8 Castle Street (*qv*), by one less confident, and architecturally degenerate relatives are to be seen in the upper part of 3 Castle Street and at 39 - 41 Castle Street (*qv*).

Before 1865 number 38 The Borough belonged to the Eyre (*qv*) family, from whom it was bought by the London and County Banking Co. Ltd. They opened in Farnham at 11 West Street (*qv*) in August 1860. Henry Goujon, its second manager, who became prominent in the town, was appointed in 1862. He retired 36 years later. Eyre's was a neat three-bay house with Georgian-type shopfronts, central pedimented door and three dormer windows with pitched roofs. Apparently an 18th century house, but judging by its chimneys, much earlier in origin.

In 1901 the adjoining property was acquired from Thomas Eyre, reconstruction being completed in 1904 by Tompsett, with Cheston as architect. 1909 saw the London and County amalgamated with Westminster under their joint names. The title was contracted in 1923 to its present one from London, County and Westminster, having in the meantime absorbed Parr's Bank.

The building previously here was used in the 'nineties by the International Tea Co., and before that it was the office of John Nash, auctioneer and surveyor. In the 1820s Bewland, a tailor, had his shop here. Peter Pixley occupied the house in the 1780s.

The young Sturt writes happily of a fishmonger, John Hackman, who had a shop here. From his back garden ('to think of it is like walking into some sunny garden of old Germany or old Holland') came the first red and yellow tulip Sturt had ever seen.

Eyres had connections with Farnham district before Charles I's reign. Catherine Eyre gave £50 to buy a communion cloth and ornaments for the church in 1783 and various Eyres traded in the town as chandlers and glass dealers. Thomas himself had a grocery shop at 37 The Borough (*qv*) until about 1900.

40 THE BOROUGH (Elliot's)

A shop of two bays on three main floors, built principally of timber, brick and tile. A main ridge runs parallel with the street. From this two gables (one heading each bay), with uncarved barge boards, face N.

Fenestration: Ground floor, in bay two a bow shop window and, above it, under a jetty, an oriel window four lights wide with three more unprojecting lights either side. Above, each bay is centred by an oriel of five lights. Together with these, eight other unprojecting lights span the façade. Under each gable apex is a twin leaded light. All oriels are supported by two corbels, one of which bears carved initials 'G.I.W.' Façade windows, apart from those on the ground floor, have rectangular leaded panes.

Door: Adjoining east end of bow shop window.

Other features: Bay one contains an archway leading to the rear. Its timber head is supported by two curved wood brackets, back and front. The façade generally is of exposed timber framing infilled with brick and plaster.

A yard, with sets, leads from the arch. To its west is a series of extensions to the main building. The main interior, showing signs of extensive alteration, is galleried.

The date of construction has been stated to be *c*. 1660, although the general character of the façade is typical of what was built rather earlier elsewhere, and buildings to the rear may incorporate fabric of considerably earlier date. As the front has been restored, considerable changes in detail now appear, despite very careful work. This was carried out by H. Falkner (*qv*) in 1911 under the patronage of C. E. Borelli (*qv*). The general character of the building has been restored, although (in the 1820s, if not before) there were no oriel windows at all. The main first-floor windows were simple three-light casements and there were probably gable finials earlier. There was, too, a massive brick chimney with a heavy crown. It rose from the ridge of a third gable, facing south, a little back from its junction with the main east-west ridge. The chimney was multi-flued but simple in plan; of the style still to be seen at Firgrove Cottage (*qv*), but of more monumental size and proportions.

Edward Hassell's drawing of 1828 (see 'Farnham Inheritance') shows the ground floor with a Venetian window to the west. Later, there were two similar. The present shop-front is modern and the inside is mainly a reconstruction.

Some time about 1870 the building was grossly mal-treated. The front was, it is said, covered with floorboards and roughcast (imitating what they buried), the chimney decapitated, eaves cut back and bargeboards disappeared. In the 1911 restoration great care was taken to regain the appearance of the earlier structure. Much of what is exposed today only needed uncovering.

Early reference to the house has not been found, but it is known that Daniel Bristow (*qv*) leased it in 1782, and that Daniel Bristow, junior, bought it, together with what is now known as 41 The Borough (*qv*), for £700, from a Great Ormond Street merchant named Samuel Turner. He sold it for double the price 29 years later.

John Nichols, senior (*qv, b* 1766*) bought the property in 1827. He started the post office here and with 41 and 42 (*qv*) next door, established a printing and bookbinding works. Although they retained the latter two premises for some years longer, the Nichols family sold number 40 in 1865. It became a beer house called The Goat's Head (*qv*), the licence and name having been transferred from another house demolished thenabouts. Perhaps it was at this time, on the first change of use and hands in 40 years, that the house was so clumsily altered. It was the right time for such activities. It is not known on what evidence the claim that this 'originally was probably a cloth merchant's house' is made, but it is not unlikely.

George Wroth was a draper. Nathaniel Wroth once occupied premises adjoining the east side of 43 The Borough. There is no proof though to connect G.I.W. with George Wroth (*qv*).

It was during John Nichol's postmastership that his stormy correspondence with William Cobbett (*qv*) blew up. It arose over the 1d. delivery surcharge to Cobbett's house at Ash. Nichols enforced the extra payment. Cobbett, of course, did not give way. It ended happily with neither losing face, as Cobbett arranged to have his own man collect the letters (possibly at several times the normal cost). Later, Cobbett called on Nichols. He '. . . drove over in his old gig, not worth five pounds'. In future, he sent to Nichols, free of charge, vegetables from his own garden at Ash. The letters which Nichols accumulated as a result of this contact with Cobbett were considerable in number, but he lost nearly the lot when his office was invaded by souvenir hunters, many strangers to the town, on the occasion of Cobbett's funeral. His tomb is near the north door of St. Andrew's church.

Nichols' owned or were connected with a considerable number of central Farnham properties, including 4 Castle Street, 6, 118, 120, 121 West Street, The Bush Hotel (*qv*), and 23 Downing Street. There was later in the century a post office at 24 The Borough, but John (presumably one of John the Elder's two sons — Robert and John) opened a new post office at 114 West Street (*qv*) in the 1880s. Robert Nichols (*qv*, *b* 1801*) was later postmaster in The Borough. With him were his wife Matilda, and daughter Jane (*b* 1827*).

For about 45 years after the 1911 restoration, 40 The Borough was known as the Spinning Wheel (*qv*) antique shop.

41 AND 42 THE BOROUGH (Boots)

A shop on three main floors, built with a front displaying timber framing, two jetties, leaded lights and a double shop-front, all under a single gable and tiled roof.

Built about 1930, replacing a three-floor three-bay shop with stuccoed face and slate roof. It is said that evidence of an early building, found on reconstruction, determined largely the present appearance.

The property is closely associated in more recent times with 40 The Borough (*qv*) through ownership from 1827 of the Nichols family, the tenancy of 42 being taken up by Francis Sturt, George's father, in the late 1870s

In 'A Small Boy in the Sixties', George Sturt relates, '. . . my friendship with Arthur Nichols continued. . . . Moreover, within a year, the Nichols's had offered, and my mother and father gladly accepted, the tenancy of an old family book and stationery shop Mr. Nichols owned at 42 The Borough. The house was roomier — and we had begun to need more room — and the shop, too, would admit of extension of business which had been beyond my mother's reach before. In short, while 18 The Borough had been only a little poky tenement, on the other hand, 42 The Borough was an opening to considerable middle class comfort. The change was decidedly an advantage for us.'

Frank Sturt (*b* 1859), George's brother, carried on their father's business at 41, and 42 for 46 years. He died at Newnham's in October, 1930. F. Sturt Ltd., stationer, is in the arcade of the Town Hall Buildings today. There were many Sturts living in Farnham and district, and they have done so for several centuries at least. No fewer than nine were charged Hearth Tax in 1664, although old George Sturt (*b* 1784*) was born at Haslemere. This may once have been the house of Nathaniel Wroth (*qv*) and later of Samuel Wright. If not, both once occupied a house, probably number 43.

In 1851 old John Nichols, born in Norfolk about 1762, and his wife Elizabeth (*b* 1774*) were still here. He had been the bookseller. A grandson, John (*b* 1827*), was a printer, and John Nichols (*b* 1803*), who lived at 103 West Street (*qv*), was by that time the active book binder and seller. His wife was Lucy (*b* 1805*). They had daughters Lucy (*b* 1835*), Jane (1837*), Ellen (1839) and Emily (1844*).

43 THE BOROUGH (Silver's)

A shop of two bays and three floors. Built of brick and part of timber, with a stucco façade — corniced and parapeted, under a slate roof.

Fenestration: Ground floor, a double shopfront with central glazed door flanked by bow windows; First floor, bay windows containing three sashes, each of 2-4-2 panes, corniced and flat topped; Second floor, flush architraved sashes.

The immediate interest of this building is its '18th century' shopfront, but it was not made until 1932 — when the premises were generally improved. Plate glass windows were replaced on upper floors too, and a dull Victorian shopfront was removed. The bay windows and façade above are of Victorian appearance. Further reconstruction work at the back was carried out in mid-1961.

This is one of the earlier, and better, pseudo-Georgian fronts fitted in Farnham this century, although some will say that if they are bogus there's nothing to choose between them. Since this was fitted there has been a heavy crop, some later ones very coarse in detail, out of scale, and historically maladjusted, if identifiable. In fact, of the thirty or so 'Georgian' bay and bow shopfronts in the town which can be immediately recalled, about six pre-date this one. Of those, only one is pre-twentieth century, in situ. Two more have been well restored according to evidence found during reconstruction. The one at 43 The Borough is modelled on Fribourg and Treyer's existing shop in the Haymarket. The proportions and overall appearance, though, are very different. There, to enter, one steps up: here, one steps down. However, the improvement is great and the shopfront no longer disowns completely what is above it. The conversion was one of those directed by Charles Borelli (*qv*).

Inside there are considerable remains of a timber framed house with some herringbone brickwork infilling. At the east part may have been in the form of an archway with rooms over, as at the Spinning Wheel.

In the early eighteen hundreds this was one of a pair of houses inherited from his father by Daniel Bristow, junior (*qv*) and in 1805 it was sold to James Bennett, for the use of Thomas Birch (*qv*), carpenter. Bennett's son, Charles (*b* 1806* or 1801*), inherited the house in 1850 on his father's death in that year. James and Charles Bennett were renowned as makers of agricultural machinery and as inventors of the (a?) corn winnowing machine and the grass seed machine. Charles, with his wife Mary (*b* 1802*), employed two men when they took over the business. They also made toys and potato grinders. James died in 1850 and Charles in August, 1871. Sturt refers to 'old Charlie — maker of machines'.

From shortly after Charles' death until well into the 20th century James Williamson's stationery shop was here.

49   T H E   B O R O U G H   (Timothy White's Ltd.)

Here once lived William Portello (*qv*, *b* 1806* or 1811*), apothecary, and Mary Portello (*b* 1811*). Other chemists — William Higgins and, later, Louis Cullingford (*c* 1890) — followed.

CASTLE STREET

Castle Street presents the town's major visual climax, when looking up or speeding down. It runs uphill, northwards, to be crowned by a Castle on its nest of trees. Street elevations are from the 17th to 20th centuries, about half dating from the 18th century alone. They are remarkable for their variety, yet they conform. Very few, above a cluster of shops where Castle Street and The Borough meet, are fakes.

This is a splendid approach. The Grange is glimpsed across fields, through gates. Then the steep, heavily wooded and dark chilly descent swinging round a moat bursts into the light and space of a wide, formal street. The surprise is held to the last: the effect heightened by a forced perspective as the street slowly funnels south to be stopped by a big white house. Reversed, this perspective also plays its part in the architectural drama of an outstanding country town street.

CASTLE STREET, looking south.

2 CASTLE STREET (The Coach and Horses)

A timber, brick and tile building on two main floors, with dormer above.

The Coach and Horses existed in the early 19th century, when it was one of James Knight's houses, but the building as seen from Castle Street today is a recent reconstruction in a pseudo-Tudor style with yet another set of 'Georgian' bow windows — these of early 1962 origin. Apparently the reason for the building's present form is to make a symmetrical block with its neighbour. But, at least as far back as the mid-18th century, there was no such precedent. At that time the building (from outside) was typically 18th century. Before the recent reconstruction the building was still of Georgian character, but with later stucco. Much early history is shared with 10 The Borough (*qv*). No inn named The Coach and Horses is listed in a manuscript of places having accommodated troops in the mid-18th century.

Very near here must have been The Golden Horse Shoe, which was described in 1775 as all that house, formerly two, the greater part of which had been recently built and converted into an inn. The two houses had formerly been occupied by William Mabberly, Richard Smither (*qqv*), and John Bartholomew and were at that time the property of William Dowden (*qv*) of 104 West Street. The Golden Horse Shoe was 'in Castle Street near the Market Place on the west side'. It was probably higher up than number 2, but there is as yet no proof. Other early pubs and inns of Farnham not positively located at the time of writing include The Crooked Billet, The Green Dragon, The Angel, The Horse and Jockey, and The Three Pigeons. All existed in the mid-18th century.

In 1664 the Bailiffs paid over ten pounds to a Mr. Mabberly 'when the Lord Bishop's Buck was spent'. Two years earlier he had supplied 33/8 worth of salmon for the Bishop. A 17th century token is inscribed 'Francis Mabberley, Farnham, Fishmonger'.

3 CASTLE STREET (Alexander's Ltd.)

Once a house of Thomas Falkner's (*qv*), occupied by Ann Falkner and Richard Baker, later William Vine's, then John Povey's, George Ransom's (*qv*) and E. Kimber's — all grocers or greengrocers. In the 1950s a pseudo (though hardly deceptive) Georgian shopfront was added.

4 CASTLE STREET

Two bays on three levels. The building is of timber and brick, has a stuccoed façade, and a tiled roof behind the parapet.

Fenestration: Ground floor, a double shop front; First floor, two 1-3-1 wide-boxed sashes; Second floor, two 1-3-1 wide-boxed half-sash windows. These are glazed, but blind.

See 4A Castle Street.

4A CASTLE STREET (Baverstock and Son)

A three-floor, three-bay building of timber and brick, with a stucco façade and a tiled roof of quadrangular plan and central valley. The façade is finished with moulded eaves cornice and is accentuated horizontally by plain string courses dividing the storeys.

Fenestration: Ground floor, a small shop window centrally placed between doors; First floor, sashed, wide-framed windows three panes wide in bays one and three. The centre one (1-3-1) has four panelled pilasters and cornice decorating the box. The window in bay three is blind; Second floor, as those below, but of three-quarter height. Those in bays one and three are blind.

Door: In bay one, has two finely fluted free-standing columns supporting an unpedimented entablature with carved feather frieze. The rectangular fanlight has curvilinear tracery. A plainer door in bay three gives rear acccss by a side covered passageway.

4 and 4A together are reconstructions of timber-framed houses which still remain, greatly altered, behind the newer façades. A small but elegant staircase, and general treatment of façades and interior details, suggest that the reconstruction took place early in the 19th century. Buildings dating from the Regency which also use the feather in capitals or frieze decoration may be found elsewhere in England.

Particularly good is the pillared front doorcase, which, with its partner (and in relation to number 4 before its simple centrally placed door was removed), was sufficiently emphatic to leave no doubt as to which was the most important one, and yet was carefully related in shape, proportion and character to the others. Secondary doors were also carefully detailed as can be seen in the delicately moulded architrave and cornice remaining. Early timber framing is clearly seen in the passage wall, and is plentiful inside.

The façade of 4A is of subtle design, gaining considerable strength from the interplay of strict horizontals and verticals of varying strength. Partly by necessity (as it is a veneer) and partly by design, this is very much a composition in two dimensions. Yet it retains an elegance with its austerity. Visually the pair is pleasing, but as works of highly moral architecture they are not so praiseworthy, both façades being untrue to what they profess. They are not external expressions of what lies behind them.

Number 4 has two floors. Not three. Upper windows really camouflage a very deep parapet which hides the roof of asymmetrical W-section (the apex being between "windows"). Then there are three blind windows in number 4A. But this house has three genuine floor levels. Inside, the solution of conversion has been equally ingenious.

It is possible to trace the earlier houses here. Considerable remains of the former roof of number 4 exist and many structural timbers remain throughout both houses. From what evidence there is it appears that the buildings had gables overlooking the street, and that by the mid-18th century the houses had been converted to business premises. After the 19th century reconstruction 4A looked almost as it does now, although its shop window was removed in the late nineteen fifties. It was similar to the one immediately above and was, at the time of its removal, intact. Number 4 had unusual semicircular windows—one either side of the door. They had simple radial tracery and the appearance of re-used doorcase fanlights. There is a good barn with basement at the back of the premises.

Henry Nichols, senior (*b* 1773*, *d* 1848) and Elizabeth (*b* 1774*), had two sons, Benjamin (*b* 1806*) and Henry (*b* 1810*, *d* 1874). Both Henrys were wine merchants, and Benjamin Nichols was a solicitor. Henry, junior, was, in addition, a hop planter who occupied land and kilns at Beaver's. There was also more than one Benjamin (*qv*). The elder bought The Bush Hotel. The younger was quite prominent locally. In 1834 he was one of those appointed to the committee of the newly formed Gas Company, which soon built its first tiny holder in East Street. Only four years earlier new oil lamps had been installed in Farnham Streets. Some at least were lit by gas in 1834. An era ended when, in 1953, gas manufacturing in Farnham stopped.

Sarah Nicholls, wife of Benjamin, died in 1795; James, a bachelor, in 1800; Thomas, the son of Thomas and Elizabeth, in 1812; Elizabeth, wife of Henry, in 1856. Henry, junior's, wife was Mary (*b* 1817*).

There were many other Nichols' trading in Farnham. Joseph and Jane were fishmongers in Downing Street. There were the printing Nichols' (*qv*). There was a hairdresser, a postmaster, shoe warehouse man, and professor of drawing—perhaps the inn-sign painter who advertised. Eggar recorded in about 1920 that the late John Nichols' father painted many public-house signs, e.g. The Fox and Hounds and The White Horse. Another writer, recalling the 1830s, remembers 'A rather superior stationer's shop kept by Nichols. Old Nichols served only the tip-top ranks of Farnham society, having a shop woman for others'. See 41 The Borough.

As Henry Nichols, senior, owned the freehold of this house in Castle Street from at least the 1820s, it is possible that he made the conversion at 4 and 4A Castle Street.

5   C A S T L E   S T R E E T   (Stevens and Bolton)

An asymmetrical four-bay house on three floors with slate roof and deep eaves with paired brackets.

Fenestration: Ground floor, in bays one, two and four recessed sashes two panes wide; First floor, four similar, four panes wide; Second floor, four recessed half-sashes, three panes wide.

Door: In bay three, with flanking side lights, all under a depressed three-centred arched fanlight with radial tracery. Plain stone case with mouldings at springing points, topped by a cornice, but no pediment.

Other features: Adjoining the north, a two-bay parapeted block on two floors with a lunette on first floor and side access below. The roof is tiled. To the rear the wing extends west from the north end of the main block.

A house, the façade of which has a character similar to 9 The Borough (*qv*). It probably dates nearer mid than early 19th century and is possibly the result of the industrial activities of John Lidbitter (*qv*) at Factory Yard. He lived here at the time when much of this property is likely to have been rebuilt, leaving parts of an earlier house on the site. Stylistically, at least, it is early Victorian rather than Regency. The Renaissance hold on proportion and disposition of parts is relaxing, but still under control. Despite its width, the doorway retains some elegance. A few years later similar ones were built higher up Castle Street, on the same side, but they became clumsy in proportion, coarse in their detailing, and awkwardly related to the façades of which they form a part.

James Stevens was here as a solicitor later in the 19th century, as were Drs. Ealand and Coad. Edmund Yalden Knowles (*b* 1813*), a doctor born at Thursley, and his wife, Mary (*b* 1815*), probably lived here after Lidbitter had gone.

In the Second World War the Red Cross had a local centre here and during the period immediately after the war when things even remotely Regency in style began to enjoy reappraisal and commercial popularity, The Regency House Restaurant and Club opened. A misnomer? Perhaps.

6 AND 7 CASTLE STREET
(Robert Dyas Ltd.)

Shop premises of three principal bays on two floors with dormers above, built mainly of brick and timber under a tiled roof.

Fenestration: Ground floor, number 6 is a double fronted shop with plate glass windows. Number 7 has a large single shopfront with glazing bars. The door of number 7 divides these shopfronts; First floor, sashed, recessed windows, four panes wide; Second floor, flat-roofed dormer windows with sashes.

Other features: Number 6 shopfront is contained between two wooden three-quarter columns. Number 7 is pilastered. Together they support a simple miniature iron balcony running the total length of their cornices. A diminutive parapet and wood cornice with paired modillions runs the front's length.

This brick front might be dated *c.* 1820, generally, with later shopfronts. Again, this is only a façade, earlier buildings being timber-framed. Then much of this early building was demolished and rebuilt in 1958 behind the façade and under the roof which is still there.

With so many text-book and Christmas Card examples of 18th and early 19th century shopfronts about the town, it is refreshing to find an early one (even if not as elegant as some imitations) which is the real thing, more or less intact. Ninety per cent of the others are fakes. The cornice and first floor windows, as well as details of brickwork, help to date the façade.

As early at 1868 the two messuages formerly here had been thrown into one. Earlier still, it is said, the premises were an inn — named the Fleur de Lys. A mural painting, still visible until recent alterations, in an upper room, gave weight to this report. Tradition has it that the decoration was made by monks in return for lodging when this was an inn.

Allowing tradition to be well founded we can refer to an otherwise unlocated property in Castle Street which, in 1738, was the subject of an indenture between John Mayne and Elizabeth, his wife, and Henry Mayne, of London. Property known as The Fleur de Lys, together with a house adjoining on either side, houses near Church Passage, The White Lion in Castle Street, and hop fields, were sold for £600. The inn was occupied by Widow Piper. The fact that George Mayne lived at what is now 8 Castle Street may, of course, be only a coincidence, but suggests that tradition is probably sound.

The Tily family has long associations with Farnham. They occupied these premises for about a century. Earlier, John Lidbitter (*qv*) was the owner, and Thomas Simmons was here before him. John Tily, patten and brushmaker in 1826, had earlier been a heel-maker.

In 1773 Simon, son of John Tily, died. Thirty-three years later Elizabeth, wife of John, died. James (*b* 1817*) and Mary Tily (*b* in Crondall 1790*) were brush makers. James' wife was also a Mary (*b* 1816*) and their daughter (*b* 1847*). Mary had retired from the craft by 1851 and probably lived with her daughter Rebecca (*b* 1832*) at 7 Castle Street; the rest of the family — James and Mary Tily, with their other children, John (*b* 1840*), James (*b* 1843*), and Lewis (*b* 1845*) — in number 6.

By 1855, still under Mrs. Mary and James Tily, the business had taken on more of its present character, having developed into an ironmongery. James later carried on alone. He died in 1898. Another of his sons, Walter, who inherited, died in 1923. M. and J. Tily had another shop at 117 West Street from which they withdrew in 1933. Earlier they had taken over Hart's ironmongery there. The Tilys had associations also with 27 and 39 Castle Street (*qv*).

Hart's ironmongery had been long-established. Charles (*b* 1801*), a cutler, and Charlotte (*b* 1806*), his wife, were in business by the 1820s. He was probably the son of Joseph Hart (*qv*) of Castle Street and had himself a large family including sons Thomas (*b* 1831*, *d* 1906), Leonard (*b* 1839*), George (*b* 1843*), and Frederick (*b* 1850*). Frederick Hart, ironmonger, died in 1904.

8   CASTLE   STREET

A three-bay, three-floor house with an elevation symmetrical except on the ground floor. It is brick built and painted, roofed with slate and the eaves have paired modillions.

Fenestration: Ground floor, bay three, a plate glass window with decorated architrave; First floor, three plate glass sashes, architraved and pedimented; Second floor, three large paned sashes with architraves and key blocks. Prominence is given to the first floor.

Door: In bay two a door with key block, architrave and bracketed flat hood.

Other features: Two major horizontal subdivisions are made by string courses which underline the windows of both upper floors, the lower course being stopped by double-bracketed corbels and having a dentil-like moulding. A gateway in bay one gives rear access.

1869-70. Pevsner and Nairn estimate *c* 1850. Visually, the ground floor is disconcerting, an otherwise balanced façade having the ground floor openings arranged haphazardly. Earlier Farnham builders would have found a visually more successful solution to the problem of gaining rear access through a façade of classical inspiration. Here the gate, rather than off-centre door, has become the focal point. However, the house has certain pictorial qualities which are enhanced by its immaculate paintwork. It is one of a number built or refaced about 1870, in which similarities are apparent. Westminster Bank (38 and 39 The Borough, *qv*) and, to a lesser degree, in 79 West Street (*qv*), and above fascia-board level in a group of shops at the junction of West Street and The Borough. In all of these there is a distinct loosening of the firm grip still apparent in upper parts of, say, 118 West Street (*qv*) which has the appearance of being earlier.

The house was built for Charles Hazell (*qv*, *b* 1825*, *d* 1894) by Goddards. It replaces an earlier building once occupied by George Mayne, Richard Lunn, then William Meere, which in the 1830s was owned by William Lockerbie (*b* 1791*). To the west of his yard, running behind number 7, were his malthouses, and beyond them his garden. The Lockerbies (*qv*) followed various trades, of which more will be found elsewhere in this book. William, of 8 Castle Street, was a hop planter and maltster, and may also have been the William who was earlier a tailor, draper and fellmonger. In the 1790s William Lockerbie, senior, had a farmyard at 28 East Street (*qv*), which later became one of Sturt's wheelwright shops. The family fades from the Farnham scene, generally, about mid-century, although Elizabeth (*qv*) died here in 1875. She was the sister of other drapers and hop growers, James and John Darvill (*qqv*). The William Lockerbie, of 8 Castle Street, married Sarah Warner (*b* 1791*), a widow, about 1831.

A small plaque on the present building is inscribed 'CH 1869'. There was an entry in the day book for 1870 of Goddards, the builders, recording an appointment for 'meeting Mr. Hazell to discuss the new house in Castle Street'. It is likely that Hazell, a maltster, occupied offices behind the house for some years before he bought from Lockerbie in 1858. Hazell's wife, Harriett (*d* 1915), and daughters, Ada and Mary, continued the family's possession of the house until 1927.

The Hazell's were not a Farnham family, but were prominent in the town for many years. Charles' father, born at Hampstead, had a drapery in The Borough. It appears that his sons were brought up in the trade, John (*b* 1827*) later taking over the shop when William moved to Ivy House (*qv*). Charles had another brother, David (*b* 1810*). His uncle, David Hazell (*b* 1811*), was also one time at the shop.

9   CASTLE   STREET

An almost symmetrical five-bay brick built house on two main floors, with tiled roof and miniature parapet.

Fenestration: Ground floor, four recessed sashes, three panes wide; First floor, five similar; Above, two flat-topped dormers with casements.

Door: In bay three, a pedimented wood case with plain pilasters supporting a broken entablature. This contains a depressed arched fanlight with keyblock and scroll tracery fanlight with lantern. Capitals are of Corinthian proportion, but not detail. A door giving side access is to the north of bay five.

Interior: The central hall contains a pine staircase with turned banisters (two to a tread), and depressed arch with keyblock and pilasters. South-east ground floor room, half panelled. North-east ground floor room, chimney piece with coupled fluted shafts. Front windows have folding shutters except first floor bays three to five.

The façade is one of Farnham's neatest and is more homely than some of the academic ones. The unusual door-case acts as a focal point, capitals having more of an Egyptian than a Corinthian flavour. The subtly depressed arch shape is rare in Farnham doorcases although found frequently in early 19th century fanlights in some other parts of the country. Its shape here may have been decided in part by the ceiling level, as this is a brick refronting. By 1730 a 'great messuage' here had been converted into two dwellings. By 1797 they had been made again into one, and by *c.* 1960 the house was once more divided into two, a new staircase being added to the north end, a modern carved chimney piece to the south-east front room, and extensive reconstruction carried out generally. Farnham Conduit (*qv*) was once in the street hereabout.

In 1730, the house which had once belonged to Edward Peck and then to William Piggott (*qv*), senior, was sold by Anna Child, of Guildford (widow of John), to Thomas Leigh (*qv*), surgeon, for £1,300. The garden had once been planted with hops but had been walled in not long before this transaction. Later the house was John Hollest's (*qv*). He sold to James Moore Molyneux (*qv*) of Loseley Hall in 1797 although Molyneux had occupied the house before he bought. He also owned what is now College Gardens (*qv*). It is recorded that a John Child and John Stevens lent the Borough £200 at 3% in 1673.

The Crump (*qv*) family were glovers and fellmongers and had connections with 4 Downing Street (*qv*). The William Crump, junior (*qv, b* 1775*, *d* 1852) was, among other things, a hop planter. His wife was Mary (*b* 1797*, *d* 1868), his brother, Richard (*qv, d* 1848?), his sisters, Martha and Anne (*b* 1773*, *d* 1851). A Richard Crump owned over 200 acres round Farnham in the 1830s, and an Ann Crump (*b* 1786*) lived in West Street ten years later. William was not a Crump name which had been in fashion just in the 18th and 19th centuries, for William, son of yet another William Crump, was christened in 1696. By mid-century William Crump, of 9 Castle Street, was described as a linen draper. His family included Elizabeth (*b* 1816*), Mary (*b* 1818*), Ann (*b* 1824*), Emma (*b* 1826*), James (*b* 1828*), Louisa (*b* 1830*), Henriette (*b* 1832*), Harriett (*b* 1835*) and Frances (*b* 1837*).

William Crump, senior, died in 1808, and Elizabeth, his wife, in 1833. James Crump lived here later in the 19th century. Crumps had been freeholders in Farnham since the 17th century. The daughter of Joseph Crump died in Farnham in 1662.

Thomas Leigh (*d* 1776) must have been a very rich man for on his death he left properties not only in Farnham in trust for his daughter, Mary (then to his granddaughter, Mary Leigh Willis, *qv*), but also in Southwark, Frimley and Binsted. These included an additional 74 messuages, 20 warehouses, 16 stables, 3 slaughter-houses, 3 dye houses, 4 wharves, 50 curtilages, 10 gardens and 300 acres of farmland; and more. He was possibly the Thomas, son of Thomas Leigh, who was christened in Farnham in 1691. His wife, Mary (*b* 1719*), died in 1799.

A symmetrical five-bay brick built house on two floors with area basements and a slate roof with central well. Bays one to three project. A moulded string divides floors. Front, colour-washed.

Fenestration: Ground floor, four almost flush wide-boxed plate glass sashes; First floor, five windows, similar.

Door: Central, above stone steps, fanlight lantern, under a porch with twin freestanding Corinthian columns and bracketed but unpedimented entablature.

West elevation: Two dormer windows, brick elevation, coved eaves.

Interior: A staircase with oak banisters and rail, deal treads. Strings decorated with carved foliated scrolls. Main banisters fluted Doric; others with twists. The north-west ground floor room is fully panelled as is the first floor south-west room.

Other features: Iron fenders to lower front windows, and railings guarding areas. Wrought iron gate to entrance and railings on low walls flanking the gate.

Still retaining the essentials of the fine house which Thomas Piggott built about 240 years ago, this building has suffered a number of modifications, the sum of which would have incapacitated a lesser house. It has been re-roofed in slate, front eaves have been altered, glazing bars removed, and the façade painted. Inside, the greatest single change is seen immediately. The double-doored entrance hall is divided by a panelled wall which has been moved from its original alignment in order to enlarge the south rooms. As a result these are no longer symmetrical. The spacial organization has been badly upset, and the fitting in of an extra room has added to the cramping. Space around the staircases of Sandford and Willmer Houses, Castle Hill and The Grange (*qqv*) allows display of their magnificence and contributes to the sense of scale within being compatible with that outside; even enhancing it. With grander still staircase here, the lopping off of space around the stairs is most unfortunate. In short, the house has suffered typical 19th century misadventures and a few others too.

The gates are said to have come from Moor Park House. They have recently been re-hung on brick piers. The robustitude of the house and vigour of the cresting rather overpower the small stone pommells.

Thomas Piggott (*qv*), of Kingston, was a London grocer who inherited the site from his father — probably John or Nathaniel Piggott, both of whom were Farnham freeholders in 1719. In 1661 William Piggott was a woollen draper in Farnham who was taxed on four hearths in 1664. He once owned 9 Castle Street (*qv*), and had died by 1730. Thomas Piggott, who built the house, was here by 1730. Mary, wife of Mr. John Piggott, linen draper, died in 1709, another Mary, widow, in 1713.

The house seems to have been built from scratch, and stands on a place which probably saw many fortunes won and lost during Farnham's first boom days, for here were The Corn Rooms — 'several structures or buildings' — which, as the boom was still on, presumably next occupied new quarters elsewhere. Were they stores, a market, or exchange? In the manuscript the name is written with capital initials.

Thomas Piggott's interests were not limited to 10 Castle Street. He inherited two houses in West Street adjoining The George (*qv*) and bought from Elizabeth, widow of Robert Bicknell, and from John Bicknell (*qqv*), land in Long Garden, which linked his Castle Street garden with the West Street back sides, barns and kilns. This largish holding was devoted to the culture of hops and to the income of rents from his tenants. When, by 1763, he sold to John Randall, a cheese-monger, it was all let off.

John Bradley, the father of Bristow (*qqv*), later bought the house, which passed to his son. On Bristow Bradley's bankruptcy in 1814 the house was sold to William Samways Oke — a local surgeon who was an extra-licenciate of the College of Physicians, receiving his doctorate in 1828. A colleague, John Drinkwater (*qv*), helped with the purchase and a few years later the house was occupied by Robert Clarke (*b* 1800*), another doctor. His son, Alfred (*b* 1835*), was trained as a doctor. In the 1720s a Charles Clarke had been established as a Farnham apothecary, although Charles Clarke was born at Poole. A medical partnership in Farnham in the 1820s was Oke and Clarke; in the 1830s, Clarke and Bury. By the 1850s Robert Oke Clarke (*b* 1827*), G.P., was in Castle Street.

14   CASTLE   STREET

In the later part of the 19th century and early 20th century, Mrs. Swayne's Middle Class School was here. See 74 Castle Street.

Typical of many smaller Castle Street houses in its earlier 19th century outward appearance, this was of a group of eleven adjoining, six of which were sold to Joseph Hart (*qv*) in 1809. With the group, in 1809, was an additional dwelling at its south end which had been converted into a coach house and stables — then in the occupation of Bristow Bradley (*qv*). He also occupied Home Garden, a hop ground of three-quarters of an acre lying behind the houses which included 20 Castle Street (*qv*).

20 CASTLE STREET

A three-bay, two main floors house with symmetrical brick elevation and tile roof. A brick string course runs between floors and is broken above the door case. Eaves have paired modillion brackets.

Fenestration: Ground floor, narrow framed recessed sashes four panes wide; First floor, bays one and three, as below. Bay two, similar, three panes wide. All three have outside louvred shutters.

Door: Slender fluted pilasters and triangular pediment contain a semicircular fanlight with curvilinear tracery.

Interior: Symmetry here is only skin deep. Although superficially a formal plan is apparent to the depth of one room from the deceptive façade, this is a house developed from earlier building.

The façade probably dates *c.* 1820 rather than later 18th century. Visible clues to this (but no proof) include the light doorcase with very slim and elegant pilasters, four-pane wide windows, the modillions — here retracted almost to flat brackets — in quite widely-spaced pairs. At 88 West Street they are lighter; and deeper and flatter at 5 Castle Street (*qqv*). By the time 39 and 40 Castle Street (*qqv*) were built the brackets had evolved as something very different from their Grange paired forebears.

Eaves brackets can be seen in many later 19th century houses which hanker after the classical style. They vary between simple rectangular horizontal blocks and ornate vertical brackets of considerable height. Generally, spacing between pairs becomes greater and modillions, or brackets, tend to change their major axis from vertical to horizontal over the two centuries. This is no rule. There are many exceptions.

There are several buildings with modillion treatment closely resembling that at 20 Castle Street. For example, 6 and 7 Castle Street, 88 and 112 West Street, 6 and 7 and 16 The Borough (*qqv*). At the last mentioned pairs and trios alternate.

If at 20 Castle Street a double shopfront has some time been fitted (as appears from outside), the brickwork has been very carefully restored. It is difficult to reconcile Victorian shopfronts with timber studding of the earlier building still visible inside — where the windows would have been.

The irregular original plan has been adapted in later times to suit a different way of life. The house can be divided into two major parts, both timber framed. The south part is larger, and included, as one room, the present entrance hall. There was a similar room above. This part of the house was more highly finished than the rest. Perhaps there were two smaller houses here and it is therefore possible that Joseph Hart (*qv*) converted two of 'the six messuages lying together in Castle Street', which he bought in 1809 for £1,100 from Elizabeth Mayo. Such a pattern of development is not unprecedented in Castle Street, and the house serves well to illustrate what happened many times about the town to bring earlier cottages into line with Georgian standards of design and living.

What is now number 20 was Hart's house. His executors sold it to John McDonald (*qv, b* 1791*, *d* 1860), a gardener, in 1832.

On the death of Harriett (*b* 1801*, *d* 1862), John's widow, instructions were left for all to be sold. Then George McDonald (*qv*), the West Street manufacturer (one of John's sons), bought 20 Castle Street in 1871. He left 19 - 22 on his death in 1903.

The ownership of 20 Castle Street, with its immediate neighbours, malt house and hop ground, can be traced to 1684 when they formed a moiety inherited by Robert and Joan Lusher. By 1775 the property included eleven messuages, and a hop ground known as Home Garden (*qv*).

Elizabeth Mayo was once the wife of John Restall. A maltster of that name died in 1784 and occupied kilns near 41 West Street (*qv*). Another was a hop planter and freeholder forty years later. A Francis Mayo, of Minchinhampton, in Gloucestershire, married an Elizabeth Restall, widow, of Farnham, just two months after the said John Restall of Farnham had died.

A family of Restalls lived in a neighbouring house in the 1840s. Members included Charles (*b* 1799*), a painter, and Charles (*b* 1820*), a tailor in The Borough. Another Charles died in 1825, yet another in 1768. There was also a series of James'.

32 CASTLE STREET

One of the houses of William Birch (*qv*), this was in use during the 1880s as Miss Josephine Reynard's School for Ladies. She moved here in 1879 from 38 Castle Street (*qv*).

33 AND 34 CASTLE STREET
(Alley Between) Lowndes' Buildings

A terrace of brick built cottages on two floors with slate roof.

They presumably take their name from Thomas Lowndes who included the land, if not the cottages too, in his will of 1833. There was certainly a row of buildings on the same site seven years later, and these are referred to as Lowndes' Buildings before mid-century. 34, 35, 36, 37 Castle Street were also owned by Thomas Lowndes. The holding was offered for sale in lots in 1877. George Harding (*b* 1806*) who lived higher up the street mid-century and was described as a landed proprietor, married Elizabeth Lowndes (*b* 1800*), who had a daughter, Elizabeth Lowndes (*b* 1827*), and a grand-daughter, Elizabeth Lowndes (*b* 1849*). He also had a son, George Harding, who was born in Farnham about 1840.

38 CASTLE STREET

An asymmetrical three-bay house on two floors with slate roof.

Fenestration: Ground floor, two wide-boxed almost flush two-pane-wide sashes; First floor, three similar but smaller windows.

Door: In bay three, open rectangular fanlight between engaged Tuscan columns and under unpedimented entablature.

A very neat little house built possibly about 1830 on to a timber framed one. The front is of two builds. The south bay is later than the rest, say 1860. Among clues to this extension having been made is a joint running down the chimney stack. Another is the wide spacing between bays one and two. The robust and slightly austere doorcase has something of William Birch's (*qv*) touch about it and the richly coloured brickwork is worth close examination. A form of pointing has been used, the only reason for which seems to be imitation of fine gauged work such as at Willmer House. Commonplace earlier brickwork had, later, much care lavished on the jointing, the result of which can apparently alter the bond from, say, English to Flemish and at the same time give seemingly finer jointing. The old mortar joints are dyed red, some new ones actually cut into the brick faces, and on top, almost mechanically it appears, an extremely fine but entirely superficial line of mortarlike substance scribed.

There are several other examples of this treatment and variations of it; one opposite at 48 Castle Street (*qv*), and others at Longbridge House, Sandford House, 10 Castle Street—west front (*qqv*). Usually the brickwork is of un-natural colour—a plummish red—like the front of 114 West Street (*qv*). The fashion must have provided a status symbol in the same way as suggested by the window treatment at 112 West Street (*qv*).

Behind the house (and at the back of the west end of Lowndes' Buildings) was an early Non-Conformist chapel, approached by a gateway alongside the (then) unextended house. The small L-shaped chapel disappeared in mid-19th century, presumably at about the time of extending the house. The chapel was there in 1839.

In 1879 Miss Reynard's School moved from this address to 32 Castle Street (*qv*) in order to increase accommodation, at which time the house belonged to Ralph Ainsley who sold in 1887. His father, Thomas (*qv*), appointed F. C. Birch (*qv*) a Trustee.

39, 40, 41 CASTLE STREET

Three attached, two-bay, three-floor, grey-brick-fronted houses under slate roofs, deeply eaved with widely spaced paired brackets.

Fenestration: Ground floor, a square large-paned sash; First floor, windows have balconies with cast-iron fenders; Second floor, windows are underlined with a string. All front windows are large-paned, recessed sashes with architraves and key blocks.

Other features: Outer corners of 39 and 40 and all three doorways are coigned.

William Birch built Zingari Terrace (*qv*). He married Henrietta (*b* 1802*) and in his day was the leading local builder. Zingari was finished by February, 1862. F. C. Birch (*qv*, *b* 1833*) built 41 Castle Street in 1866, 39 and 40 being finished a little earlier. An engraving dated July 13th, 1866, shows all in a finished state. Perhaps F. C. Birch, the son of

William, did not actually design the Castle Street houses, but these two examples show clearly how rapid, in terms of the Georgian, the aesthetic standards were changing at that time; how the dying generation of builders (William Birch died in 1863) took with it most of that sensibility passed on by the builders of 18th century Farnham. Everything which had just started slipping at Zingari, has, at this group in Castle Street, slipped. Detail is coarse. Materials are clumsily dispensed. In their ground floor windows is demonstrated the demise of a Georgian (1-3-1) success. Despite all this, they are not without character and judgement on such styles has softened noticeably in the past few years.

All three were built for Thomas Ainsley (*qv*), the Bishop's steward. He bought the then cottages in 1857 and died just before completion of the rebuilding of 41. Its front was recently painted white.

45 CASTLE STREET

A symmetrical five-bay brick house on two main floors under a gabled tile roof with moulded wood eaves cornice. Brick strings run above both main ranges of windows.

Fenestration: Ground floor, four three-pane-wide sashes with wide moulded frames, almost flush; First floor, five similar; Above, three leaded dormer casements with tiled hoods and moulded eaves.

Door: In bay three; wood pilasters with entablature broken over, supporting a triangular pediment which breaks the lower string.

Interior: Ground floor north-west room, full pine flat-panelled and chimney piece with inverted shell and foliated scroll flanked by arched recesses. The hall has a segmental arch with keyblock. Main windows have folding shutters.

Other features: In front of the house are spearheaded iron railings.

A façade, much as one might expect to have been built in Farnham about the 1720s, but one unaffected by the London Fire Acts fashions which had by that time reached Farnham; at least as far as eaves treatment was concerned. Here it is of the earlier unparapeted type, unlike Longbridge House of 1718. Window frames are still of the wide architraved type, in common with Longbridge and Willmer House of 1719 and flush with the outer wall surface. It is, in any case, a reconstruction, as much behind the façade (particularly upstairs) is timber framed. The house had been extended eastwards and in 1957 lower south rooms were thrown into one. The doorcase is of character popular a hundred years after the here-supposed date of the façade. Single course vertical headers over upper windows are unusual. Pilasters to the arch which spans the entrance hall appear to have been removed.

Sarah Williams (*qv*) owned this house and 46 Castle Street in 1839 when they were in the occupation of Mary Miller. At this time a George and Elizabeth Miller (*bb* 1771**) were living at Castle Hill (House), just above. The Williams family sold in 1867 to James Burningham. The house was offered for sale in 1905 with number 46 and (as then) 5 and 6 Park Row, and again in 1934. See 122 West Street.

47 CASTLE STREET

An asymmetrical two-bay brick and timber built house on two main floors with attic above and tiled roof.

Fenestration: Ground floor, in bay two, a 1-3-1 sash, recessed; First floor, two similar windows; Above, a flat topped dormer window with sash.

Door: In bay one with bracketed flat hood.

A timber framed house of considerable age, apparently part reconstructed at about the turn of the 18th century. It is convenient to consider this and number 48 (*qv*) as one, for they were both owned by a man named Lowe who separated them in 1746. A pump then stood in the street. Number 47 went to a carpenter named Samuel Hare and 48 to John Knight. Both houses were owned successively by George Eldridge and John Hunt, maltster, before Lowe bought them. In 1746 the house adjoining the north side was Robert Gardiner's, number 47 having been devised to his daughter, Joan Hunt, by George Wisdom in his will of 1717. Outwardly, both appear to have been altered at about the same time. The similarity of fronts only suggests that one person was responsible, but the fact that they were next held by one person—John Newell—only between 1810 and 1812 may be of some significance in dating the reconstruction. He disposed of them separately and could have bought them as a speculation.

48 CASTLE STREET

An asymmetrical two-bay house on two main floors with attic above and tiled roof.

Fenestration: Ground floor, bay one, a 1-3-1 window recessed; First floor, bay one, similar window.

Door: In bay two, brackets supporting an open pediment hood.

A much altered house with timber framing, closely associated with number 47 (*qv*). Front brickwork has features in common with some other Farnham houses, for example 38 Castle Street (*qv*) opposite. See 47 Castle Street.

50-52 CASTLE STREET (The Nelson Arms)

Asymmetrical, on two main floors, and built mostly of brick, with a tiled roof.

Fenestration: Ground floor, front, leaded casements; First floor (Castle Street) is lit by three-pane-wide recessed sashes. Simple wood casements open to Park Row.

A public house has been here for over two hundred and twenty years, but (as one might presume) not always under this name. Early in the 18th century it was The Hand and Pen, occupied by Francis Parker, and owned by John Tanner, of Haslemere. In 1739 the name changed to The Baker's Arms. This name was used well into the 19th century. Whether the first name was originally from an inn sign is a matter for speculation as The Pen and Hand sign was used by scriveners.

Originally only the north part was a pub. By degrees it has spread to occupy two former dwellings and to extend round the corner of Park Row (until about 1840 known as Bear Lane). One of the houses on this site was built between 1729 and 1738 by a carpenter named Robert Knight, who bought The Hand and Pen in 1729 and also owned The Bull and Butcher (69 Castle Street, *qv*) by 1739. In that year 50 Castle Street passed to the Bunch family (*qv*) who held it until 1805. There was once a hop kiln to the rear and the house adjoining which was sold with the pub was described in 1739 as divided into five tenements.

1926 saw general restoration. 'Tudor' windows are the result of 'modernisation' which was completed in more recent years.

53-60 CASTLE STREET (Windsor Almshouses)

A symmetrical terrace of eight houses on two floors built of brick, timber and tile. A continuous roof ridge runs parallel with the street. From this five gables project west; four have carved bargeboards and finials. The centre one is stepped and displays a carved tablet of dedication over the gate it contains. This gives rear access.

Fenestration: Ground floor, eight wooden casements, in pairs (headed with hood moulds) under four gables; First floor, four wooden casements, centred, one to each of four gables.

Doors: Eight, each with bargeboarded and finialled hood echoing the shape of main gables.

The terrace was built by Andrew Windsor in 1619 as almshouses for eight poor, honest, old, impotent people. The picturesque terrace gives a touch of contrast to its more formal and dignified streetmates, as does its scale and architectural style. The display of gables is a miniature equivalent in brick of the more familiar displays about the country at large of its timber framed contemporaries. The building is of additional interest for having earlier, positively dated, brickwork.

Andrew Windsor lived at Bentley. He was one of at least four Andrews and his memorial tablet in St. Andrew's Church depicts him kneeling in prayer. The inscription reads, 'The table was set up at the cost of George Windsor, Esq., that the almshouses should not be lost. Near this place lies buried the body of Andrew Windsor Esquire, Grandchild to ye Lord Andrew Windsor, and founder of the almshouse in Castle-street, in this town, who departed out of this life in September, 1620'.

George and his wife Margaret (*m* 1615, *d* 1631) lived at Bury Court, Bentley, which appears to have been the family home. He left 6½ acres of land to the poor. George Windsor, gent, died in 1641. 'Ye Lord' was probably Sir Andrew Windsor (it is said born 1467, made a baron in 1529, died in 1543). A Mr. Windsor still lived at 'Berry Court' in 1666, an Andrew Windsor having been leading inhabitant of Bentley in 1621, according to records printed in Owen's 'Bentley' (1909).

Andrew, the Farnham benefactor, also endowed the almshouse inmates to the extent of 1s. 8d. each week from the income from land at Buscott. But thirteen months after his death his brother, Peter, refused to pay. Two inquisitions held (1624 and 1625) found him to be at fault. The bailiffs' accounts for 1624 record 'Item, paid for rushes for the towne hall, and for fier fuell when the Earl of Holderness and the Lord Bishop of Winton, with other commissioners for charitable uses were in Farnham, 16d'.

In the meantime the bailiffs had to find eight shillings in 1623 '. . . left unpaid of 5 Almshouses', and they paid rents in 1619 as well. All the same, they thought it worth while spending another 7s. 10d. in order to give Mr. (Peter?) Windsor a sugar loaf and pottle of sack. Further benefactions helped to strengthen the Trust's funds, including a small gift from Daniel Bristow in 1819, and a legacy of Thomas Beddus Mill's (*qqv*).

John Byworth (*qv*) had also endowed four almshouses near the church gate. He died in 1623 and the houses were by then in being. In 1597 'Old Alice Searle of the Almse House' died. Which almshouse it is not possible to say. Other alms-houses were established later by Sampson, McDonald and Trimmer (*qqv*).

61   CASTLE   STREET

A symmetrical brick built house of three bays on ground floor and of five bays above, on two floors with tile roof. An interrupted painted string course at first-floor window head level, and a continuous one below the plain parapet. Bay three projects.

Fenestration: Ground floor, two four-pane-wide recessed sashes contained within brick arches with five centred heads; First floor, four three-pane-wide recessed sashes, and in bay three a semicircular leaded window with radial tracery and painted key and springer blocks.

Door: Pedimented case with semicircular architraved fanlight and radial tracery contained within fluted Doric quarter columns, which in turn are contained by panelled Doric pilasters which support the pediment and rosetted frieze.

A façade with a difference. Informed opinion has dated it from 1720 up to about 1775. It might even be later. Stylis-tically it bears a relationship with 90 West Street, 29 East Street and 2 Downing Street (*qqv*). It seems to fit, in this context (but not chronologically) between the first two. With the first it has much in common in the upper half. With 29 East Street it shares a projecting bay to contain a doorcase and window with arched head; also four-pane-wide ground floor windows. Then there are the eliptical recesses, or arcades, to contain these. Shapes as these were popular in the early 19th century, and on this façade they prophesy the breakaway, which was to come, from the strictly classical formula; a step nearer 5 Castle Street and away from 41 West Street (*qqv*).

90 West Street was 'newly built' in 1810. 29 East Street

was not built before 1840. 1790 might be nearer the mark for 61 Castle Street.

The doorcase is particularly interesting as it is of a type not to be found elsewhere in the town. It has a lot of individuality. An interior wall can be seen overlapping the south corner of the fanlight. It indicates a small but unexpected degree of internal asymmetry, probably the result of retaining a sturdy earlier wall when rebuilding. It is thicker than its counterpart.

There are some Victorian additions at the back. It is likely that when built all ground floor windows were four panes and upper ones three panes wide.

Like much of the property on this side of the street below Windsor's Almshouses, it was, early in the 19th century, part of James Stevens' estate. His hopfields were between East Street and the Park, and the property included an old cottage in Bear Lane, lately altered. About mid-19th century, the large brick and tile twin-ridged hop building, now a store, was built on Stevens' frontage to Park Row. It did not appear on a plan of the later 1830s.

The Stevens family had too many members in Farnham during the 18th-19th century to be listed in full. They included Rev. James Stevens (*d* 1843), Alfred (*d* 1855), Rev. W. H. Stevens (*d* 1855), James (*d* 1850), Elizabeth, neé Watts, wife of James (*d* 1845), Louisa (*b* 1816*). One Elizabeth was born in 1781*, another in 1786*.

About mid-century Alfred Stevens (*b* 1817*), his wife Elizabeth (*b* 1816*) and children Elizabeth Amelia (*b* 1845*), James (*b* 1848*) and Alfred Henry (*b* 1849*) were living in Castle Street.

62 CASTLE STREET

A symmetrical five-bay brick built house on two main floors, with attics, under a tile roof. The parapet has five panels relating to windows below, but no cornice or string courses. Front in heading bond.

Fenestration: Ground floor, four three-pane-wide recessed sashes; First floor, five similar.

Door: An open pediment over a semicircular fanlight with scrolled tracery and keyblock. Fluted Doric pilasters support a broken triglyph frieze and dentils.

A good example, compared with, say, 45 Castle Street, of the influence of London Fire Acts on the Farnham house. Here, there is not known to have been any law preventing the use of heavy wooden eaves or wide-box frames flush with the outer wall surface. It is most unlikely that such a law existed. In London, from the first decade of the 18th century, one did. And here is a Farnham house which conforms. There are, of course, many other examples in the town. But as this is an isolated building, the cubic effect is well seen; also the slenderness of windows, those of the ground floor being of unusual proportion for Farnham. The house is depicted in a painting by G. Shepherd, dated 1818, in the collection of the Department of Western Art of the Ashmolean Museum.

Parapets brought visual problems as well as solving practical ones imposed by the Acts. What was to be done with the five or six feet of brickwork left above top window heads? Here we have one answer — to relieve the emptiness by recessing brickwork to make blind panels which continue the pattern established by windows below. Another answer was to add a cornice, not of wood. It is said that the one at Sandford House (*qv*) is of plaster. Being concerned with fashion rather than Fire Acts, some Farnham builders still used wood cornices above the windows, on parapets. As if to make quite sure, some used cornices, parapets, and panels, for example at 121 West Street (*qv*).

The detachment of 62 Castle Street is also helpful in assessing the visual quality of heading bond which it uses. It can be seen detached, yet is easily compared with number 61. The textural difference can be easily seen.

This was a property of the Stevens' (*qv*) family and was probably occupied during part of the first half of the 19th century by Elizabeth Stevens, a spinster, and her niece Louisa (*b* 1812*).

69 CASTLE STREET (Ransom's)

Symmetrical two-bay shop premises on two floors with a flat-topped dormer above. The tiled mansard roof has a decorative ridge and the eaves are bracketed in trios.

Fenestration: Ground floor, a double shopfront with central door; First floor, two 1-3-1 sashes, recessed; Above, a sashed dormer.

The building appears to have been fairly recently re-fronted, as the return faces of coigns on the north side can be seen protruding from behind the brick front. The roof has been altered and shopfront fitted. The façade was earlier stuccoed and the first floor had three windows with heads and keystones in relief.

Here was once a pub, The Bull and Butcher, which is mentioned in an agreement of 1760 concerning Sarah Knight and her brother Robert Knight — the children of Mary and

Robert Knight, carpenter. Robert Knight senior bought The Hand and Pen, now The Nelson Arms (*qv*) in 1729. Mary Knight, widow, sold a house in Castle Street, abutting the north side of The Rose and Crown (*qv*), to Robert Knight, carpenter, in 1725, and Robert Knight owned The Bull and Butcher by 1739. So it looks as though The Bull and Butcher was one of Robert Knight's enterprises, he opening the pub here between 1725 and 1739.

The property is mentioned in the will of James Knight, brewer, of 1868, being offered for sale by Farnham Brewery in 1891 when it was still a going concern. Its amenities included a skittle alley and market room. When for sale again ten years later it was 'until recently carried on as a fully licensed public house recently known as The Bull and Butcher', and then owned by R. S. Nicol who probably bought it a year before.

George Murrell (*b* 1781*) was for many years landlord, from at least the 1820s, then, by mid-century George Lee (*b* 1817*).

70 CASTLE STREET

A five-bay symmetrical brick built house on two floors, with tile roof behind a shallow parapet — a string below.

Fenestration: Ground floor, four three-pane-wide sashes in wide flush boxes; First floor, five similar.

Door: Semicircular fanlight with keyblock and rococo-gothick tracery, under an open pediment supported by scrolled brackets and panelled pilasters.

Built by George West the elder about 1775; certainly not more than two years earlier although perhaps a little later. He bought from Dr. Thomas Leigh (*qv*) three houses (acquired by him in 1721 from Richard Coldham) forming an inn then called The White Hart. The northern two houses were demolished and West rebuilt them to form 70 Castle Street. On the site of the third building now stands number 71 (*qv*). The small house adjoining the north end of 70 was constructed about 1930, where a gateway and side entrance had been until then.

This house and its neighbour make an interesting pair as they are post-1772, retain wide flush sash boxes and have a style of doorcase once popular in Farnham. Although a number of variants on this pattern have gone, a few others remain. Number 70 adds to the 18th century group fronted in heading bond — supposedly rare but in fact not uncommon in Farnham, for example at Castle Hill, Old Roof, 62 Castle Street, 104 and 121 West Street (*qqv*).

Sometimes, supposed headers are not bricks but cleverly set tiles. These deceive the eye and evaded Brick Tax. Precisely moulded and hung tiles are 'pointed' by their joints being filled with mortar. The upper part of a Middle Church Lane house appears to have these special tiles. There may be others still deceiving.

It has not been found possible to say when The White Hart became an inn. Presumably it was after The White Hart, later The Hart and then The Lion and Lamb (*qv*) changed its name. But even before number 70 Castle Street had been named The White Hart it was an inn — then named The Rose and Crown. In 1638 Christopher Newland was charged four shillings 'for standing and hanging of his figure post for the Rose and Crowne'. Probably, then, his inn sign stood in the street. The name was still current in 1721 but had changed by 1725.

Probably most notable of those who have lived here was the family of George West the elder (1734-1823). He is said to have established a Farnham Friendly Society and to have had three sons, one of whom, John (*b* 1778, *d* 1845) was for three years a minister in Canada. George West the younger (*b* 1768, *d* 1831) was the youngest son (by his father's first wife). He was born at Farnham and became Rector of Stoke (1795), Perpetual Curate of Seale (1823) and Chaplain to the Earl of Oxford. He married Sarah, the only daughter of Francis Crueze of Woodbridge House in 1797, Crueze being High Sheriff of Surrey (1788). George West was remembered as being 'the poor man's friend' and author of 'Observations of Friendly Societies', according to an obituary notice in The Gentleman's Magazine. The Rev. George West was listed under 'Gentry living in Farnham' in 1796 and as resident of Weybourne House (*qv*) in 1826. William West (*qv*), the remaining son, is said to have inherited his father's property and hop-growing business. He owned property in West Street in 1839.

A George West married Mary Novell in 1766 and Ann West married Charles Pink (*qv*) of Winchester in 1757. George West senior was a carrier and hop planter. Robert Trimmer (*qv*) was, apart from being a brewer, maltster, hop planter and brandy merchant, a carrier too. A firm—West and Trimmer—advertised as carriers, their waggons leaving their warehouses Mondays and Thursdays at 10 a.m. for The George Inn, Snowhill, London, during the 1790s. Loads were taken at 1/6 per hundredweight.

At about 70 Castle Street in the mid-19th century lived William West (*b* 1780*, *d* 1855?), a farmer then employing six men, also his wife Maria, daughter Caroline (*b* 1820*) and son Charles. Caroline West (who probably inherited her father's estate) married L. Austwick (*c* 1858) and Lancelot Austwick (*b* 1819*, *d* 1910) was living at this address in the 1890s. He advertised earlier as a wine merchant. See 71 Castle Street.

71 CASTLE STREET

A two-bay brick built and tiled house on two floors with shallow parapet — a string below.

Fenestration: Ground floor, in bay two, a four-pane-wide flush wide-boxed sash; First floor, two similar, three panes wide.

Door: Open pediment, containing a semicircular fan-light with radial and festoon tracery, supported by plain scrolled brackets and panelled pilasters.

Built by George West the elder after 1772 where formerly part of The White Hart stood (see 70 Castle Street).

Although the house is similar to its neighbour, the ground floor window, being four panes wide, is unexpected. It might be later. The house, which retains some long bricks, has later builds behind.

72 CASTLE STREET (Westminster Wine Co.)

A symmetrical brick and timber built shop of two bays on three floors with slate roof. Eaves are supported by paired brackets. The front is rendered.

Fenestration: Ground floor, a multipaned projecting shopfront; First floor, two four-pane-wide unrecessed sashes with wide boxes; Second floor, two similar.

Doors: Flanking shopfront, under a common fascia and cornice.

A timber-framed house appearing to have had two major frontal transformations — one when the timber façade was bricked over and jetty filled in; the other by piecemeal altera-tions to shopfront, windows and by rendering, etc. Inside there is a good Adamesque chimney piece with central plaque, allegorical scenes with figures and festoons, all painted very dark brown.

Here was once part of The Bell and Crown, earlier The Lamb and Flag, and once The Lamb (see 73 Castle Street). The premises served for many years as Charles Smith's saddler's shop, until his son George Smith moved to South Street in 1911. Seventy years before, Henry Smith (*b* 1803*) was harness maker in The Borough. His wife was Caroline (*b* 1806*). Their several children included Henry (*b* 1833*), William (*b* 1834*) and Thomas (*b* 1840*).

Early in the 19th century this house was owned by the Wilkins family and premises to the rear were let to John Lidbitter (*qv*). One John Lidbitter died in 1843, and was presumably the same (Leadbeater) who, about 1830, was described as chief draper in Castle Street, put out of business by Beal's who opened up a more fashionable store in West Street. Lidbitter expanded to Factory Yard (*qv*) in 1831. The family held property in Castle Street including 5, 6 and 7. John Lidbitter, haircloth factor, born in 1782*, was there in 1841. John Stevens from Reading is believed to have started a cloth factory here about 1825. Lidbitter took it over. In 1839 a James Stevens (*qv*), weaver (*b* 1782*), lived in East Street.

Jane and Louisa Stratford (*qqv*), schoolmistresses, once lived at 72 Castle Street and had their boarding school here. William Patrick, John Cook and Abraham Briggs had also been occupants, Knights selling to the Smiths in 1888, at which time the property was described as a brick built and tiled house and shop.

73 CASTLE STREET (Now demolished)

Here was The Bell and Crown Inn. Until earlier in the 20th century this was a house of 18th century elevation, stuccoed, and of three floors height. To the middle floor had been added two bay windows. The low pitch roof was slated .

In 1745 The Lamb was here. It belonged to William and Charity Nash. Their daughter Charity married and in 1786, with her husband, Daniel Newland, currier, sold to John Wilkins, currier, several properties in Castle Street, for £800. Newland was son of Daniel Newland, senior, currier, and Hester Searle of Farnham. By mid 18th century the inn had expanded to embrace what is now number 72 (*qv*) and the name had been changed to The Lamb and Flag. With it went a currier's shop stables and hopkiln. There is another Lamb (*qv*) in Abbey Street. During Wilkins' occupation the name changed again, and by 1799 was known as The Bell and Crown. By 1845 the houses seem to have been sold separately, 73 passing to Charles May, currier, and from him to Florence Knight in 1889.

In the street outside these houses was once The Butchers' Shambles, which were probably demolished about the middle of the 18th century.

William Wilkins, currier, was born in 1791*, his wife Martha in 1796*. Their daughter Caroline married William Harding (*qv*), surveyor. John Wilkins came to Farnham from

Warminster. In 1764 John Wilkins, of Rotherwick, was married in Farnham to Sarah Collyer.

Farnham has produced few painters (in the past) likely to be long remembered. The Elmers (*qv*) have secured a firm place, but Farnham seems to know nothing of the Smith family. This may not be surprising. It is most unlikely that they ever painted the Farnham scene as they worked in the Cotswolds. It was only through the chance finding of one of their paintings in a Gloucester shop that the connection was made. Francis Dallett, Librarian to the Athenaeum of Philadelphia, is an authority on their work. He writes that Daniel Smith was born in Farnham in 1791, the youngest of nine children of Thomas Smith and Charity, daughter of Daniel and Charity Newland. Thomas Smith (*d* 1810), he adds, was a patent saddler, who moved to Bond Street. About 1807 Daniel Smith entered William Burgess' drawing academy at Chelsea. He exhibited at the R.A. in 1813, had married in 1811 Elizabeth Gardner, and with her and their son Alfred (*b* 1812) moved to Gloucestershire where he free-lanced and taught, producing in particular portraits and landscapes. He died in Cheltenham in 1839. Alfred Newland Smith was, by then, also an established painter and after a successful local career died also at Cheltenham in 1876. His brother, Edward (*b* 1820, *d* 1893), was also a painter like two of Alfred's sons. Examples of the Smiths' work can be seen at Stroud Museum. Others are in the collection of Mr. Dallett who wrote an illustrated booklet on 'The Cotswold Artists Smith', published in Philadelphia, 1959.

7 4   C A S T L E   S T R E E T   (Eggar & Co.)

A five-bay brick house on two main floors with panelled parapet and half-hipped mansard tile roof.

Fenestration: Ground floor, in bay two a five-pane-wide shop window with pilastered case and an entablature. In bays four and five recessed three-pane-wide sashes; First floor, five similar; Above, behind parapet, two flat-topped sashed dormer windows.

Door: In bay three, Doric pilastered case with triglyph frieze and open triangular pediment containing semicircular architraved fanlight with keyblock and radial tracery. Ribbon-work decorates the entablature soffits. In bay one a secondary door with arched brick head.

A good façade with doorcase of robust palladian character such as one might expect to find in a mid-18th century joiner's copybook. In fact details of the entablature adhere very closely to an example in Batty Langley's 'Builder's

Jewell'. Although like the case of 88 West Street (qv) it is crisper and more sturdy. It shares qualities to be found also at Guildford House (qv) in its back doorcase.

The 18th century building was on to remains of an earlier house. Its timber framing and some other parts are to the back south-east corner and rear of the house. Recent alterations include blocking the main door. The secondary one is now the entrance. It was probably in the late 19th century that the south dormer window was added. There was a shop here by the 1830s.

This was almost certainly the house of Andrew Bristow (qv) in the later 18th century. He could have rebuilt it. By 1839 it belonged to William Wilkins (b 1791*) who was a currier like others of his family (qv) who owned property hereabout. Mrs. William Swayne advertised her Middle Class School at 14 Castle Street (qv) in 1891 and is said to have transferred her establishment later to 74 Castle Street. From there it developed into Farnham Girls' Grammar School (see 25 West Street). Mrs. Emma Swayne sold 74 Castle Street to Watney's brewery in 1909. She probably opened after John Baker left the premises for he as leather cutter and currier, carried on the connection with Wilkins' trade till late in the 19th century and advertised from this address in 1878. Eggars have been here since early in the 20th century.

The Bristows of Farnham were many and they were diverse in their occupations, ranging from 'gentlemen' to glovers, bankers to brewers, barbers, drapers, and wool-merchants. They could also boast a proprietorship of Blissi-mere Hall hopmarket at Wey Hill and provide an innkeeper. Many early Bristows came from around the town. One, John Bristow of Debnall (Dippenhall), left instructions in 1485 to be buried at St. Andrew's. He left one penny to the Mother Church of Winchester and residue to Katherine, his wife. Richard and John of Frensham were woollen merchants a century later. None was named, though, in the Hearth Tax Returns for Farnham in the 1660s.

Andrews, Thomases and Daniels (qqv) figured promi-nently in Farnham in the 18th century. One Andrew, son of Andrew, glover, of Alton, was apprenticed to Roger Snitwell, a frequently encountered Farnham periwigmaker, in 1714, while Samuel, son of Samuel, of Alton, clothier, was appren-ticed to a Farnham barber — Andrew Bristow — in 1724. Andrew Bristow, gent, died in 1782. An Andrew died in 1797 while one Elizabeth Bristow, wife of Andrew, died in 1753; another, also wife of Andrew, in 1808. Thomas Bristow (d 1697) was probably the husband of Margaret (d 1693) and father of Mary and Elizabeth, christened 1689 and 1691. It is recorded in the Parish Register that a stranger died in Thomas Bristow's house in 1577. Thomas and his wife Julia owned a messuage, garden and croft in Farnham in the mid 16th century and Thomas Bristow was a Farnham innkeeper at about that time. There were also several Daniels. Daniel Bristow, senior, died in 1800, two years after another bought the Spinning Wheel (*qv*). He was probably the banker-draper.

75 CASTLE STREET

A five-bay bank building on two full floors of basically symmetrical façade. It is brick built with decorative features and coping of stone.

The building was opened by Lloyds Bank Ltd. (*qv*) in November 1931. Their architects were Guy Dawber and Wilson. It was built by Mardon & Ball.

To be a poshish pastiche standing between two thorough-bred (even if not grandiose) neighbours must be a little style-cramping. The building is typically bankers' neo-georgian of the 1930s: secure, deeprooted, correct. It has material quality and is very refined in comparison with most Victorian counterparts, for example Westminster Bank (38 and 39 The Borough, *qv*) and Norman Shaw's bank building which previously stood here, in Castle Street, on this same site. It is rather for reasons of indirect association with Shaw's bank and, in turn, with Farnham hop-growing days, than for its architectural distinction that this account is given.

Shaw's building was John and James Knight's Farnham Bank. Some think it Farnham's most outrageous 19th century building. Shaw certainly let himself go. He produced a four-floor Elizabethan giant two and a half times the height of its neighbours. Timber framed, jettied, bargeboarded and tile hung, it stood for half a century a dominant in lower Castle Street, replacing what appears to have been a timber framed house with a miniature parapeted and stuccoed Georgian front. The flavour of its 'Elizabethan' replacement can still be savoured from the two brick chimney stacks which have been rebuilt — one on the Town Hall Buildings, the other at the Bush Hotel (*qqv*). Lloyds were reluctant to demolish such 'a landmark in our architectural history'.

In 1886 Knight's were taken over by Capital and Counties, and then they amalgamated with Lloyds in 1918. Knights themselves had bought out James Stevens' Bank established by 1806. Knights sold for £9,000, Capital and Counties giving one of the family management at £400 per annum.

These two families — Knight and Stevens — have their histories intimately woven into the growth and prosperity of Farnham. Between them they have owned half the most important houses and good hop land of Farnham, as well as maltings, breweries, and other businesses. James Knight (the elder), banker and brewer, died in 1868. John Knight, solicitor, of Vernon House (*qv*), had two sons — James (the younger) and John — who ran the banking business until Capital and Counties took over. In 1891 James Knight was named as branch manager.

THE FREEMASONS' HALL,

A six-bay building on two floors, of symmetrical façade except for bay one, which contains only the main door. A pediment with mouldings and dentils in brick tops a shallow projecting bay containing the three centre windows of both floors. The hall is brick built under a tiled roof, and at the back is in heading bond. Behind is a massive brick chimney stack and brick of a different quality.

Fenestration: Ground floor, recessed sashes three panes wide; First floor, five similar with round heads and radial glazing bars.

Door: Pilastered with triangular pediment. There is another door in the north end.

A biggish building of forthright character which has remained almost unchanged in appearance for at least 140 years. Dating probably from the third quarter of the 18th century, it might have been converted with subscriptions raised in 1813 to start a National School. The property was probably leased from the Bishop for 900 years from 1820. It was certainly known as The School two years later. A new National School (*qv*) was built next to St. Andrew's Church in 1860.

In 1877 a charity was created. It was known as 'The Working Men's, or Castle Street, Institute', although the premises had already become known as the Working Men's Institute well before that date. The hall was also used for church meetings. Trustees offered the property for sale in 1909 and recommended it eminently suitable for a museum or motor garage. However, the Education Committee continued to use it until *c.* 1950, when it became the Freemasons' Hall.

Among the teachers employed at the school here were George Phillip Hamilton (*b* 1791*), Edwin Buddick Brice, Miss Susannah Shephard and a Miss Stratford (*qv*). See Castle Hill. See also 80 East Street.

A brick built house mainly on two floors, finished with a parapet. The plan is not symmetrical.

All fronts are bound by a deep wooden cornice supported by paired consoles. These are scrolled with foliated decoration. Four brick pilasters give vertical emphasis to main fronts. Their protrusion from the façade is responded to in the cornice. Brick panels — recessed and in relief — on the parapet relate directly to these pilasters and the windows which the latter contain. North, east and west fronts are bound also by two plain brick string courses — the upper one at first floor sill level, the other a course above lower window-heads.

Fenestration: Wide-framed, almost flush, three-pane-wide sashes, with the exception of one, lower west front, and some two-pane-wide replacements. Above the main doors, windows have semicircular heads, the circumferences of which are broken. These two sash boxes are finished with a central shell ornament immediately below the key bricks. Sills on the east front do not project.

Doors: East front, of wood. Corinthian pilasters supporting an eliptical pediment. Entablature mouldings break at the centre, sweeping upwards into foliated scrolls — inward-turning to embrace a high-relief garland of interlaced foliage and a festoon. The architrave is enriched by leafy carving; West front, a flat wooden hood supported by two scrolled and foliated console brackets; South front, flat hood supported by scrolled and foliated brackets.

Other elevations: North, symmetrical, of three bays; South, very different from the others. It has three floors, is asymmetrical, has two- and three-light casement windows with wooden frames mostly leaded, in four principal bays. String courses return from main fronts to end abruptly. Receding some feet the east end of the front contains a blind upper window, fragments of other string courses and of brick panelling (see illustration).

Interior: Both main doors are connected by an entrance hall. From this (east end, south side) lead the main stairs. The hall, spanned by an eliptical arch, is raised-panelled throughout in stripped pine, doors leading off having bolection architraves. The arch is supported by pilasters with foliated caps. Spandrels have carving similar in character to the east door garland. Soffits are panelled and keyblocks bear a mask.

Stairs are of oak with panelled wainscot and turned, fluted banisters are two to a tread. Strings have scrolled foliated brackets, to the lower contours of which the under-side of treads conform.

Painted murals decorate the stairwell. Three main allegorical scenes are contained within 'marble' Corinthian pilasters, festoons and a cartouche. Subjects include (1) Venus, Cupid and Apollo; (2) Vulcan and Mars, forging the arrows of Love; (3) Ceiling, an oval frame, cloudscape with goddesses and cupids.

All main rooms are panelled or part-panelled and have folding window shutters. The landing is also panelled, and from it a second staircase leads to the three-floor south side.

Other features: The grounds are walled and include some decorative ironwork. The east gate wrought iron is particularly notable. It is set between panelled piers of rubbed-brick. Outbuildings include cottages (converted from hop buildings) and a barn.

The greater part of this house was built by Mr. Forbes about 1710, although part is earlier and part is later. The Grange and its lands were once part of the bishop's property, and references to a building known as The Grange have been traced by others to the early 13th century. It is not claimed here that any dwelling house stood on this site at that time. There was, however, a malthouse and other offices when in the 1590s '. . . the new Grange with farmland' was held by John Hardy, senior. As late as 1680, when the west barn and Castle Field was leased by Edward Goodyer, of Dogmersfield, there is no mention of a house, although it is probable that one was there as, 65 years before, the bailiffs of Farnham had contributed to Mr. Langford's supper at the Grange, and again later for wine.

Towards the south side of the house the building contains timber framework and three floors. The south and west doors are of earlier character than most of the house, and, together with intricacies of plan, suggest that in Restoration times additions were made to an earlier structure. The problems attending the satisfactory fusion of two with three floors at one corner are considerable. Aesthetically, they have not been completely resolved.

In 1710 this part of the Bishop's land was disparked and would have been available for private development. Not long after this date it was written that there was 'a good modern built house erected by one Mr. Forbes called The Grange, situated behind the Castle'.

It appears that a door has been removed from the centre bay north side. The whole building south of bay five on the west front is modern; probably Edwardian. This extension may reflect the appearance of the former (later 17th century?) south front, re-using the door hood and some other fabric. But the cornice which now binds this side is also new, as formerly, it just turned the corner then stopped short after two brackets. The parapet here was plain. These alterations did much to unify this side of the house with the other three but did nothing to improve the already awkward west front fenestration. The difficulty of producing the two brick strings along this front was not overcome. A guess at what the south front was like pre-18th century can be made from what evidence can still be seen at its east end — where the blind window, broken string course and partly obscured panels back on to the space now exhibiting Venus, Cupid and Apollo. The side had projecting rooms before the recent extension.

The Grange, as a house, is among Farnham's best. It is unique, locally, in having classical mural paintings (good enough to be typical of a far greater house) and its gardens. There is no evidence of a more successful attempt in Farnham town to unify the outside of a house with its interior and immediate environment, although Moor Park (*qv*), on the town's outskirts, might have made a serious challenge for some years after Sir William Temple's death.

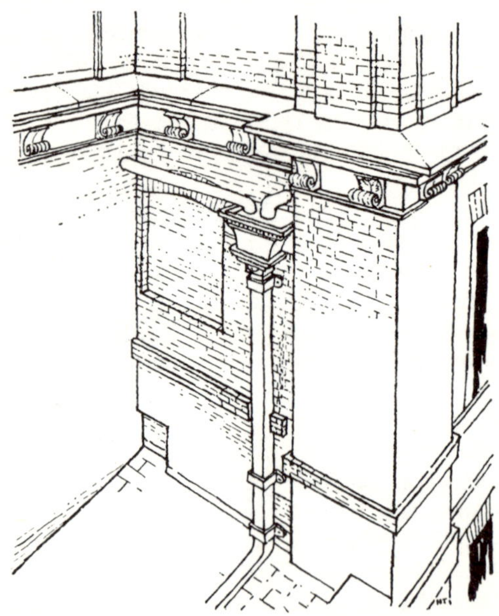

THE GRANGE, CASTLE HILL. A detail which shows where alterations have been made to the house at various times. The blind window is backed by a stair-well mural painting believed to be dated c 1720-1740.

The east front is best. Its symmetry is not much impaired by the extension, and the door case is Farnham's finest. Although not elaborate, the interplay on this front of horizontals and verticals is subtle. The arched centre window-head with broken circumference is interesting but fussy and was made necessary, it has been suggested in an article elsewhere, by using bricks intended for a larger arch. If Mr. Forbes could afford the panelling, staircase, murals, doorcase and carving that he could, it is unlikely that an accident like this would be let pass, especially twice — at the centre of both main façades.

Supposed connections with Wren as architect and Thornhill as decorator seem optimistic. The east front proportions are perhaps based on a modular formula.

Restoration of the mural paintings has been carried out recently. The restorers estimate their date to be 1720-1740.

The Granges, according to an account to be found in "Mediaeval Farnham" were completely rebuilt after the French left Farnham Castle in 1217. Senex's 1729 map of Surrey marks the Grange and names its owner — Mr. Forbes. By 1792 it had passed to William Asheton, of Lancaster, who leased it to John Knowles, yeoman, of Farnham. He died in 1814 and the property passed to his son John, who, before his death in 1831 had contracted to sell for £1,800 to his tenant, Samuel Andrews (*qv b* 1772*). On Samuel's death in 1842 The Grange passed to his son Charles, farmer, and it remained in his possession for 64 years, until he died there aged 91. It was he who bought Castle Hill House (*qv*) in 1872. In 1844 Charles Andrews married Mary, daughter of Thomas Lidbitter (*qv*) of Downing Street. She died six months later at The Grange.

Samuel had a large kiln in Potter's Gate early in the 19th century and as a result of his having eleven children — most with business connections in Farnham — the family's property and renown was widespread in the later 19th century. Children of Samuel and Harriett (1774-1859), of The Grange, were Harriett (*b* 1795), Ann (*b* 1797), Samuel (*b* 1798), John (*b* 1800, *d* 1877) butcher, Jane (*b* 1802), Richard (*b* 1804) solicitor, Catherine (*b* 1806), Susan (*b* 1807), Kesiah (*b* 1808), Frederick (*b* 1810) farmer, and Charles (*b* 1815). Frederick and Richard lived at one time in East Street, the latter with his wife, Hannah (*b* 1809*), and son, Samuel (*b* 1832*). Andrews' were so plentiful that only a few are mentioned here. It may be helpful though to add a few more details of those who figured more prominently in local affairs. These include John (above) also a hop planter, who married Catherine (*b* 1815*).

Their son was John (*b* 1834*) and daughter, Catherine (*b* 1837*). Frederick (above) married Ann (*b* 1818*) and had children — Frederick (*b* 1836*), Andrew (*b* 1838*) and Harriett (*b* 1840*).

Coxbridge Farm, The Goat's Head, 90 West Street, 14 Downing Street and 77 Castle Street (*qqv*) are also directly connected with the Andrews' family.

The Knowles' connection with The Grange was perpetuated until *c*. 1950 when Knowles Lane was renamed Old Park Lane after the Bishop's land, so named, before disparkment.

By the time of Charles Andrews' death the house was in poor repair. It was creeper-clad, cornices were rotten, window heads sagged. After the sale it was repaired and extended to the south. In 1919 the house was bought by Sir Edward Perceval who did much to put it and the grounds into excellent condition.

CEDAR COURT, CASTLE STREET

This Tudoresque house was built in the 1890s it is said, by one named Marsden. An earlier house, known as The Cedars, was demolished beforehand. It was on two main floors, parapeted, stuccoed, and had architraved sash windows. It had a rather bleak appearance outwardly and was of 18th century character. Elizabeth Penfold (*qv*) was its owner in the earlier part of the 19th century.

CASTLE HILL, CASTLE STREET

A five-bay house of two main floors, built of brick with a tiled roof. The main building has a symmetrical parapeted façade in heading bond. There is no cornice, but horizontal emphasis is given by two brick string courses which stop short of the building's length. Extensive cellarage is in the semi-basement, which helps to give a modest piano nobile effect to the front. On the north is an extension in brick with gabled tiled roof.

Fenestration: Ground floor, four recessed sashes three panes wide; First floor, five similar; Above, a single gabled dormer.

Door: In bay three. A case of unpainted stone is decorated with an eared architrave. Consoles support a segmental pediment, and it is approached by steps with slightly convex leading edges.

Interior: The main floor-plan is roughly quartered, the largest (north-west) 'quarter' containing stairs and entrance hall. A passage extends from the latter to separate back rooms and leads to the garden door.

The staircase is of mahogany and oak, in a pattern used in the best Farnham renaissance houses, and is the least elaborate of them. Banisters rise two to a tread, wainscotting is pilastered, and the square strings are carved. All doors leading from the hall have eared architraves. Half-panelling, an egg-and-dart cornice and arch decorate the hall. The arch, with fluted Doric pillars, foliated capitals and rich carving, accentuates the transition from hall to passage.

Raised wood panelling extends the height of the front room. It is finished with a cornice of dentils, modillions and rosettes. A richer, Roman, cornice with acanthus decoration is in the south-east room. This, and the other back room, have bay windows. All main windows on both floors have folding shutters, and all principal bedrooms were panelled in wood throughout. The front one is now half panelled.

The house probably dates in the main part from about mid 18th century. It is a building of high quality, of more elaborate decoration and detail inside than out. It has one of the very few, if not the only, 18th century natural stone doorcases in Farnham and is unusual, though not alone, in its extensive use of heading bond. This gives a fine texture to the façade. The main staircase fits the house in a more convincing way than another similar one does at Willmer House, and as well as being the simplest of its type it is probably the best locally.

Bay windows projecting from the back are later additions; nearer the date of the extensive 19th century building at the north end. Like the dormer window this is unfortunate in style, but the quality of materials is good and they are generally sympathetic to those used earlier.

A characteristic of some Farnham 18th century houses is the presence of small two-pane-wide windows in return walls near their junction with the façade. Here, at 62 Castle Street, and at 104 West Street, they are glazed; at Guildford House, 10 Castle Street, and 41 West Street (*qqv*), they are blind.

It is possible that Thomas Baker built this house. He certainly owned it shortly after it was built and as a hop planter, solicitor and Justice of the Peace, might well have aspired to building a dignified high quality house, secluded yet close to the town centre. As early as 1719 a Thomas Baker had been J.P. in Farnham, and the John Baker who was taxed on seven hearths in 1664 was probably a man of substance. Thomas Baker, solicitor, was living in Farnham in 1726, and Thomas Baker, J.P., was here in 1791; a sufficient span of time to suggest father and son. John Bakers married into the Bicknell and Longhurst (*qqv*) families in the 18th century and a William Baker married Mary Andrews in 1784. Charles Andrews (*qv*), of The Grange, bought Castle Hill in 1872. After his death in 1906 both properties passed to Mrs. Bertha Gough and from her to Howard Jackson.

Where the Musick House which Mr. Baker built in 1753 was is not known. It was a big enough affair to house later a large organ which he erected there; perhaps a connection with the organ which Thomas Baker's executrix bought for the church and was installed there in 1800? Could Mr. Baker's Musick House have been the building opposite, now the Masonic Hall (*qv*)? It is possible.

GUILDFORD HOUSE, CASTLE STREET

A house with symmetrical façade and built of brick. It has a tiled roof, five bays, two main floors and dormer windows behind a parapet with balustraded panels. Angles of the ground floor bay windows are coigned, as are outer corners of the façade in applied composition stone.

Fenestration: Ground floor, two bay windows with three-pane-wide sashes; First floor, four sashes, three panes wide. In bay three an oriel with ogival roof and gothick glazed sashes. Above are sashed dormer windows with flat tops.

Door: This is placed between the bay windows, under their connecting cornice and balustrade. It has two free-standing Doric columns with responders which contain the fanlight. This is semicircular and, in its turn, contains a lantern.

East elevation: Mainly unpainted brick. A low parapet exposes the hipped mansard roof from which open three dormer windows. This elevation is divided into three main parts, two large bay windows capped by depressed ogival domes which rise to parapet level and between them an oriel at first floor level, similar to the front balcony window. Ground floor windows are sashed, 1-4-1 with single-piece headstones. Above are four-pane-wide recessed sashes. Under the gazebo, set back, is a door with Doric pilasters and a semicircular fanlight, traceried radially.

Interior: Stairs occupy the north-west quarter. They are of pinewood and lead from the entrance hall with its plain modillion cornice. A passageway leads off the hall to connect with the garden door.

This is a much altered house possessing great charm in its outward appearance. The core is probably very late 18th century. To this additions had been made on all sides.

If one were looking for a Regency façade in Farnham which has the spirit of that period, Guildford House would be hard to better. Here are classical elements unpompously used, a confident handling of basic forms with subservient decoration, a touch of Brighton Pavilion, a reminder of Strawberry Hill, an effect of stucco with applied 'stone'. There is a feeling of gaiety, yet restraint is still apparent; of romantic fancy held firmly within bounds by a classical symmetry. In fact, a Regency treat. But it probably isn't; not entirely anyway. Some major features of this façade are almost certainly not earlier than 1853. The same can be said for the back, although wings previously north and south were early, in the main. There were a few fragments within the south extension (now demolished) of one of the two houses which were formerly here.

The garden front, with its big and deep windows, painted window-heads and, until recently, large square panes of glass, was more typically mid-century. The remodelling did not all happen at once. Parapet and doorcase indicate the earlier eastern limits of the house, and at one time the oriel jutted directly from this wall. It is possible that it opened on to a balcony over bays then extending from ground-floor rooms only, as at the front. Then, if these were built upwards to enlarge bedrooms, it would have been necessary to bring the gazebo more into line. This would account for the dwarfing of the doorway which has become engulfed and on a totally different plane from the gazebo, once probably directly above it.

Inside is disappointing architecturally. Most of Farnham's best houses have relatively austere façades and some riches within. Here the normal is reversed. The staircase is of a similar basic pattern to those of the best houses, but only in pattern is it comparable; not in materials, craftsmanship, or detail.

The Rev. J. S. Utterton seems responsible for enriching the façade and garden front. It would have been a happy coincidence if John Leigh Williams, of Exeter, who sold the house to Utterton, had done it. He came from Pennsylvania Park which is amongst the finest of smaller Regency suburban projects. But the transaction took place a year or so before what appears to be the date of this façade, or at least before some parts of it were built. By 1856 it was finished, the porch and bays having been built on land which had not been legally made over to the property until 1853.

During 1961 the house was restored to its present excellent condition by the architect/owner C. V. Tillett. Unsightly wings to north and south were removed, four-pane-wide sashes fitted at the back and the whole house carefully brought into line with present-day standards. This realistic approach is an alternative answer to making good (but large) houses into offices, flats or shops.

In 1824 Guildford House was sold to Miles Penfold (*qv*). He died in 1837, aged 91. The property passed to his wife, Elizabeth, whom he married in 1786. She died in 1842, aged 96, and at that time was one of the largest landowners in Farnham, holding over three hundred acres. As daughter of Peckham Williams (*qv*), she had a link with what was probably Farnham's largest house, Badshot Place (*qv*). Peckham Williams was responsible for introducing the white bine hop to Farnham and was a proprietor of Blissimere (at Weyhill Fair). Elizabeth Penfold owned the original Cedar Court (*qv*). See 122 West Street.

Guildford House (known one time as Castle Hill House, like its neighbour) was bought by J. S. Utterton in 1853. Utterton was Rector of Farnham and became Archdeacon of Surrey six years after. A century later we are reminded of him by the chimes of St. Andrew's. It was through his effort that the tower acquired its perpendicular crown and the chimes in 1865. Without his work it is unlikely that this visual focus of the Farnham skyline would be here to enjoy.

South Street, looking north from below Station Hill, in the late 19th century. The Corn Exchange tower and Norman Shaw's Castle Street bank building can be seen pushing above older roof tops, left.

PLATE 1

PLATE 2

The Borough. A late 19th century view from its junction with Park Lane (now Bear Lane) and South Street. George Sturt lived in one of the houses on the right. It is recalled in *A Small Boy in the Sixties.*

The Borough, looking east from its junction with Castle Street, drawn by John Hassell in 1822. Passmore's, now Boots, is on the right. Number 40 is shown as it was before two extensive remodellings.

PLATE 3

PLATE 4

25 West Street, The Master's House. Farnham Grammar School, before part-demolition and reconstruction. These buildings are now part of Farnham School of Art.
Page 145.

Bridge Square, showing (left) the Tanyard house, drawings of
which by Hassell and Shepherd are also reproduced. Premises
on the right are shown before conversion to a shop. Page 93.

PLATE 5

The Bush Tap. This was presumably the ancestor of the
existing one in South Street, on the site of which a pub existed
by the early 1870s. Ten years before that there was a Bush
Tap in Farnham. Page 19.

PLATE 6

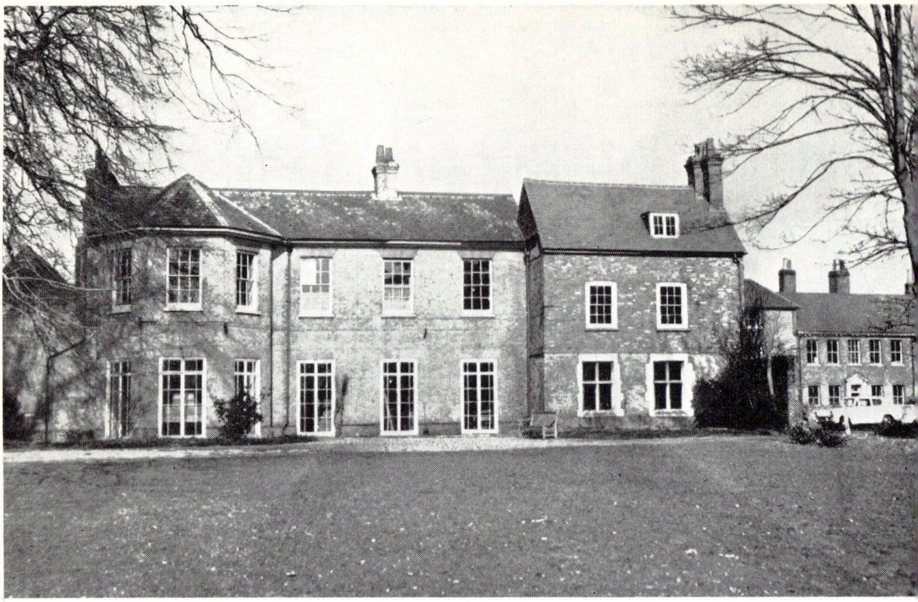

PLATE 7

Vernon House, 28 West Street, from the garden. Most seen in this view is of late 19th century build. Even before that, the east part did not appear wholly at one with the rest of the house. Page 153.

PLATE 8

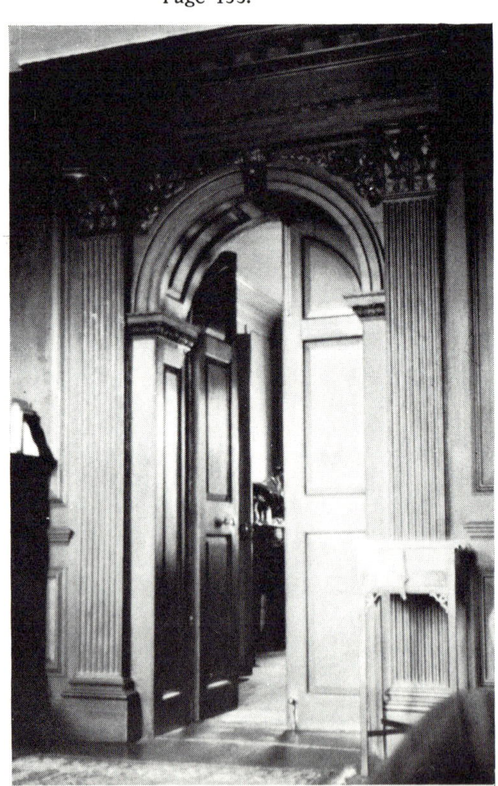

Willmer House, 38 West Street. This Corinthian oak doorway connects what were front and back reception rooms. Page 166.

PLATE 9

The Workhouse, drawn by Hassell in 1822. Like many such institutions of similar date, it was built outside the town. Many became infirmaries, hospitals or connected with homes for the aged. The block shown here has been extended and is part of the hospital. An earlier poor house is said to have been in Upper Church Lane.

PLATE 10

Willmer House, 38 West Street. A notable staircase, possibly not in this place at the time of the house's building in 1718. Page 166.

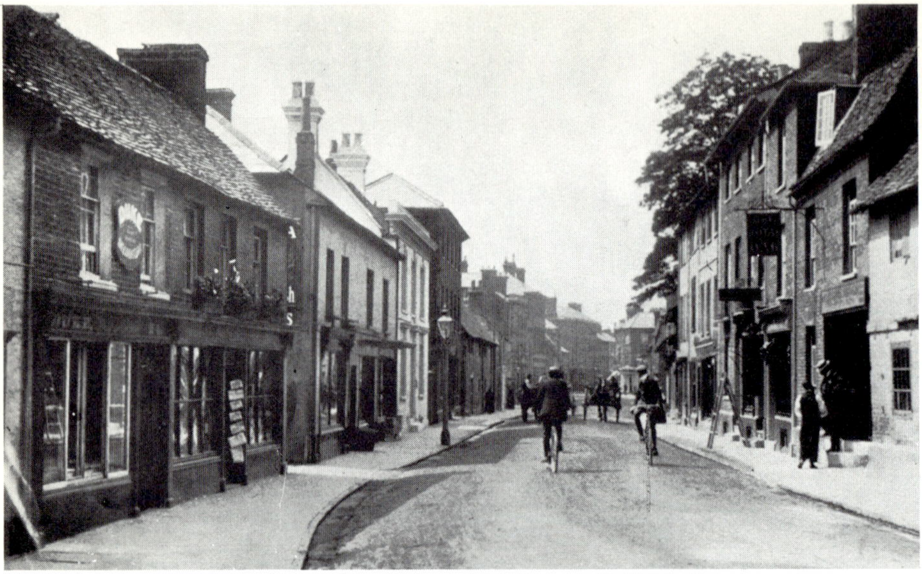

PLATE 11

East Street. An early view looking towards The Borough. The Royal Oak, long gone but in name, is on the right. Frontages cleared for the Regal Cinema are visible.

PLATE 12

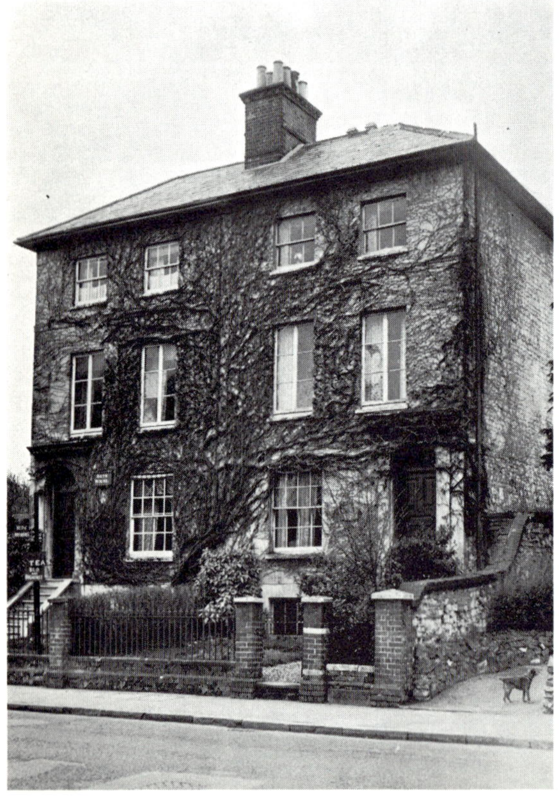

Bath Terrace, East Street, built by Patrick about 1847. Merton House (right) has been painted white. Page 120.

Dippenhall, drawn by J. Hassell in 1824. The house, shown on Seller's map of 1680 (qv), has long been demolished but the district retains its name. This drawing is the only likeness of the house known to exist. Page 233.

PLATE 13

PLATE 14

Church Lane. White paint, hung tiles, rugged brick and plaster give high visual value to relatively humble houses.

65-68 Castle Street is part of a typical Farnham group displaying a happy mixture of formality and irregularity with colour and textural variety. Light and shadow, warmth and coldness, patterns of fenestration and variations in skyline add to the richness of Farnham's traditional scene. Consideration of scale, proportion and materials help give form to the whole.

PLATE 15

PLATE 16

61 Castle Street. An excellent, probably late 18th century façade, displaying much in common in its upper parts with 90 West Street. Page 49.

PLATE 17

Brightwell, off East Street. A sedate house of earlier Victorian
appearance but of earlier origin. It stands in a small public park,
once part of its private pleasure garden. Page 113.

PLATE 18

The Liberal Club, South Street. This is an early Lutyens work,
designed soon after he set up in London in private practice.
Page 106.

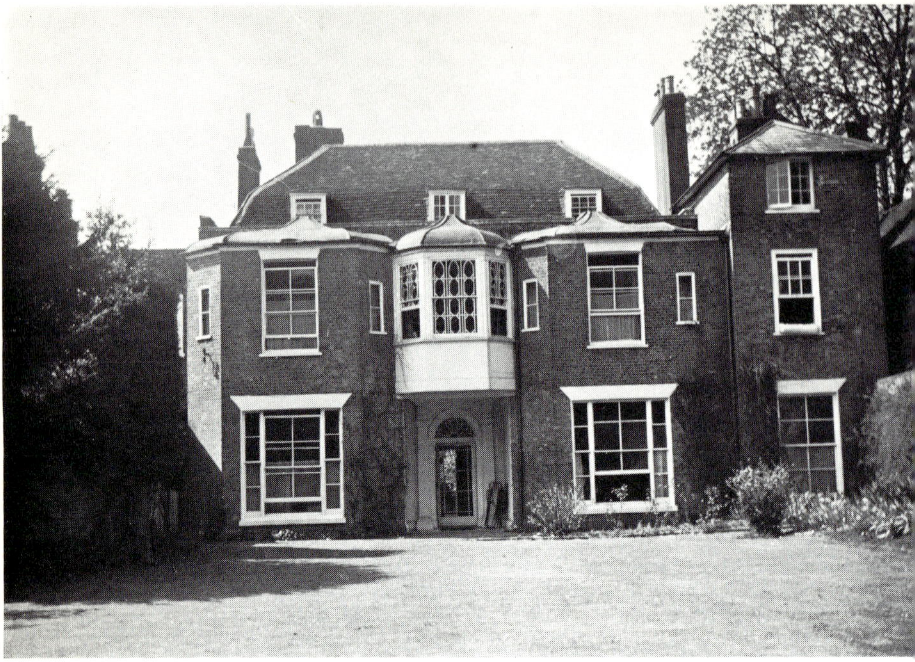

PLATE 19

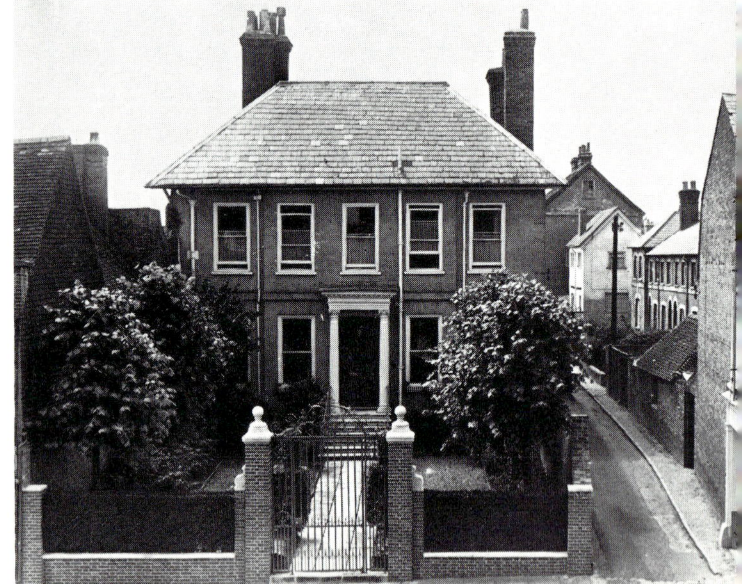

Guildford House, Castle Street. The garden front before recent improvements which included demolition of flanking blocks and refitting windows with small panes. Page 66.

PLATE 20

10 Castle Street. Built by Thomas Piggott about 250 years ago, this house has suffered many alterations but still retains considerable strength of character. Page 39.

80-97 West Street, including an exceptionally fine group of mainly 18th century house fronts in brick.

PLATE 21

Castle Street, by G. Shepherd, 1818. This water-colour from the Ashmolean is almost the same as another at the British Museum. It shows the original Cedar Court (right of centre) and suggests that the upper west side of Castle Street isn't quite as Georgian in its fronts as often supposed.

PLATE 23

The Old Market House (1666-1866), drawn by Hassell in the 1820s. It shows the Castle Street
entrance to The Goat's Head courtyard. Page 15.

PLATE 24

Farnham, from Firgrove, by G. Shepherd. This drawing from the Ashmolean Collection, appears to be one worked up by the artist from his more freely executed one at the British Museum. It shows Old Roof and Tanyard (apparently then still a tannery) and the low church tower. Extensive hop gardens cover The Hart. This drawing was made in 1818.

PLATE 25

Bourne Mill Village, by John Hassell, 1822. Bourne Mill was occupied at this time by the Simmonds family — also some time at Weydon, Froyle and Willey Mills.

PLATE 26

Lower Church Lane, Waggon Yard and Lower Downing Street seen from St. Andrew's tower. A method of invisible roofing behind parapets can be seen at 3 Downing Street. Alterations to the main roof of 4 Downing Street (compare back and front) are apparent.

DOWNING STREET

Downing Street shelves south from its junction with West Street and The Borough. The three were once knotted by the Round House — long gone. Downing Street curves, to turn abruptly east towards Longbridge and ends its identity as a street where Union Road begins. The view down Downing Street's length is stopped by a big brick house. Several alleys lead off the street. Few hold interest now, although Ivy Lane harbours a good house and Church Lane is a very pleasant detour on busy shopping days.

37 and 38 DOWNING STREET. A partly conjectural reconstruction of its original façade.

*   1   DOWNING   STREET

At the time of writing, this extensive site was being re-developed to convert the yard, late of Mills, builders, to a County Police establishment.

In its state of semi-dereliction the site possessed considerable charms and was potentially an area which could have brought new life into the town as an integrated part of it, as well as offering a site for some fundamental amenities which the town still lacks. It was one of the very few remaining undeveloped central areas. It has a river frontage, it is adjacent to a park and close to the meadows. A great opportunity has been missed. Attention was drawn to the possibilities in the Press four years before re-development began. It was only in mid-1961 that the public generally queried the wisdom of the then irreversible plan.

In 1752 the property passed from Samuel Lutman of Bentley to Richard Knight, yeoman. Occupation remained by that family until well into the 19th century when land and buildings were surrendered by Margaret and Sampson Sampson (*qv*) to F. C. Birch (*qv*), builder, who had been hereabout since 1861. Until the 1950s it remained a builder's yard — of Birch, then Tompsett and Kingham, Mardon and Mills, and finally Mills and Son.

When the house (which until lately stood near to 2 Downing Street and is now demolished) was first built is not clear. There was certainly a dwelling with the site in 1819 when land, including Hydes, passed on the death of George Knight (*d* 1819), yeoman, to his son George (*d* 1880). Charles Knight owned and occupied a barn, stabling and house here twenty years later. The inelegant grey (Paines) brick and slated house, which we remember was built on the site of a sizeable earlier building. The recent house had a look shared by 39-41 Castle Street (*qv*), suggested that its origin was about 1865 and that its builder was F. C. Birch. At one time this house, as is number 3, was called Longbridge House.

George Knight the younger had a niece, Margaret, who married Sampson Sampson, the Bridge Square maltster. Sampson's kilns and house were immediately across the river from this property and later became part of Barrett's Brewery.

The Lutmans, a notable Bentley family, lived at Jenkyn Weelys, later Jenkyn Place. Gilbert White remarked upon their regiment of tombs in Bentley churchyard.

Other Lutman-Farnham connections were through the marriages of Elizabeth Lutman of Farnham to John Manwaring in 1784, and of Elizabeth Lutman to Richard Drinkwater (*qv*) of Farnham, in 1761. One Samuel Lutman married Mrs. Mary Holloway in 1715 and Samuel Lutman Esquire was buried at Bentley in 1756.

Richard Lutman of Rogate (near Liss) gave financial help to a Farnham butcher, Edward Smith, and his wife Joan, in 1659. Their house, barn, slaughterhouse and stable were 'in the Borough North Side of the High Street near unto the Fish Cross' (*qv*).

2   DOWNING   STREET

A symmetrical three-bay, two-floor façade of yellow-grey brick divided horizontally by a string course and cornice of stone. This is supported by a pair of consoles at either end.' The main front projects as a bay between these brackets. There is a parapet, stepped up over the centre bay. The roof is part tiled, part slated, of complex structure.

Fenestration: Ground floor, two 1-3-1 sashes; First floor, three four-pane-wide sashes in slender frames, the centre one of which is arched. All windows have wide, moulded architraves.

Door: With semi-circular fanlight and contained within a coigned rectangular recess. Tracery is radial.

A façade of strong character which, although Victorian, stands near the end of Farnham's genuine Georgian tradition. A possible relationship to Zingari Terrace (*qv*) has been noted, also the stylistic relationship with 29 East Street (*qv*) and other houses. The front might be dated about 1860. Pevsner and Nairn say *c* 1830. It is untouched by Gothick or other romantic agents which were already established else-where. A guess would put the façade to the hand of William Birch (*qv*) of Castle Street. This concerns only the front. There is also the greater part of an older red brick building, the front of which was some feet back from the Victorian one. Most of the roof is tiled. Over the front addition it is slated. Until recent years a forecourt garden was enclosed by a simple, pretty railing on a dwarf wall.

This was once known as Rhama House and as Morley House. What is now the adjoining shop was until quite recently its garage. In 1839 the property was occupied by Thomas Paine; before that by one named Milton. The Paines (*qv*) owned many Farnham properties and were allied through marriage with most of the more prosperous local families. Apart from those living in the town there was a family at Frensham. This included Richard (married Lydia Trimmer 1781). He has been described as a yeoman-hop planter. He had a contemporary of the same name at Seale. There were still representatives of the family at Frensham in the late 19th century.

3   DOWNING   STREET   (Longbridge House, Wey Valley Water Co.)

A symmetrical brick built house of five bays on two floors with a tiled roof behind panelled parapet and moulded brick coping. Bay five is broken forward, the moulded and dentilled cornice being surmounted by a brick pediment spanning this projection. A string runs between floors and stops at the projecting bay.

Fenestration: Ground floor, four recessed sashes three panes wide; First floor, five similar, the centre one contained by a double raised architrave and apron.

Door: In bay three, the case in cut brick. Panelled pilasters with double-scroll foliated brackets support a dentilled cornice above a frieze decorated with a shell and fleur de lys.

1717 is the date incised on a brick panel contained by the pediment. The initials over the door are presumably those of John Chitty who rebuilt the house. As a prototype English renaissance house in Farnham of the Grand (country town) Manner, it set a high standard. It was soon to be surpassed at Willmer House (*qv*) in size, cratsmanship, grandeur and design. But few local buildings could have measured up to its standards at the time it was built. It has been stated that this and Willmer House were undoubtedly by the same hand. If so the hand-owner's eye learned much in the few months which separate their dates of building.

Some of the cut brickwork here is of richer quality than Willmer's, where there is not the freedom seen in the doorway decoration of Longbridge. They share though the fleur de lys motive, but this is unlikely to have been an emblem of both owner-builders as they were apparently of different families. A builder's mark, it has been suggested. Has it been found elsewhere in a similar context? The brickwork is good and stands between the sophisticated of Willmer House and relatively rustic of Ivy House (*qv*) though all, technically, are far removed from more traditional work seen in the early remains at the Bailiff's Hall (*qv*). At Longbridge someone seems to have made an effort later to catch up on Willmer House by using a method of superficial repointing and secret jointing seen well at 38 Castle Street (*qv*).

John Chitty did not make a complete rebuilding. He constructed what was almost a brick box to encase the earlier timber framed house. Extensive alterations were made from 1948. Much of the earlier inside was removed, Chitty's encasing remained, glazing bars were restored to front windows and additional accommodation was built.

The house, and what was once its hopground, had been occupied by some of Farnham's leading families. These included Piggotts, Drinkwaters, Paines, Lockerbies and

Darvills *(qqv)*, as well as the Chittys. Ownership can be traced back to John Fielder's and later to Nathaniel Piggott's who owned it before the 1717 rebuilding. It was Thomas Piggott who built 10 Castle Street *(qv)* at about the same time. Elizabeth Lockerbie *(qv)* who owned 3 Downing Street until her death in 1875, was of a family connected with many town properties.

There appear to have been two groups of Piggotts: those who lived in the town and those who lived near Hale. Of the latter, Elizabeth, wife of John, died in 1714, his daughter Ann the year before. Nathaniel, the son of Nathaniel, was christened in 1692. William Piggott, draper, died in 1698. David Piggott had sons William *(d 1714)* and Henry *(d 1718)*. Henry Piggott Esq., of Petworth, was buried in Farnham in 1713. A David Piggott was apprenticed to John Fry, a Farnham corn dealer, in 1722. Mr. Piggott was charged tax on two hearths at Badshot in 1664.

In April, 1904, Longbridge House was sold to Mme. Desmaret. She represented the sisterhood which established a convent (sometime known as Longbridge Convent) here and about 1930, ten years after the Sisters sold the house, there was a time when this nearly became a cinema.

The Chittys were a notable and prosperous family with many local representatives in the 18th century. A few are mentioned here as a guide to the dates and occupations of the more prominent. Chrusophilus had an interest in 13 West Street *(qv)* and a C. Chitty was among the possessors of 3 Downing Street. Richard owned it later. It was a Richard Chitty of Farnham who married Emma Billinghurst in 1764. Henry and Chrusophilus were mercers and drapers, Manwaring Chitty an auctioneer and appraiser. Chrusophilus I died in 1737, a successor in 1771, and Chrusophilus III in 1808. Sarah *(d 1694)* was wife of an early Chrusophilus Chitty. They are unlikely to have been a prosperous Farnham family long before building 3 Downing Street as none was charged Hearth Tax in the 1660s or '80s. Land behind 69 West Street *(qv)* was known as Chitty's. Many of the family were hop planters. In 1809, foreign Chittys — Christopher of Lewes, brewer, and Bartholomew of Leatherhead, tanner — were two of the ten proprietors of Weyhill's Blissimere Half Acre. This had very direct Farnham connections through the hop trade. The children of various Chrisophilus' included Martha *(d 1699)*, Jane *(d 1704)*, Joan *(d 1706)*, Charles *(d 1788)*, Phillip *(b 1785)*, William *(b 1786)*. There were very many more of this name living in Farnham from 17th-19th centuries.

A symmetrical five-bay façade of three full floors built of brick with a part slate and part tile roof. Floors are separated by plain brick string courses. The roof has a main ridge running east to west with the north eaves supported by paired modillions. Secondary ridges run at right angles to this above gables at the back.

Fenestration: Ground floor, four recessed, three-pane-wide sashes five panes high; First floor, five similar; Second floor, five similar, four panes high.

Door: In bay three, two freestanding wooden fluted Doric columns with responders support a portico without pediment. The whole is mounted above three steps.

Other features: On either flank of the house is a two-floor block of one bay, set back. The west one shields a limb of the house which extends southwards. This is a two-floor timber-framed building. Behind this, extending south again, is attached a range of brick buildings.

An article published twenty years ago states that the house is dated 1737 and that the top floor is a 19th century addition. Pevsner and Nairn date the house early 19th century. The slate and general character of the eaves suggest that the front was re-roofed at least. But the rest of the roof is tiled and of different earlier character. If the upper string course is original, it is not likely to have been put just there on a two-floor house, and from the back, which is three floors high also, one is hard pressed to imagine that it was only two floors high early in the 19th century even if the roof were new.

4 DOWNING STREET. A detail of the eaves treatment, north corner.

The lower floors have exceptionally tall windows for a Farnham house, and there were other openings of similarly slim proportion (though smaller) at the back. There have been frequent and extensive alterations, re-affenestration and additions to the south front.

Traditionally the property was known as Bartlett's Garden and, with a hop field, it belonged to Farnham Manor, to which it was surrendered by Edward Tilby (or Tilley) in 1748. Bartlett had already given his name to the hop field by this time. Eleven years after Robert Manwaring was in occupation Ann Manwaring (widow) leased the house for 21 years. After sixty years' occupation by William Crump (*qv*) and his family, it was sold to John Manwaring Paine for £750 in 1841. It was the property of Thomas Eyre (*qv*) and then Charlotte Eyre from 1889 until 1920.

Ann Manwaring, daughter of John, died in 1783. There were not less than three successive William Crumps. One died before 1760, one in 1808 and another in 1852. They were, by trade, fellmongers, glovers and drapers, and also owned 9 Castle Street (*qv*). There were Crumps in Farnham by the 1660s, and the second of these Williams was one of Farnham's two bailiffs in 1762. William Crump was described in 1790 as a Farnham woolstapler. Crumps had hop kilns at Beaver's and behind the Mitre Café.

The family were not newcomers to the Downing Street quarter of Farnham for Richard occupied a place (at present unlocated) described in 1744 as 'that messuage now in five tenements with the barn stable workhouses . . . hop ground . . . near to the church gate on the south side of a street or land there called Church Street leading to the river'. This was part of an estate which included 114 and 115 West Street (*qv*) and must have been very close to Bartlett's Garden.

The Eyres owned a lot of land in this quarter of the town. The site on which Westminster Bank stands was theirs (38 and 39 The Borough, *qv*). A Thomas Eyre was once joint holder of the Conduit (*qv*) and a Thomas Eyre bought the Round House (*qv*). Thomas Windsor (connected with Andrew, of Windsor Almshouses, *qv*) of Bentley sold Long Mede to a Thomas Eyre in 1613. About that time a family called Eyre is frequently referred to in the Bentley Manor Court Rolls.

5A DOWNING STREET

Mid-19th century dwellings in brick and tile altered in the mid-1950s. At this time the large Downing Street window and a door were added; also leaded lights in Church Lane. As a result the Church Lane house is now in Downing Street (see illustration). It occupies the site of the east end of Richard Smither's (*qv*) malthouse which stood here in the first half of the 19th century. He lived a house or two further up Downing Street.

5 AND 7 DOWNING STREET
(The Toy Shop)

Two 1930s Tudoresque shops of timber and brick construction. These replaced three earlier houses, which were, from south to north, a brick built earlier-19th century house, and a timber framed and jettied picturesque pair (see illustration). The first of these three appears to have been a recased genuine Tudor house. It was rare in having simple recessed sashes five panes wide, but they were clumsily disposed on the façade. Their placing was perhaps a result of their relationship to a timber structure.

5A - 7 DOWNING STREET before alterations to 5A were made and the other houses demolished.

17 DOWNING STREET (G. Hopkins)

A shop of 20th century pseudo-Tudor character in timber, brick and tile. The Sun Inn was here. From the street, a humble two-floor building of brick, with small early 19th century type casements and a simple door with flat hood and brackets. At the north end a gate with room above led to stables. It is probable that a timber framed building was masked by the façade. There were extensive buildings behind it.

This pub went by the same name in the early 1820s. It was for sale in 1888 and disappeared from accessible records by 1895.

In 1890 Downing Street, with East Street, was to have been paved by the Board with blue brick. Victoria stone was thought more suitable for The Borough and West Street. The scheme was the subject of an enquiry and was not carried out in full. Blue bricks are still to be found around Downing Street. Most pavements before this date were of ironstone cobbles.

18 DOWNING STREET (Little Soho)

Once a small house, but for many years a shop, this has an early bay window of note because it is not a fake. For very many years this was Baker's butcher's shop. William Baker (*qv*), sausage maker, was in Downing Street in 1845, and Alfred Baker, sausage maker, at number 18 by the 1870s, if not long before. Then Alfred and Harry; and in the 1950s they were still here.

22 DOWNING STREET (Sarah Stuart)

Converted from a private house with pedimented doorcase and overhanging eaves to its present form. Additions included the parapet, oriel and shop windows. The reconstruction was carried out in 1949 to the design of G. Maxwell Aylwin.

An indenture relates to unidentified property near here, possibly a few houses north of 22 Downing Street (Tithe Awards 480 and 481?). Although undated and anonymous it provides some interesting facts and names. The property passed from Sarah Roak, widow of Richard Roak of London, and mother of Richard, to Richard Stillwell of Brook. Richard senior had lived in one house, a second had already been sold by the recently bereaved Roaks to a man named White. Both houses were fronted by Downing Street and had the Parsonage garden to their west. They were bounded on the north by a passage way leading from the street to a Nicholas Turner's malthouse and barn.

35 AND 36 DOWNING STREET

(John Goodridge)

A shop of 20th century pseudo-Tudor character, in timber, brick and tile, abutted by an older structure at its north end.

Here stood The Cricketers Inn, at one time occupying both premises. When it was demolished about 1930, the building had not been used as a pub for some years. It had been a small cottage-type building on two floors, with tiled roof and probably a timber frame beneath its brick façade. The property was described as a house in the 1830s, when it was owned by William Baker (*qv*) and occupied by John Lickfold. A William Baker who owned freehold property in Downing Street was at that time living in West Street. Edward Windibank (*b* 1815*) was a victualler living hereabouts in 1851.

IVY HOUSE (Ivy Lane) DOWNING STREET

A brick and tile house of eight bays and two full floors with dormers above. It is of a shallow E-plan and is asymmetrical in that the doorcase is in bay five. Eaves are moulded and dentilled. At ground floor level a conservatory encloses bays three to six.

Fenestration: Ground floor, mixed, bays three, four and six rectangular and sashed, bays seven and eight wide boxed sashes with semi-circular heads; First floor, three-pane-wide flush boxed sashes; Above, four sashed dormers.

Door: Plain pilastered, topped by an arched hood.

The house is of a style likely to have been built about 1700. If it was, it would have been one of Farnham's largest town houses of its day and an immediate ancestor of the relatively highly-polished and sophisticated (but still provincial) Longbridge House of 1717 (*qv*) and of Willmer House of 1718 (*qv*) which were to set the architectural pace in Farnham for many years to come. There is still about Ivy House a rustic air. Perhaps its seclusion, ruggedness and variegation of brick colour, and its boldness of style contribute to the atmosphere. 10 Castle Street (*qv*) is rather nearer the early 18th century town house mark. In fact, when it was built, Ivy House had uninterrupted views of the countryside to the south-east with fields and meadows up to the garden wall.

The house has been altered and added to. The block adjoining the east end is of recent date although an extension had been made at that end beforehand, about 1880.

Mrs. Hay died in 1775 and Ivy House went to her husband William, they having owned it probably for over twenty-five years. From him it is said to have passed to Thomas Beddus Mill, who died in 1828. It then went to John Grant, James Darvill (*qv*) senior, and in 1855 was bought by William Hazell. By this time it was known as Ivy House. His Executors sold the property to The Farnham Working Men's Conservative Club in 1894.

Even if Mrs. Hay had owned the house for thirty years it is unlikely that she had it built, although it is possible that her father or father-in-law could have done so if he held the land before she did. There is a clue. In deeds relating to 43 The Borough (*qv*) that property is described as being bound on its south and west sides by 'the capital messuage and garden late belonging to Alexander Hayes and others and late belonging to James Woodyer'. That was in 1723. It almost certainly refers to Ivy House although there could have been another capital messuage fronting The Borough. In 1660 a Mrs. Hayes left 20/- for bread to be distributed to the poor on St. Matthew's Day at The Bush Inn (*qv*).

Thomas Beddus Mill was connected with the Mill family of The Welches, Bentley. In 1775 John Mill, of Bentley, owned a house in Farnham occupied by Widow Green. The Mills had been at Welches since at least 1716 and voted in Farnham during the century.

Thomas Beddus Mill (his wife was named Sophia) who died in 1828, owned Dippenhall Farm and considerable estates in the Runwick area. They were mostly occupied by William Pinke Paine (*qv*), and Mill devised them to John Frederick Mill, oldest son of John Mill. He also left to John Frederick Mill a share in Blissimere Half Acre — the Weyhill hop market. To John Mill, John Frederick Mill's brother, Thomas Beddus Mill left all his lands — in several occupations — at Wrecclesham. Other children of this John Mill were Mary Sophia and Sarah Ann Mill. Living at the same time in Downing Street was Sarah Mill, the daughter of John Mill the elder of Froyle.

A prosperous man, T. B. Mill left handsome recognition to the children of his friend John Hollest (*qv*) and one of his Executors Joseph Richard Williams (*qv*). He owned also a house in East Street which he gave to its occupant, Joseph Johnson, a minister of the Dissenting Meeting House in

Farnham, while his own house passed to (the above) Mary and Sarah Mill. Another house, somewhere in Downing Street, was left to William Mason, its occupant, conditionally. Two more houses in Castle Street went to Joseph Thomas Williams, son of Joseph Richard Williams. (See 122 West Street.) John Frederick Mill owned about 200 acres around Runwick and Dippenhall about ten years after Thomas Beddus Mill's death. It was occupied by William Pinke Paine and John Manwaring Paine (*qqv*). Thomas Beddus Mill and John Manwaring (*qv*) were Commissioners for Land Tax late in the 18th century.

Between 1693 and 1713 two Anns, two Thomas' and two Johns Mill — all children of Mr. John Mill — were buried in Farnham. John Mill, a Farnham churchwarden, married Sarah (*d* 1720) the daughter of John Manwaring (*qv*) the elder. Their children were Mary and Ann. John Mill was Overseer at Bentley in 1727. Perhaps he paid Ogden the two shillings 'for heving Ann Mills to Docking field'. The Mill-Manwaring family produced four children which, one source says, all died young. They included Mary, Ann and John.

Apart from Thomas Beddus Mill, there was Thomas junior, who died in 1703. Thomas Mill, Gent, followed him three years later. In 1730 another Thomas Mill, son of George Mill of Farnham, Gent, was apprenticed to Spencer Man, a cloth worker. Mary Mill and Thomas Child, both of Farnham, were married in 1766.

One other Mill — George Esq., a churchwarden — has left a record of himself for having exceeded his rights in 1727. He built himself a new pew at St. Andrew's, at the front, in what appears to have been the best position. This was with disregard for those already entitled to sit in that place. An enquiry was held. The Lord Bishop, the vicar, two George Vernons, John Lampard and John Stevens (*qqv*) met on the spot. George Mill moved his pew to behind those which he had so imprudently displaced. Theirs were moved even further forward to make room. Humble pie for Mr. Mill.

An undated (probably late 18th century) manuscript concerning the Mill family is quoted under Runwick House (*qv*).

William Hazell (*b* 1805*) was established as a Farnham draper in 1839 as was John Hazell (*b* 1827*) of 32 and 33 The Borough in the '70s and '80s, and later of 4 Corn Exchange. Charles (*b* 1825*), maltster and hop planter, built 8 Castle Street (*qv*), and James, his brother, lived at Rock House. William Hazell bought Ivy House in 1855 and ran a

corset factory in outbuildings there. He followed the occupation then of John Bailey (*d* 1781) and Andrew Merriott (*qv*,
d 1805). The venture nearly lost the house when it was
damaged as a result of a fire in his factory.

According to the June, 1901, edition of 'Ladies' Realm',
an outdoor rifle range for ladies was opened in the grounds.
Arthur Hart, the secretary, 'gave generous encouragement
to shooting among women'. Dramatic scenes are conjured
up. First to join, in response to Lord Salisbury's appeal to
produce shots to resist possible invasion, was Lady Mary
Arkwright, daughter of The Earl of Stafford.

In 1887 The Farnham Conservative Club Company was
formed to acquire premises for The Farnham Conservative
Working Men's Club. Many townspeople bought shares to
secure this house already on lease to The Working Men's
Club. William Hazell's Executors sold it to the company
in 1894, since when it has served the same purpose, as The
Conservative Club.

37 AND 38 DOWNING STREET
(Farnham Coffee House)

A four-bay, two-floor pair with painted stucco façade and
slate roof. Bays are marked by five unfluted giant Ionic
pilasters. The two centre bays have blind arcades. Three
pommells decorate the parapet.

Fenestration: Ground floor, bow windows in bays two
and three. In bay four a three-pane-wide sash; First floor, in
bays one and four a deeply recessed and architraved square
window.

Door: In bay one.

This vigorous façade probably dates from *c* 1855, being
built at a time when some 18th century refinements were
lost, but when there was enough architectural sensibility
left to produce a well-proportioned and vigorous classical
façade. A relatively light Victorian hand composed these
Renaissance elements. This was more apparent when the
building was in its original condition. It was then more
virile than now. (See illustration, page 69.)

As built, each arcade contained a round-topped window
with Ionic pilasters. Alterations to the skyline have tamed
earlier boisterousness. The once pierced parapet has been
filled and refined pommells replace the big, Brussels-sprout-
like pineapples which punctuated the parapet.

The 1950 alterations by G. Maxwell Aylwin (*qv*) restored
favourably an ill-treated façade. The bow windows then

inserted, decorative plaques, filled-in rustications (still trace-
able alongside the windows) and other alterations did, though,
tip the scales a little backwards stylistically. Once robust
Victorian has now a gentle Regency flavour. Market houses
built in various parts of England between 1850 and 1865,
and some earlier railway stations, have much in common
with the spirit of this façade.

The door of number 38 has been replaced by a window
and the premises made into one. Original details bear comparison with the upper part of 26 and 118 West Street (*qqv*).
Number 37 was a butcher's shop for many years in the
19th century, but the building seems to have been filleted
later and converted to a fishmonger's. Number 38 was known
as The Coffee Tavern more than seventy years ago and the
two premises combined to retain this link in their recent
renaming. Before 1855 there was a hop kiln here. It was
occupied by Francis Mathews — probably the veteran hop
planter of that name (*b* 1740*) who died in 1841 at a Longbridge house called Paradise. Francis Mathews senior (*d* 1778)
occupied kilns to the rear of The Nelson Arms (*qv*).

43   DOWNING   STREET

Now, with 42, at the time of writing, is being altered for use
as a supermarket.

Here stood The Bird in Hand, although a garage was on
this site before the present one was built. In the 1750s there
was an inn called The Bird in Hand in Farnham. Ann Bicknell
was the occupant. 43 Downing Street was used as a pub of

43 DOWNING STREET. A partly conjectural reconstruction of The Bird in Hand.

this name by the 1820s. Twenty years later the pub was owned by John Hawkins and occupied by Joseph Baker. It was offered for sale by Farnham United Breweries in 1928.

The building was of four bays, two floors, and had an asymmetrically placed door with flat hood and brackets. Apparently brick built and tiled, it was in fact timber framed. (See illustration.)

It is said that hereabout was a house once called Hoggate.

46 AND 47 DOWNING STREET

Paired brick houses totalling five bays on three floors under a tiled hip roof with eaves brackets.

Fenestration: Ground floor, in bays one and two, four and five, plate-glass shopfronts; First floor, four three-pane-wide recessed sashes with a blind recess in bay three; Second floor, three three-pane-wide recessed half-sashes with blind recesses in bays two and four.

Door: Twins in bay three, contained between two engaged unfluted Doric shafts, a third shaft separating doors centrally. The whole is under a single segmental arch with metal fanlight and radial tracery.

Particularly interesting for its rare doorway, this façade may date from the early 19th century. The twin treatment, part of a solution to the problem of considering two houses as a unit (seldom exploited as successfully today), is now unique in Farnham but once had companions in 100 to 103 West Street (qv). They were built by Daniel Batchelour in 1812, and were possibly later austerity variants on 46 - 47 Downing Street. The present shopfronts here were fitted in 1922. Original window arrangement could scarcely have repeated exactly what is above. Perhaps four-pane-wide windows were fitted, one either side of the double doorway. There was probably a house here before the present one was built.

In 1876 William Blake (d 1909), Farnham Excise Officer, bought this property, it is said, from the Nash (qv) family, solicitors and hop growers.

Earlier, this and neighbouring houses were owned by Thomas Baker (b 1786*), auctioneer. 'J.N.B. May 1st 1843' is incised in a wall. The inscription possibly commemorates James Baker's (b c 1821) coming-of-age. Robert Baker (b 1821*) was in partnership with his father. This is probably the same Baker family, once Farnham curriers. James Baker

was a currier, also John Baker of Castle Street, born at Wool
in 1811*. Thomas Baker of Downing Street was a currier too.
In his will of 1785 James Forth left to his cousin Robert
Kempe his house in Downing Street, then in the occupation
of Francis Baker.

The Nibletts lived hereabouts in the early 19th century,
possibly in one of these houses. They were solicitors whose
names rarely appear on local documents; more frequently
as clerks to another solicitor. Charles William Niblett was
practising in Farnham by 1823, as well as in Guildford, and
Charles William (*b* 1815*) was still practising in Downing
Street in the mid-fifties. Elizabeth Niblett was born in 1781.
Charles Niblett junior's wife was Charlotte (*b* 1818*) and
his son William Charles Niblett was born in 1844*.

48, 49 AND 50 DOWNING STREET

A symmetrical five-bay brick built house on three floors
with tiled roof and moulded eaves supported by paired
brackets. The main house has two-floor abutments to north
and south with shopfronts and arched brick doorheads. Both
of these wings have a recessed 1-3-1 window above.

Fenestration: Ground floor, two multi-paned shopfronts
in bays one and two, four and five; First floor, five recessed
three-pane-wide sashes; Second floor, five similar of three-
quarter height. Windows in bays two and four are blind.

Door: Engaged Doric oval columns with fine reeding
support a broken entablature with paterae and open triangular pediment. This contains a semicircular fanlight with radial
tracery.

Eaves treatment and some doorcase details suggest that
this is a late Georgian house. The shopfronts were inserted
into the main block in the mid-1950s to replace four windows
similar to those above them. The flanking wings have had
shopfronts for very many years — perhaps a century or more.

The block was sold by the Nash (*qv*) family in 1906.
They had long been Farnham hop planters and mealmen.
The remains of their kiln are still at the back of the yard
adjoining to the south, which property, together with a house
belonging to it, was owned by John Nash in the 1830s.

There were several families named Nash frequently
encountered particularly in 19th century Farnham. The
Downing Street family who lived probably here as well as
in neighbouring houses were most prominent. John and Anne

senior were grocers who were in business by the 1820s at the latest. John and Ann junior (*bb* 1811**) had sons John (*b* 1846*) and Alfred Nash (*b* 1848*). Their father was a hop planter and brickmaker. James, hop planter, (*b* 1818*) and his wife Elizabeth lived nearby.

Thomas Baker (*qv*) is named as owner of the property in 1839. In more recent times it became The Carlton Hotel, by which name it was known until about 1954.

6 3 AND 6 4 DOWNING STREET
(The Hop Bag)

A brick built public house with tiled roof.

There appears to have been no pub here in 1732 when the property was the subject of a mortgage. By 1755 there was one, known as The Adam and Eve. There were two houses occupied by Jonas Jennings who was tenant of William Whittingham, carpenter, who in that year conveyed the property to one named Shorter. The houses were not joined. The eastern one was part-built by Whittingham's father (William also) where a barn had been.

Jennings received part of the King's Bounty (*qv*) for lodging troops in 1755. By 1794 the name had been changed to The King of Prussia. That did not last long. It was soon altered to The Hop Bag (alternatively known as The Pocket of Hops). In the 1830s and '40s George Rivers (*b* 1801*) was there.

A fire nearly destroyed the whole place in 1868. The barn (probably one which in 1850 stood at the back of number 63) was burned down, the house damaged. Farnham Brewery offered the place for sale in 1891, G. C. Knight of Runwick House (*qqv*) having bought it from Samuel Lewcock, confectioner, in 1827.

The building to be seen today is almost all, if not entirely, modern. A thorough-going reconstruction of the earlier two floor cottage building was made in 1906. A barn-like building east of the gateway was in fact a house — probably the one built by William Whittingham the elder as a conversion from the barn, before 1755.

CHURCH LANE

Church Lane leads off Downing Street, to its west, from two points and follows three sides of a ricketty square. It should not be missed. It not only has qualities of its own, but leads to St. Andrew's Church and the Old Vicarage in its yard. In the south-west corner of the churchyard is a tiny alley which connects with water-meadows and the River Wey. St. Andrew's School is to the north of the church.

Church Lane is frequently divided into Upper, Middle and Lower, although this has not long been so. The little south-west spur was once Lower Church Lane and a map less than seventy years old names the two upper members Lower Church Lane, the third, Church Lane.

Church Lane, especially the middle section, contains a fascinating variety of vernacular details and façades, mostly in their natural state as, perhaps surprisingly, it has not yet become a fashionable backwater. No doubt it will do.

THE RECTORY, CHURCH LANE
(Upper)

A symmetrical five-bay brick façade on two main floors with dormer windows in a tiled roof. Eaves are moulded and decorated with scrolled brackets and in part by alternating roundels. A painted string course divides floors. The whole stands high on a plinth and extensions have been added to this main block.

Fenestration: Ground floor, four three-pane-wide sashes with wide boxes and segmental heads; First floor, five similar; Above, two dormer windows with casements and gables, the open ends tile hung above windows.

Door: In bay three, above steps and with a gabled porch. The door is framed by an architrave with segmental head. This contains the fanlight with metal tracery.

Interior: A hall, to the west of which a room with raised wood panels, dentil cornice and Adamesque chimney piece. To the east a similarly panelled room. First floor, front bedrooms, one panelled, contain fitted cupboads with architraves decorated in the Adamesque manner. All principal windows have folding shutters.

Other features: An earlier building was timber framed and parts remain particularly to the back north-west. Rebuilding and possibly extension have taken place to the east and on a small scale to the west.

A good brick 18th century front with some locally unusual details. It has been defaced by its later porch and by dormer windows. Major reconstruction has been carried out resulting in rebuilding the east end; rebuilding rather than extending, as various 19th century (small scale) plans from the 1830s show the house to be of similar size and disposition.

A description written in about 1948 states that there were the remains of sawn-off Doric columns under the porch, and that the fanlight was plain. It dates the east extension, porch and dormer windows as *c* 1900. Asymmetry of eaves decoration suggests a part-rebuilding of the roof.

Perhaps the entrance hall was never decorated. It is unusual though to find a house with such well panelled rooms upstairs and down (and once distinguished façade) without a good staircase and handsome hall. The former is inconspicuously placed and relatively mean; the latter bare. Articulation of these parts of various date is not typically accomplished for an 18th century reconstruction.

Early 17th century indentures relate to the lease and holding in trust of the rectory or parsonage of Farnham and the manor or mansion house of the same and all the barns, buildings and privilege pertaining to the rectory and manor. They were during that century held by Sir Thomas White (*qv*) and in 1671 John Pearson, Archdeacon of Surrey, leased the same to Thomas Vernon (*qv*), merchant, of London. He sublet. It was customary to lease for three lives. The tithes passed to Anne, wife of Sir George Woodroffe (d 1779), of Poyle. Thomas Walker later sold to Henry Halsey of Henley Park. Henry Halsey is mentioned in a conveyance of 1790, and one of that same name is recorded as occupying the Rectory fifty years later; also large kilns in East Street where the Regal Cinema now stands. Mr. Halsey is now remembered for having given the altarpiece painting by Elmer (*qv*) to St. Andrew's Church, and for having given up his ground rent on the parsonage barn and yard when St. Andrew's School (*qv*) was built on the site adjoining The Rectory in 1860. A second Mr. Halsey? It may be that Miss Milne's School was here. It was in or near Church Lane 1851-55 at least (see The Old Vicarage). The tithes were not relet after 1864. As they fell in they were redistributed among neighbouring parishes.

In the Bodleian Library Department of Western Manuscripts (Wilberforce Papers) is a list of the chief rents
belonging to The Rectory in 1726, together with a query,
and opinion, concerning the powers of the Archdeacon of
Surrey in granting a lease of The Rectory in 1762. The list
contains names of thirty-one people, of which many are
familiar. But apart from The Antelope (*qv*) no house names
are mentioned.

4   UPPER   CHURCH   LANE

From at least mid-19th century hereabout was The Baker's
Arms. Property, 'late The Baker's Arms', was offered for sale
by Farnham United Brewery in 1928.

28   LOWER   CHURCH   LANE

Hereabouts was The Feathers, which existed in the later
19th century.

*   28-30   (Between)   LOWER   CHURCH   LANE
(Mardon, Ball & Co.)

This extensive builders' yard retains old light-industrial
buildings. Their forms and skylines are vigorous and varied
(see illustration). There is also the appeal of picturesque
decomposition of the oldest ones.

Lamport's Waggon Yard was here in the 19th century.
George Lamport (*qv*) was probably also at 10 The Borough.
In The Wheelwright's Shop it is recorded of waggons coming
down the Hog's Back into Farnham that '. . . though still
three miles away they were audible to my grandfather at his
gate. . . . The waggons got to Farnham, where it was his
duty to look to them, at about 10 o'clock at night. The
place where they put up is now Messrs. Mardon and Ball's
"Waggon Yard Joinery" '.

Lamport was a carrier by 1820 and George Lamport
(*b* 1791*), corndealer, was son of James Stewart Lamport of
10 The Borough (*qv*). Robert Lamport (*qv*) of Longbridge, was
a woolstapler in the early 19th century and Thomas Lamport's (*qv*) widow, Eleanor (*d* 1859*), married George Knight
(*qv*) *c.* 1834.

30 AND 31 LOWER CHURCH LANE

(Trusler's)

A house and shop of timber framed construction, on two main floors with tiled roof. The front is brick built with recessed three-pane-wide sash windows.

A large house of considerable age. It has been much altered and refaced — apparently in two stages — recently, to cover a once oversailing front. The house is of several bays depth, and has been claimed to be among the oldest in Farnham. A good chimney piece dated 1623 was at 31 Church Lane till about 1900 when it was sold to Lord Eldon and removed. The carving was heavy and elaborate with grotesque caryatids, lion masks and smatterings of renaissance details.

Tradition also holds that this was Byworths, a house connected with the family of that name and later with the Vernons (*qv*). Evidence that the place called Byworths was not here in fact is strong. Henry Vernon's will reads, 'all that messuage or tenement late Byworths barns other buildings and gardens backsides there adjacent near West Street on the north and the New River on the south'. This description does not say 'late of' or 'formerly of John Byworth'; 'late Byworths' suggests the name by which this West Street property was known. It does not exclude 30-31 Lower Church Lane from being connected with John Byworth. Almshouses for which he left money were very near. But as deeds of the property were burned years ago facts are difficult to establish.

WAGGON YARD, Lower Church Lane. Old buildings in the functional tradition still standing and now used as builder's stores and workshops.

The date 1623 on the removed chimney piece suggests a link, for in that year John Byworth (born in Kent) died in Farnham. Further, in 1622 he had recently bought from Thomas and Agnes Over a house 'next to 'the river' which he quickly set about repairing and in part rebuilding by March of that year. One godson, Thomas Horsford, inherited the newly-built part, with half the yard, barns and with a grass plot. Another godson, Byworth Horsford, inherited the other moiety which included the repaired part of the house. If 31 Church Lane is that same place the chimney piece could well have been either part of John Byworth's re-fitting, or a memorial to his passing fitted by grateful beneficiaries.

Petronel Byworth (née Mower) died in 1628. She left a house, already in his possession, to Robert Horsford. It was in West Street. Was this Byworth's? It was partly occupied by 'Old Chaffer and Mrs. Moore' and included a dye house, vats and furnace. She left conditionally to Robert, the son of Robert Horsford of Wrecclesham, another house near Longbridge (also possibly 31 Church Lane) next to the tenement of one called Fygge, her house then being in the possession of John Bridle. More property in Fanshawe Street, London, went to the Fyvens.

Mrs. Moore, above, was related to George and Oliver Moore. They benefited from Petronel's will. Oliver and Elizabeth Moore's children included Thomas, Richard and Mary. George and Ellen Moore's children included Sarah, Joan, John and Petronel Moore, Mrs. Byworth's goddaughter, to whom she left a 'little silver bowl that goeth about the house'. Her other goddaughters were Petronel Legg (probably daughter of Joan Legg, a cousin) and Petronel Horsford. It is interesting to find that in the early 19th century 30 and 31 Lower Church Lane were owned by James Moore, still being occupied by Mary Moore, dressmaker, Ann, her sister, and Lydia Moore in the 1850s. But this, like the dated chimney piece, may be coincidental. Were Moore and Mower synonymous?

The Byworths were an important family of which very little has been recorded previously and of which few relationships seem to have been established. Bearing in mind that 'cousin' could cover a fairly wide range of relatives the following may prove of value to researchers. Of John Byworth (*d* 1623) Daniel was a brother with daughters Alice, Martha and Ann; Thomas Horsford a cousin whose wife was Elizabeth; Christopher Fyvens a cousin with a sister Ellen; George Moore a cousin, also Oliver Moore, his wife being Elizabeth; Robert Wybart, a cousin, like Augustine Phillips; Joan Parkins, his daughter-in-law. Petronel Byworth's relatives also included Robert Baynard, her brother-in-law, and Joan Legg, her cousin; Christopher Stickland, her brother; Mrs. Parkhurst of London, her daughter; Robert Gary Horseford and Michael Gary, cousins.

The Byworth-Gary (or Garie) connection is of interest as Christopher Gary, draper, married Joan, the daughter of Robert Bicknell (*qv*). He was the son of Michael (*d* 1658), woollen draper, and Elizabeth Gary. Petronel Byworth left Christopher Gary 'the bed brought from London' which was in the green chamber of her house. Michael Gary's house has not yet been located. It was left to his wife — remembered by Petronel who left to her the furniture 'in the chamber where my husband's picture is'. Michael Gary also left a house in Castle Street, another in Downing Street and one more in The Borough, which was let to widow Joan Thompson in 1654. Michael and Elizabeth Gary's children were Christopher, John, Robert, Nathaniel, George, Michael, Ann, Elizabeth and Jane. Elizabeth (the mother) had a brother, William Mower of Cranley. In 1689 William Mower, a Farnham weaver, and Barbara Mower, of London, sold property at Windlesham. At the Minet Library is a manuscript concerning a legacy of Jane Gary, daughter of Christopher and Joan Gary, the daughter of Robert Bicknell deceased.

John Byworth asked to be buried at Farnham Parish Church and to have erected there a marble stone costing £7 or £8. He left £10 for a silver-gilt Communion Cup and money for Nicholas Manweringe the elder 'that dwelleth against me . . . to buy him leather'. See Manwaring.

The house at 31 Church Lane, with hop land to the rear, was offered for sale at The Bush Hotel on instruction from Mr. Lambert in 1877 but was not sold on that occasion.

THE OLD VICARAGE, CHURCH LANE   (Near)

An asymmetrical brick and timber built house on two main floors with a tile roof. Projecting north from a main east-west ridge a gable, partly with carved bargeboards, closed with hung tiles and containing three upper casements and the main door.

Fenestration: Irregular, mainly leaded casements with a gabled dormer facing north, to east of main door.

Interior: Particularly in the upper parts considerable timber work, including a collar beam roof and a door frame with four-centred head and mouldings.

The house has been substantially altered over many

centuries. The list of Buildings of Historic Interest dates main parts as 14th century with 16th, 17th, and 18th century and modern alterations. It states that the house consisted originally of a single hall with open timber roof and a room for the priest over the north porch. This room was reached by a ladder from the hall. It adds that the first floor was probably inserted in the 16th century and that the attic floor is of later date.

One is struck by the enormous expanse of roof on the north side. This is largely accounted for by extensions to the original building. Various changes of roof pitch suggest this and the manner in which bargeboards end indicates the extent to which the porch has been widened — it is said, in this century. The front, east of centre, was certainly altered about mid-19th century and a range of outbuildings, to the east again, demolished not very long afterwards.

Trees line the path to the church door — for many years sealed but lately reopened. In 1739 John Cartwright and Thomas Rivers were paid 4s. 8d. for 'planting the trees in the church yard', and a further five shillings was paid to a gardener and three men for taking up and planting Mr. Smithers' trees there. Not that it is confirmed here that this avenue is 223 years old. There are other trees too.

Until recently the Old Vicarage was Church property but it is now privately owned. Few facts have come to light about its past, although it appears once to have served as a private school for, in the 1840s, Laura Barrett (*b* 1821*?), a governess, and Anne Savage (*qv*, *b* 1811), her assistant, were at the Old Vicarage. They had at least eight pupils named Beldham (*qv*) and others including an Elizabeth Barrett (*b* 1837*). Barrett and Beldham (*qqv*) were a brewing partnership having their brewery in Church Lane before moving to Bridge Square, and at about this time John Barrett was tenant of the Old Vicarage, Henry Warren holding the Vicarial Glebe.

By 1851 'Church Lane Vicarage' was occupied by Thomas Pearcy (*qv*, *b* 1808), a bricklayer, his wife Maria (*b* 1814*) and son Charles Pearcy (*qv*, *b* 1841*), while a school in or near Church Lane was run by a Gloucester-born mistress named Ann Milne (*b* 1825*), the daughter of Susannah (*b* 1801*) with a brother John (*b* 1827*). She had a flourishing establishment catering for girl boarders. Whether this school succeeded Barrett's, was at the Old Vicarage or at The Parsonage, has not been not been definitely established, although it does seem likely to have been at what is now The Rectory (*qv*).

BRIDGE SQUARE

Bridge Square is by the river, off centre, approached via Downing Street or South Street from the town. Here meet Longbridge, Firgrove Hill, Abbey Street, Red Lion Lane and the Wey. This is the focal point of what was a little suburb, south of the river, and until recent times only fields lay between it and The Borough and Lower Downing Street. There were about sixty cottages in Abbey Street, Bridge Square and straggling down the south side of Red Lion Lane. A century ago they, with a couple of houses, were dominated for various reasons by the brewery, Firgrove and The Jolly Farmer. Taming the river has made the place less damp, although it is still liable to flood, and the Square has only lately lost the long familiar smell of malt.

1   BRIDGE   SQUARE

Here was The Bridge House, a pub which existed in the later part of the 19th century. It was offered for sale by Farnham Brewery in 1891.

Most of this corner of Bridge Square was demolished about 1900 and rebuilt shortly afterwards.

BRIDGE   SQUARE   (Red Lion Brewery,
   Courage and Barclay)

An extensive riverside site with ranges of brick- or chalk-built
industrial buildings, mainly slate roofed and on several floors.

   This block provides an exciting skyline and adds valuable
variety to the scale, shapes, character and purpose of the
buildings of central Farnham. Austere, and rather forbidding,
they are virile, functional and bold. Unfortunately big business economics have rendered them unusable for some years.
Inside, the largest buildings are impressive for their vast
floors, uninterrupted but for scores of columns connecting
them with low ceilings.

   The development of this site is complex and a long
one, but it can be divided into three major phases: 1, The
Tannery—which, early, occupied the west half of the site;
2, Barrett's Brewery, which developed on the same site from
1845; 3, Since the amalgamation of this site with the one
lying to its east, which was already the malting of Robert
Sampson (*qv*) by 1839.

   The tannery was working by 1760 (possibly long before)
under Michael Redding, and was bought by Stanley Bolen
(*qv*), tanner, in 1770, together with Tanyard House (*qv*), an
orchard and buildings. When brewing started on this site, it
is difficult to decide, for as early as 1802 it was owned by
Michael and James Page (*qqv*), who were brewers in Farnham. Yet when sold to John Barrett and George Beldham,
brewers, in 1845, the property was still described as a
tanyard, and at about that time nearly a dozen tanners lived
in Red Lion Lane. There was, however, another tannery not
far away. The yard occupied roughly the courtyard as it is
today, but extended north to the river. The buildings there
at about that time were quite small and not the kind that
one would associate with even a small brewery. Barrett and
Beldham had been brewing previously in Church Lane where
the smithy now is.

   Robert Sampson's (*qv*) maltings already occupied his
stretch of river bank and continued round the corner into
Bridge Square much as the maltings do today. He lived in
the pebble-dashed house at the east end of the terrace row,
a neat little house with nicely banistered stairs. The Memorial Sports Ground was once known as Sampson's Meadow
and Sampson created a Trust for Sampson's Almshouses (*qv*).
Sampson Sampson (b 1822), his son, maltster, lived once at
40 West Street (*qv*).

   John Barrett lived at Old Roof (*qv*), opposite Tanyard
House. Although not started here until 1845, it is said, on
good authority, that when the business was sold (and it

included many public houses) to Farnham United Brewery in 1890, it raised nearly half a million pounds. Victoria's army no doubt helped to amass this fortune as Barretts had pubs in Aldershot as well as in Farnham.

A few mid-19th century buildings remain and possibly fragments of the tannery in the south-west corner running back from Red Lion Lane. The river frontage block (west part) is said to have been built in 1902. If so, it is a rebuilding as the entire frontage had been developed by 1871. The Red Lion public house was to the left of the yard gates.

BRIDGE SQUARE (Old Roof)

A symmetrical three-bay house on two main floors, of brick with slate roof.

Fenestration: Ground floor, two three-light bay windows; First floor, three recessed sashes, with arched head in bay two.

Door: Fanlighted and pilastered.

This appears to be a house which has been partly Victorianised. The roof and additions to the front suggest it. Inside, there is a good Ionic pilastered arch in the hall, and egg and dart cornice in a back room.

Early in the 19th century Sarah Williams was owner. She may have been the Sally Williams (*qv*) who owned properties nearby and 45 and 46 Castle Street. In 1841 a Sarah Williams (*b* 1786*) was at 6 West Street, and in 1810, George, the son of William and Sarah Williams, was buried in Farnham. This Sarah was probably closely related to Anthony Williams (*qv*), Charlotte and Rosa (*bb* 1821), who was daughter of a Sally Williams (*b* 1784*). Anthony (*d* 1889) was the wine merchant who bought 122 West Street (*qv*) in 1872.

Old Roof, once Elm Grove, was later occupied by the Barrett family, who built up Red Lion Brewery (*qv*), opposite the house, from 1845. John Barrett (*qv*) had been brewing earlier in Church Lane and was in business by 1826. He occupied a malthouse and nine acres of hopland at Beaver's. John Barrett, junior (*b* 1839, *d* 1906), was at Elm Grove by the 1870s, by which time Robert and John Barrett were partners. Beldham, John senior's partner, seems to have disappeared by this time.

Extensive tunnellings run under the hillside behind. Many highly coloured stories have been told about them, for example, of smugglers, but it is supposed by the more rational that they were cool vaults for Barrett's barrels. They also accommodated many shelterers during air raid alerts in the last war.

4 BRIDGE SQUARE (The Jolly Farmer)

A brick and tiled public house of five bays on two floors.

There is no mention of an ale-house or inn in 1698 nor in 1725, between which dates a house here which had been divided into two, with a barn, stable, garden and close of land called Teynter Acre was owned by the Newberry family. The property was adjoined on the west, east and south by the Searle (*qv*) family's estate. Twenty-seven years later Henry Newberry the elder, and John, negotiated with John Bignold concerning the property described as Teynter Acre with a house and barn. The house passed to Joseph Kimber (*b* 1796*) and Sophia (*b* 1806*), and is definitely identified as a public house thirteen years before he conveyed it to Richard Balchin (*d* 1870), a Godalming doctor, in 1852. A Joseph Kimber occupied a Farnham ale-house by 1839 but not on present evidence necessarily called The Jolly Farmer. Kimber also owned the cottage adjoining the west. The east end of The Jolly Farmer was cut back some feet about the mid-19th century. In 1870 those houses adjoining the east were described as newly built.

The building as we know it is not recognisable as one depicted in an earlier 19th-century engraving. The view does not relate to an early plan of the building any more than it does to the one extant. Another engraving based on second-hand information possibly; the craftsman supplying what the topographer did not.

On March 9th, 1763, William Cobbett (*qv*) was born hereabouts, some claim in the cottage abutting the west end, some in the pub itself. His life is well recorded elsewhere and something of the funeral in this book. A terra cotta plaque records his association with the building. It was presented by the Farnham Society.

Mrs. Young paid a visit to The Jolly Farmer about 1857. She wrote, afterwards, 'The hostess of The Jolly Farmer very obligingly took me into the room where the great author of "The Political Register" first drew breath — a room on the first floor to the left of the door and looking towards the church and meadows of Farnham. The old house, she told me, was in exactly the same state as that in which Cobbett had left it. The same heavy broad stairs, the same roughly-cut wooden banisters, the same clumsy and primitive-looking doors — fixtures of 1762. There, however, all the pegs of association ended. The room had a modern French bedstead. . . . Some twelve months since, an auction took place at The Jolly Farmer, and the last of Cobbett's effects were sold, in the form of an old oak cupboard, with gilt panels, inscribed in remembrance of the first and last scene of his eventful history. . . . Madame Tussaud, it is said, has offered a large sum for the relic in question, but since its purchase by the inspector of police at Farnham, a lawsuit has been threatened for its recovery. . . . The inspector most obligingly allowed me to see it, in his children's playroom. . . .'

Cobbett produced, of course, a great body of writing. One of his projects, which seems not to have materialised, would have been a book of great local interest. It was 'The Customs of Farnham', an attempt to record the passing superstitions, festivals and rustic activities peculiar to this district.

There is a Cobbett cupboard or chest in a Downing Street house today.

George Cobbett, William's father (*b* 1741*, *d* 1792), has been variously described as a sawyer, farmer, and victualler. William's mother was Anne. The Farnham Parish Register of Burials records George Cobbett, land surveyor, died in 1792. Ann, the wife of George Cobbett, senior, died in 1788, and two Anns — daughters of a George, in 1767 and 1781. *The* William Cobbett's wife was also an Ann (*b* 1774, *d* 1848). George Cobbett was a greengrocer in Farnham in 1791, and William Thomas Cobbett owned 69 West Street (*qv*) in the 19th century.

William Cobbett died at his house at Ash in 1835. A plumber named Edwards, born in the same house as Cobbett, was ordered to build the lead coffin. A Martha Edwards lived at The Jolly Farmer in 1823. Later landlords include William Hole (1826), Richard Baker (1855), Henry Payne (1878), Charles Krafft (1882), W. Buck (1900), and Richard Jack (1915). The landlordships of most Farnham pubs could be given in some detail, but have been included only here as they may one day help to substantiate evidence, or locate relics, associated with Cobbett.

The house has recently been renamed The William Cobbett.

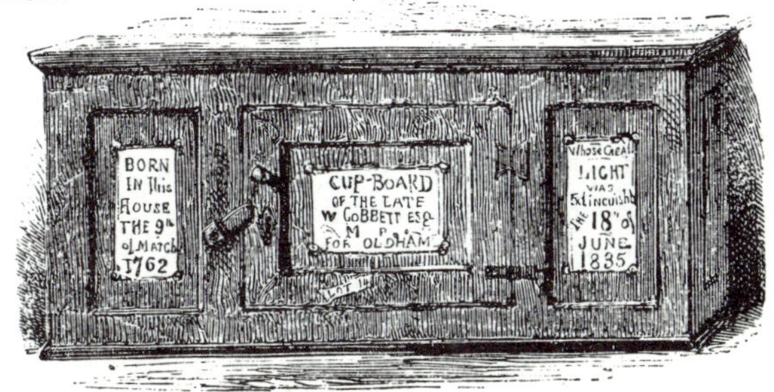

11 BRIDGE SQUARE (Firgrove Cottage)

A brick, plaster and tile house with timber frame and tiled roof. The main ridge runs north to south. From this a secondary one, barge-boarded and finialled, faces west.

Fenestration: Ground floor, leaded casements; First floor, leaded casements. On the west front is a five-light corbelled oriel window, gabled, barge-boarded and finialled, and contained within the west-facing secondary gable. Above the oriel's own gable is a small leaded window. On the south end is an oriel-cum-porch, under a gable, with carved and pierced barge-board.

Doors: On west, south and east faces.

A genuine olde worlde cottage, which has seen many changes yet retains some character of an authentic old vernacular building.

The serious research which has gone into timber-framed houses in Farnham is almost negligible. Farnham is a rich field, largely overgrown. There is little, either intact or on the surface, and what there is is generally of a relatively rugged character, with little embellishment. Few dating criteria have been established, but to put the origins of this house within the 'mediaeval' bracket would be fairly safe. The bracket is, of course, a very wide one. Little is known of the early history of Firgrove Cottage. Others have established that its first floor is an insertion into an open-roofed hall. To this, at the same time, was inserted the upper fireplace and a west-facing gable with oriel window. The once jettied west lower front has in fairly recent times been brick filled.

When Mr. Borelli (*qv*) bought the house in 1912, it was subdivided into separate dwellings. He made them one. Windows flanking the oriel were re-opened and other alterations made.

In the later 19th century the property, with other hereabout, was James Martyr Ward's. The whole block was earlier described as a six-oast kiln and store, ten cottages and three more newly-erected (those with the arched windows?).

The two dwellings immediately below Firgrove Cottage are a mid-19th century replacement for a hopkiln once owned by Olivia Searle and there was another larger kiln contained behind the block. This was completely demolished about mid-century and was probably the one mentioned above. It was owned in the early 19th century (as were several of these cottages) by Sarah Williams (*qv*). There is brickwork of an unusual quality at the north end of the block.

12 AND 13 BRIDGE SQUARE

(Tanyard House)

A house on two main floors, of asymmetrical façade, having a timber frame infilled largely with brick. Parts of the south and east fronts are plastered.

Fenestration: Windows are irregularly placed, mainly leaded casements.

The street front of this house was restored early this century, but it was not transformed beyond recognition. Tie-beam and studding follow the original pattern as does herringbone brickwork. Upper windows relate to those originally there. Elaborately carved barge-boards have gone and so has the door, once at the west end of this front.

The building extends well back from the street and toward its north end is a second massive brick chimney, less altered than the south one. It has fragments of unusual decoration. Inside, much of the original structure is clearly exposed. The house appears to have been one dwelling, known as Tanyard House, until 1760-70. By the latter date it had become two tenements and by 1827 was subdivided into four dwellings. The house is historically a part of Red Lion Brewery (*qv*) which lay to its north and west.

The brewery developed from a tannery (from which this house gets its name) and from maltings to the east. Hassell's drawing of the house shows it much as it is today.

Stanley Bolen (*qv*), tanner, who brought the Tannery in 1770, appears for the first time as a local Freeholder in 1771. He was in Farnham for many years and may easily be confused with a collar maker of the same name. A William Bolen voted in 1774. Sarah Bolen (*b* 1776*) was living in lower Downing Street in the 1850s.

TANYARD, Farnham, in the 1820s.

A brick built house on two principal floors. The main (centre) section is symmetrical, of five bays, with dormer windows above moulded cornice. The front of this section is cement cased. The roof is tiled. Substantial wings abut asymmetrically and are set back from the principal section which is as below.

Fenestration: Ground floor, four recessed three-pane-wide sashes; First floor, five similar; Above, three casemented dormers with tiled cheeks and hoods.

Door: In bay three, above steps and behind a plain portico with freestanding fluted Doric stone columns.

West elevation: Asymmetrical, of eight principal bays, part parapeted and on two floors, with a single storey bay window topped by a balustraded parapet.

The building is said to be dated 1688, and to have been refronted early in the 19th century. If one strips the house to its central block, denudes that of its Victorian additions and replaces them with probable earlier equivalents, one is left with a façade which could possibly be of that date (see illustration).

There is a vigorously carved late 17th century-style staircase of a type not to be found elsewhere in the town, although one need not travel very far to find comparable ones. This, like the marble chimney piece in the north wing, is supposed to have come from Merton Park, which was demolished about 1820. It was after that date that considerable alterations were made to Firgrove, for the house was of an earlier form in 1820. Seventeen years later the plan was much as one would have expected the early house to have had, but by 1870 it was similar to today's, including a north-west bay window shape. It is possible that an earlier plan still was E-shaped — the open side facing west.

Having sheltered for so many years behind its high wall and gate flanked by magnificent grey stone pineapples (recently restored and resited) and being guarded for at least seventy years by a quaint lodge, this house has tended to keep its secrets closely. The occupants were seldom townsfolk. Tradition, rumour and fact concerning Nelsonian association have so far proved unentanglable. Few conclusions have been drawn about the history of the house pre-1800 and much that is generally supposed of its later associations is open to challenge in the absence of documentary proof. However, it has been stated elsewhere that the house with its once extensive estate was conveyed in 1809 to Olivia Searle (*d* 1844) and was probably occupied at some time before that date by William Brereton Clerk.

Boswell and the Williamses of Badshot Place (*qv*, where Boswell was staying) went to Farnham to dine with Sir Nelson Rycroft (*b* 1761*, *d* 1827) who 'rented a place there'. Firgrove House was still Sir Nelson's seat in 1822 and probably at his death, so that the interpretation often made of Boswell's note — that Rycroft was in Farnham only temporarily — appears erroneous. It is possible, though, that he lived in Yorkshire as well. He is said to have been the son of Richard Nelson, D.D., who had assumed the name Rycroft. A monument sculptured by Westmacott was erected in St. Andrew's Church to Sir Nelson Rycroft by his family. Lady Charlotte (*b* 1766*), Sir Nelson's wife, was buried in Farnham in 1803 and she left four children.

In 1830 the Barlows were in occupation and Firgrove Hill was for many years known as Barlow's Hill after a once-illustrious member of the family, Sir George Hilaro Barlow, the brother of Admiral Sir Robert Barlow. George was Governor-General of India from 1805 to 1807, but his elevated office (in which he succeeded Cornwallis) was not brilliantly executed. Having next become Governor of Madras his policies and 'repellent manners' led him to Farnham and retirement.

At the house in 1841 were George Barlow (*b* 1766*), Frances and Anne (*bb* 1806**), Maria (*b* 1811*), George (*b* 1834*), William (*b* 1837*), and Richard Barlow. The family appears to have left in about 1847, after Sir George's death in 1846. The Dictionary of National Biography gives George Barlow's birth year as 1762. George Barlow, of Firgrove, is recorded locally as being aged 75 in 1841.

During Olivia Searle's ownership cottages and kilns at the bottom of the hill, barns and sheds opposite Firgrove House (across the road) went with the estate. Some of the farm buildings projected into what is now Firgrove Hill, which possibly accounts for their disappearance at an early date. The railway later sliced Firgrove Estate in two and the little Lodge which once stood over what is now the by-pass ended its days as an ingeniously camouflaged blockhouse, one of a chain intended to repel invading armies in the second World War.

A claim that Richard Rycroft's surname had been Nelson has been pointed out. His son's Christian name (Nelson) adds weight to this. It has also been stated that Lord Horatio Nelson's brother, the Reverend William, was married (for the second time) to a young widow, Hilaire, daughter of Admiral Sir Robert Barlow.

Lord Nelson, 1758-1805, is said to have sent a black slave to Lady Hamilton after 1798. Fatima, we gather, was baptised in Merton in 1802, and William Nelson's daughter was a godmother to her. Further, it is said that after Lady Hamilton gave up Merton Park, Fatima was removed to the workhouse in Bear Lane, Farnham. It has also long been a belief that Lady Hamilton brought to Firgrove the notable staircase and chimney piece from Merton Park; also that members of the Nelson family lived at Firgrove House.

Recently this has been disputed. 'Nelson never came to Farnham,' states one. This would seem even more difficult to prove than that he did; not that this, to the writer's knowledge, has ever been claimed. There does, though, seem very strong circumstantial evidence of at least a connection, but the correspondence between Nelson and Captain (later Admiral Sir) Robert Barlow, which is kept at the British Museum, really helps very little, hopeful as it sounds. It concerns Naval matters. At least one letter, though, written by Barlow from Bath (where his father, William, lived) hints that their relationship went a little beyond a purely formal professional one.

In 1851 more strangers to the town were at Firgrove. They were the family of Alexander Ogilvie (*b* 1812*), a Scot and civil engineer.

Trafalgar Court, a large neo-Georgabethan speculative maisonette development, was, at the time of writing, nearing completion in what has been the grounds of Firgrove House.

FIRGROVE HOUSE. A partly conjectural reconstruction of its centre block, shown here before Victorian alterations were made.

ABBEY STREET

Abbey Street is presumably so called as it was the only road from Farnham town to Waverley Abbey (centuries before South Street was made). It links South Street with Bridge Square, running approximately from east to west. Ninety years ago there were no buildings on its north side although there were two some time before that. Its south has been built-up for ages.

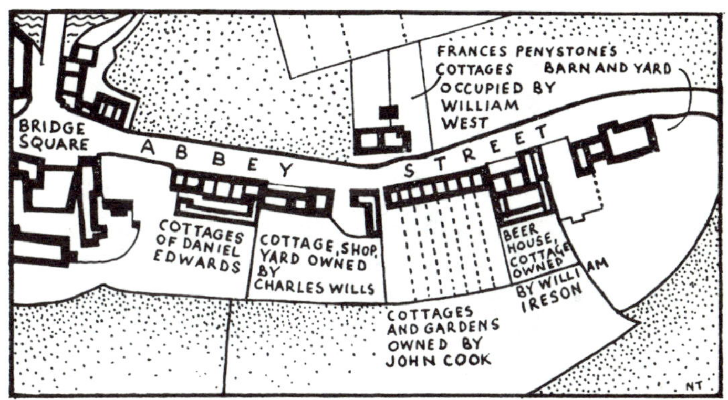

Abbey Street in 1839: a map based on W. Harding's, showing building in Abbey Street, with Bridge Square to the west. The purpose of the buildings and names of owners of the Abbey Street properties have been added.

13   ABBEY   STREET   (Demolished)

Here was The Bricklayer's Arms. A pub of this name existed in the 1830s under the ownership of William Ireson. Its licence was transferred to a new building in Weydon Lane *c* 1939, the old house being demolished *c* 1954.

43   ABBEY   STREET   (The Lamb)

An asymmetrical building with three-pane-wide flush sashes and peaked dormer windows.

This neatly-pointed brick built pub has been so named since at least 1867, not very long before which it had been converted from two dwellings. It may sometimes have been confused with The Lamb and Flag (*qv*), otherwise The Lamb, once in Castle Street. 43 Abbey Street was largely rebuilt in 1928, when bought with adjoining property by Messrs. Watneys. Their customary brown brick was used as in most of their Farnham reconstructions. Early on the pub was occupied by Thomas Matthews, then by George McDonald (*qv*).

WAVERLEY ABBEY in the early 18th century, showing a likeness of
an earlier Waverley House — probably designed by Campbell.

SOUTH STREET

South Street is quite new, although most of its buildings affect styles twice its age, or more. It leads to the station and terminates at Station Hill, having run from the point where the narrowing Borough opens into East Street. There is a park (Gostrey Meadow) with riverside walk, three Non-conformist chapels and an early Lutyens Club. Union Road connects Lower Downing Street with South Street while running along the north side of Gostrey Meadow.

When the New Road (as South Street was at first known) was to be built to make a fresh approach to the station, a committee was set up to raise funds. In six months public subscription produced over £1,000. S. Nicholson (*qv*), of Waverley Abbey, gave £100. G. Trimmer, Farnham's biggest noise, was not to be outdone by him or even by the Bishop. He gave £150 (and later owned The Royal Deer).

The Local Board's estimated total cost for South Street, including buying the houses, land, fencing and for demolition, etc., was £2,500. The bridge, with its iron and stonework and concrete, was expected to account for £415 of this sum. According to printed reports the branch line from Guildford was opened in 1849 and had been extended to Alton three years later. The Farnham-Aldershot-London line was opened in 1870. The first electric train arrived at Farnham Station late in 1936. See plan on page 108.

KILNS once at Broomleaf, near Farnham Station.

ROYAL DEER SHOPS, SOUTH STREET

A terrace of brick built neo-Georgian shops.

Another earlier rebuilding scheme of the kind inspired by C. E. Borelli's example. The group was designed to harmonise with the then recently completed Royal Deer (*qv*) adjoining. Previously here was The Assembly Room, a long, low building on one floor with stage-set stucco façade of 1880s character.

These new buildings were designed by A. J. and L. R. Stedman in 1929 — just after Leonard Stedman had joined his father's long-established practice. The firm also designed shops and flats in upper Downing Street (1929) and 49 Castle Street in about the same year. Other examples of the partnership's work are Barclay's Bank (1930-31) and 98-99 West Street (1936). The firm's office at 36 South Street was designed by A. J. Stedman in 1908, as were MacDonald's Almshouses (*qv*) in 1905-6.

THE LIBERAL CLUB, SOUTH STREET

A five-bay two-floor near-symmetrical façade of brick under a slate roof. A string course lying on key bricks separates floors. Eaves are corniced in brick.

Fenestration: Ground floor, windows in bays one, two, four and five; First floor, five windows below detached brick pediments — alternating, triangular and segmental. All front windows are wood framed, transomed and mullioned. Their four lights are glazed with rectangular leaded panes.

Door: Pilastered and pedimented, occupying bay three. There is a side door on the extreme south of the façade.

Edwin Lutyens drew his plan in September, 1894. The building was designed by him as The Liberal Club. His plan indicates Italian roofing tiles, which were used. They were later replaced by slate. Outwardly, there are few variations from Lutyens' plan although he seems to have overlooked the site's north-south decline. This has resulted in the alteration of the side door height and the making of small adjustments elsewhere about ground level.

Lutyens had connections with the district from his early days. Crooksbury House was his first real commission, in 1888. As a result he left Sir Ernest George to set up in private practice at 6 Gray's Inn Square, and it was there that he produced The Liberal Club plans very early in his career. By 1910 he was appointed to work on one of the biggest commissions undertaken by an English architect, the planning of New Delhi and the Viceroy's House. The Club is Lutyens' first-known excursion into the Queen Anne style. It is a naïve one. Although it has been stated that Lutyens built nothing in the town, drawings that prove his authorship have recently been found in Farnham. They bear his name, the date, and his London address.

F.U.D.C. OFFICES, SOUTH STREET

An integrated brick built group of public offices, including the Fire Station, on two main floors. The roof is tiled and topped by a pillared and louvred turret.

Built in 1901, in his neo-Georgian style by Paxton Hood Watson (*qv*), for about £5,000, it was officially opened in 1903. In 1956 twin arches were removed and the present higher openings to the Fire Station were inserted; unfortunate, but presumably unavoidable.

Watson was an A.R.I.B.A. from 1889-99, after which records of his Associateship end. The Council Offices are perhaps his most worthy memorial in the town. He was responsible for other buildings, notably The Institute, South Street; Farnham Grammar School, West Street (*qqv*), Silwood, West End Grove; 93 West Street; and Alice Holt Lodge. He later went to Mertsham.

17 SOUTH STREET (F.U.D.C. Treasurer's Dept.)

An early 18th century styled building in brick.

Here was once the School of Art and Science which was established in 1870. It was first built in two parts; in 1874, and then completed at a total cost of £900 in 1878. From here the School of Art (as which this building then served), moved to 25 West Street (*qv*) in 1939. A studio was retained here. The second stage of building was in about 1915 when the corner block was added by the County Architect to the design of H. Falkner (*qv*).

Farnham Art School began its life in the upper room of what has become known as The Bailiffs' Hall (*qv*) in The Borough. It was open in about 1865. Sturt was an early pupil under Mr. Offord. We have been left with a clear impression of one Victorian approach to Art education in Sturt's reminiscences.

When the school had moved to South Street W. H. Allen became Head. He was appointed in 1889 and retired in 1928. A collection of his paintings, which includes many local scenes, is in the Curtis Museum at Alton. 17 South Street and its neighbours stand along the east boundary of what was once the town's cricket ground.

1·3   SOUTH   STREET   (Farnham Institute)

A red brick, gabled and plate-glass building under a tiled roof.

Very mid-Victorian, with its heavy gables, bays, external mural decorations, colour and scale.

In 1887 Queen Victoria's Jubilee Memorial Fund was raised and the proceeds were used to build part of this institute. It was then known as The Working Men's Institute, later as The Central Club. The hall is a later addition.

Architect Paxton Watson (*qv*) submitted his plans in September, 1890, and building started soon afterwards, to begin with by Patricks. It was finished by Crosbys.

CHURCH   HOUSE,   UNION   ROAD

Built in 1909 to the design of R. B. Preston, at a cost of £2,850, by Mardon & Mills. The site was given by G. F. Romieu (*qv*). A fire in the 1940s caused considerable damage and resulted in the turret being replaced by a simpler one.

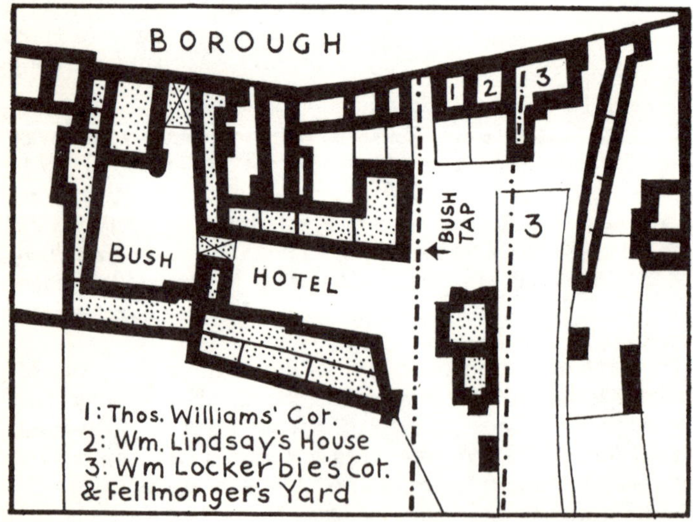

A partly conjectural plan which shows the area now partly upper South Street before the street was built. Broken lines indicate the approximate position of South Street today.

EAST STREET

East Street is a long and meandering belt of lesser buildings which extends the town towards London and projects its major axis from West Street and The Borough. Seekers of the spectacular will find only disappointment although for those interested in humbler things several small delights are in store, including some good groups and details.

The street has suffered two major reverses. The first, a hundred years of gas-making in its immediate proximity and second, several eatings into the continuity of its fronts.

Farnham has now its greatest chance to make amends. The smell has gone and several large-scale redevelopments are about to begin. Whether East Street will become as inviting as the rest depends on our own enlightenment rather than on its inheritance of buildings standing now.

88 EAST STREET. A partly conjectural reconstruction of The Seven Stars as it was before rebuilding.

4 EAST STREET (The Royal Deer)

A two-floor brick building on a corner site. The main entrance, with festooned stone plaque above, separates the north from the west front. Each is of three bays and of similar appearance. Below the panelled parapet is a dentilled brick cornice. Angles are coigned and windows sashed.

Most of what one sees from the street is dated about 1930 — when the premises were reconstructed and refaced. The plaque was carved in situ by Levison and Waite.

Another of the earlier neo-Georgian reconstructions. Part of the finished result is closely related to what was here once before. It is an improvement on the drab cement-faced building from which it has evolved, although until the mid-19th century that might have been quite good. Only half the building remains. In 1869 a new road — South Street — was being made. This was presumably the reason for demolition of the building's west part and of outhouses to the rear. A house and cottage also went, and part of The Bush Hotel (*qv*) which stood in what is now the street about 30 yards down.

Cement casing covered The Royal Deer's rough-built new west wall and also good quality bricks on the north front. Here, basic features were rather as they are now, although some details differed. There was no cornice, but the coping was rather elaborately moulded. Upper windows were the same shape, but architraved in cement. The parapet was panelled. Coigns were of the more usual kind.

The Royal Deer has a shorter history than many Farnham pubs. It was probably one of those which sprang up later in the 19th century as a result of Aldershot Camp's relationship to Farnham Station, which served it for some years. A contemporary writer stated that within twelve months during the later 1850s no fewer than sixteen new taverns opened along the route. A hint of the rapidly changing architectural scene in Farnham is also worth noting. 'Many houses are of quaint architecture, decorated with carved woodwork, and having projecting eaves, tall square chimneys, and small latticed windows, calculated to admit — well, a little dust perhaps, but certainly neither light nor air in any fair amount. And yet there is a certain character about them pleasant to behold, and the mania that obtains at present among the householders for introducing modern frontages to the town, with occasional Saracenic decorations, and red, blue, and white "Alliance Taverns", is very shocking to the eye of taste'. The reasons for Farnham Station's popularity were twofold. First, Farnborough, although nearer to Aldershot than Farnham, was connected only by a gravelly road which passed through lonely pinewoods. Second, by contrast, from Farnham there were plenty of regular horse buses if one were in a hurry and travelled at the right times, and plenty of pubs if one were not and travelled at other times. '. . . omnibuses which private speculators have transplanted from the suburban duties of Norwood and Camden Town. These vehicles make their transit in half an hour, supposing their passengers to be in the Civil Service; but if the military prevail, a certain delay, caused by thirsty sergeants, sometimes occurs. . . . On leaving The Bush where that excessively superior ostler has bowed us off . . .

we pass on, between small, quaint looking houses, now used as lodgings by dashing cavalry captains, and having seen several well-dressed people, whom we think ought to know better ascend the steps of the great red-faced inn, lately run up there, and been amused by the little iron Club House . . . we leave Farnham behind'. The Club sounds like a prefabricated cast iron structure, probably in the picturesque Alpine Cottage style. Could the 'red-faced inn' have been The Albion, unpainted?

One hundred and twenty years ago, William Lockerbie (*qv*) owned and occupied the house and fellmonger's yard behind part of which is now The Royal Deer. This extended for a considerable distance down what is now east South Street. See plan on page 108.

Fellmongering, like tanning, appears to have declined as the century advanced. There was, though, another fellmonger's yard, so described, well into the century. It adjoined the churchyard, to its south-east, and was occupied in 1839 by William Barnes (*qv*), the tenant of Robert Latter. Within thirty years the biggest buildings along the river's north bank had gone.

William Lockerbie, of 8 Castle Street (*qv*), was born about 1790. His wife was Sarah. He combined several trades — maltster, hop planter, and probably breeches maker and fellmonger, too. Presumably it was he who owned 4 East Street. If so, he probably inherited his business as he was born in Farnham and in 1823 and 1826 there are references to Maria Luckerbie and Sons, fellmongers and breeches makers. Maria Hawke married a William Lockerbie in 1784. Later, William Lockerbie was a tailor, draper and breeches maker of East Street (at number 4, after relinquishing his fellmonger's business?). There, in 1839, was a William Lockerbie (*b* 1816*), glover; probably the same one. The fact that Charles Lockerbie (*b* 1800*) and his wife Elizabeth (*b* 1808*) were in business in The Borough in the 1840s and '50s as tailor, draper and glover, suggest that Maria's other son turned from the family trade, for glovers were sometimes skin dealers also. An earlier William Crump (*qv*) is an example. A Charles Lockerbie died in 1845 and an Elizabeth Lockerbie (*qv*) thirty years later. In the '50s Elizabeth, widow, was still described as a glover, like her nephew, Laurence Lockerbie (*b* 1824*). Her sister was Caroline Beaty who lived in Downing Street.

Here was Miss Louisa Stratford's Ladies' Boarding School. It existed in 1878 and was in East Street 23 years earlier, but not necessarily at this address although it was here in 1851. In 1841 Jane (*b* 1806*) and Louisa (*b* 1817*) had a small boarding school at 72 Castle Street (*qv*), and two years earlier the Misses Stratford taught at the old National School (*qv*), in what is now the Freemasons' Hall. About 1850 Miss Louisa Stratford (*b* 1798* at Upton Grey) was governess at the East Street school. Ten years before, William True (*b* 1804*), schoolmaster, and his wife Maria (*b* 1811*), were here. There were nine little Trues and five other children in the house. Perhaps Miss Stratford carried on where the Trues finished.

What was, until 1956, the County Cinema, opened behind here as The Electric Theatre in 1913. It was built by Mardon & Mills with H. Falkner (*qv*) as architect. There had previously been a picture palace in Bear Lane, on the west side. The Regal Cinema, nearby, opened in 1933.

14 EAST STREET. A partly conjectural reconstruction of The Marlborough Head façade before rebuilding.

14 EAST STREET (The Marlborough Head)

A brick, timber and tiled public house.

This pseudo-Tudor rebuilding replaces a small brick fronted house which was partly timber built (see illustration). To the east of this adjoined a gateroom. Consent for rebuilding was given in 1929. The architect was John Howard (*qv*), of Haslemere.

A pub of this name was under the landlordship of one named Barnes in the 1750s, but for very many years afterwards it was in the ownership or occupation of one family. In 1801 John Harrison surrendered and William Harrison was admitted. Fifty years later Anne and the Reverend Dann Harrison held it, but by 1870 the Marlborough Head had passed to Messrs. Crowley. It was once part of an estate called Canterburys (*qv*). There was, a hundred years ago, a soldiers' room over the wash-house.

BRIGHTWELL HOUSE   (Behind Regal Cinema)
EAST STREET

An asymmetrical eight-bay brick built house on two main floors, under a slate roof. Bay windows, running up to the eaves, above which they are peaked with slate, occupy bays one-three and five-seven. Five plain pilasters rise full height to contain both of the bays and the east end of the stuccoed front which has a string course separating floors.

Fenestration: Ground floor, seven large-paned French windows; First floor, eight recessed three-pane-wide three-quarters height sashes.

Door: In bay four.

This house has the appearance of being early Victorian, but it is of older origin. Probably the whole front was remodelled and the west part built on about mid-19th century. To its north, where the Regal now stands, was once a vast range of kilns. These were still standing in the early '70s but had gone well before the century closed.

The house, with extensive pleasure gardens, at one time including what is now a bowling green, was owned in the late 1830s by the Reverend Richard Garth (*b* 1782*) and the house was still occupied by him and daughters Mary (*b* 1822*) and Fanny (*b* 1834*), about 1850. He kept a groom, butler, ladies' maid, housemaid and cook. In the '30s, Henry Halsey (*qv*) owned the kilns.

Colonel Patrick Paget, of the Scots Guards, lived here after the Garths, his widow, Frances (*b* 1834*, *d* 1912) still being here at the time of her death.

Brightwell's, now a Clinic, was once called Lowlands. It was probably part of an estate known in the early 18th century as Canterburys (*qv*).

26, 27 & 28 EAST STREET

Where there is an open space alongside number 27 was the entrance to Sturt and Keen's other wheelwright's shop (see 35-42 and 84 East Street). There was also a building opposite the entrance, to the south of the yard.

In the later part of the 18th century this was a farmyard. It was occupied by William Lockerbie, then by Benjamin Nichols (*qqv*), before them by William Preedy, and in 1736 by John Hole. By the time Sturt and Keen had transformed this from a bucolic to a light industrial environment it had changed hands again, and was owned by Joseph Ellis and (later) by Catherine Ellis. A Joseph Ellis was hop planter and baker in the 1820s.

In 1870 Charles Keen was here and three years later the property was described as 'sometime before G. Sturt's wheelwright shop, but now coachmaker's shop of Charles Keen'. Number 26, in 1900, was J. S. Giles' 'new extensive furniture showroom'. John S. Giles ran The Old Curiosity Shop at 11 and 12 Castle Street around the turn of the century.

Richard Hole was charged Lay Subsidiary Assessment on goods, 1593-4, John Hole was a freeholder in Farnham in the late 17th century, and Thomas Hole (husbandman?) party to a transaction at the Round House (*qv*) in 1668. The name occurs frequently in Farnham records, particularly in the 18th and 19th centuries, when David was a collarmaker, William a saddler and harnessmaker in The Borough, and George, John and two Richards all freeholders, in 1719. None was qualified to vote in 1836, and they no longer appear to have been trading in the town after 1855.

The Ellis's (*qv*) were, in the mid-19th century, quite numerous. Hereabouts, in the 1840s, were Mary (*b* 1811*), George (*b* 1828*), Richard (*b* 1838*), and Ann (*b* 1840*).

See plan on page 117.

29 EAST STREET   (Still House)

A symmetrical three-bay brick built house on two main floors with slate roof. The façade is broken forward to contain the centre bay. Eaves are unbracketed, resting on upper window-heads.

Fenestration: Ground floor, two recessed four-pane-wide sashes; First floor, three similar, the centre window having a segmental head.

Door: Engaged fluted Doric columns with open triangular pediment containing a semicircular fanlight and radial tracery in metal.

A most interesting façade for its generally being accepted as 18th century (Pevsner and Nairn estimate it to be late 18th century). This is based on its general, certainly not its detailed confromity with textbook house types. Yet it was not built before 1839. Previously there was another house here which had a cottage built into the south-west corner. In its architectural development the house seems to be happily placed between 61 Castle Street and 2 Downing Street (*qqv*). So its date and style present another example of the strong grip which the Georgian tradition had on building in Farnham. The substitution of a segmentally headed window and full four-pane-wide fenestration on the front is well handled, and the doorcase — a basic design used for decades — although here light rather than robust, holds the composition well. Eaves treatment has become lighter too, modillions and brackets have been excluded, and as at 60 West Street and Stanley Villas (*qqv*) the eaves rest closely on upper window heads. See plan on page 117.

Before domestic plate glass became popular there was a marked tendency to increase the number of panes-width of windows. Here, on the front, all are four. The five-pane type (1-3-1) is found frequently from the late 18th century. At the back of 29 East Street is an example of a rarer development in the five-pane-wide ordinary sash. There are others, mainly turned away from the street, for example almost opposite, behind the old British Schools (*qv*). There were others, facing the street, at 5 Downing Street (*qv*) and another can be seen at 109 East Street. The 1-3-1 type survived, the simple five-pane-wide type apparently having overreached itself, perhaps structurally as well as frequently visually.

A house which was here until after 1839 had been in several possessions by the early 18th century and fragments of it probably remain in the lower back parts of the present house. To the rear was a brewery. Since 1958, when it was sold, the house has been altered and much improved.

In 1736 Ellen Jackson left to her son, Samuel, 'my messuage or tenement garden orchard wherein I now dwell . . . and the little tenement at the west end thereof adjacent to the land of John Hole'. Samuel, and Ellen Jackson's grandson, Samuel, both bricklayers, inherited. By the time William Jackson passed the property to James Elliott in 1818 it was very differently described, the house just as before, but '. . . together with the brewhouse malthouse storerooms and buildings lately erected by James Elliott in the yard'. Probably Elliott had rented the orchard in order to build on it, and in 1818 'for some time then since' had agreed to buy the whole property from Jackson. His enterprise failed and on November 16th, 1819, Elliott, 'common brewer, bankrupt', faced his creditors. His property was sold at The Goat's Head to John Peacock (*qv, b* 1781*). Under his ownership the industry seems to have thrived. Twenty years after his having acquired the brewery he and his wife Ann (*b* 1791*) owned also a beerhouse at 42 East Street (*qv*), four cottages a little beyond. and stabling, a kiln and cottage behind and adjoining his pub. On his death in 1843 his son, George Peacock (*b* 1817* at Froyle), inherited. He, a brewer also, died in 1869, his widow, Mary (*b* 1824*) remarrying F. Ellington in 1873. The brewery was let to Alfred Barling, grocer, brewer and malster, and it was still in the tenancy of Thomas Bentall Barling when The Castle Brewery and house were offered for sale in 1923.

It is often illuminating to know something of people's personalities as well as biographical facts concerning them. They are easily imagined but will seldom then be accurate. George Bourne has something to say of 'A Mr. George Peacock' who called young Bourne Copper Toes. 'A curious man was Mr. Peacock. My father and mother dubbed his manner theatrical, perhaps because of his strutting walk, and his swinging his cane up to his shoulder in a gay swishing movement. He lived at the house in front of what is now Barling's Castle Brewery, of which he was, I fancy, the owner at that time'.

Alfred Barling lived at 18 East Street and carried on a grocery business for many years at 33 The Borough. A Thomas Barling (*b* 1796*) was grocer and cheesemonger in The Borough in the first half of the 19th century.

35-42 EAST STREET (Swain & Jones' Garage)

Where 38 and 39 were was once Keen's coachworks. Edward Keen, of Headley, had a son, William, who became George Sturt's partner. He also had a daughter whom Sturt married. The former of these Sturt-Keen partnerships lasted until 1826, when Keen left Sturt's shop at 84 East Street (*qv*) and set up his own carriage works. It is said that it was started here, and part of his shop remains in the turreted and half-hipped tile roofed building behind the modern showrooms. His premises were owned by Elizabeth Jones in 1839. All the same, in the year of their break, Keen was already in occupation of property owned by John Dare, of Isington, and fifteen years after his start Keen had, in addition to his small shop

and forecourt at 35 and 36, occupation of premises a little
east of directly opposite. They were larger in area than Sturt's
place, although he shared them. They, too, were rented from
John Dare. Perhaps he actually started on the north side,
not at 38 and 39. Later the business also occupied the wheelwright's behind 26, 27 and 28 (*qv*) East Street. Richard Daire,
haircloth weaver, died in 1723. Another Richard Dare, haircloth weaver, was working later.

By mid-century this must have been a busy industrial
fringe of Farnham. On the north of East Street was Sturt's, a
few yards away (in the early '40s the last developed site on
the north side of East Street) was Keen's. Opposite were their
other shops, behind 29 was Peacock's brewery, and adjoining
that Catherine Ellis's wheelwright's shop. Then, to the east
again, to the new gas works, and where the Regal is, was
Henry Halsey's (*qv*) vast battery of kilns. The houses were
occupied mainly by artisans — many sawyers — and it is
almost certain that there were other carriage builders working
in East Street at that time.

After the Sturt and Keen partnership came William
Keen's works, then Charles Keen's by the '70s, and Keen and
Heath, coach builders, by the 1890s. As with Sturt's, Keen's
business inevitably faced problems of rapid change if it was
to continue far into the 20th century. The connection
remains in Swain and Jones' garage.

The Sturts were not Farnham's only wheelwrights, and
Keen had his rivals and antecedents too. From the 18th
century Farnham wheelwrights included Henry Lunn
(*b* 1821*), Isaac Holloway (*qv*), William Berry (*d* 1729),
Richard Moth (*qv*, *d* 1786), John Taphouse (*d* 1798), John
Bradley (*d* 1782), William Grover (*d* 1825), George Draper (*qv*),
George Gates (*b* 1796*), Edward Booker (*b* 1820*), George
Swan (*b* 1817*), William Whiten (*b* 1796*), John Jennings,
Henry Knight and William Turner. Coach makers included
William Barnes, John Stokes and James Stokes (*qqv*), John
Exall (*d* 1782), James Laurence (*b* 1810*) and James Witcher.

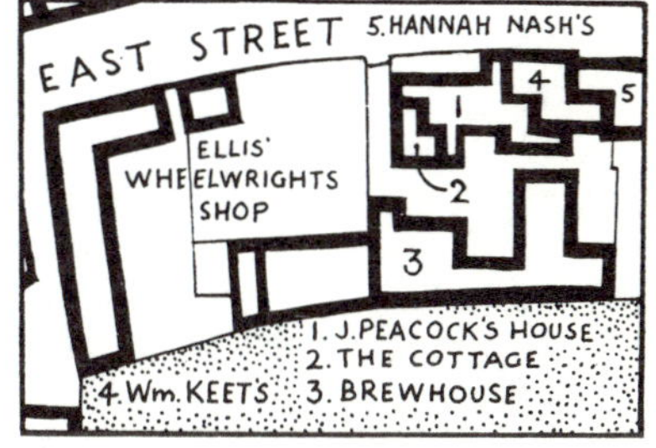

26 to 31 EAST STREET: plans based on Harding's map of 1839. 1 and 2 show 29 before rebuilding; 3, the brewhouse, now demolished. Catherine Ellis' wheelwright's shop adjoining, was later occupied by Sturt and Keen. 5, and its neighbour to the east (not shown), were owned by Hannah Nash (qv). The house, a corner of which is visible on the left margin, was Henry Nash's.

At 42 East Street was The White Swan, a pub which existed in the 19th century and was owned by John Peacock whose brewery was at 29 East Street (*qv*). In the 1830s it was called a beer house and was sometimes referred to as The Swan, not to be confused with a much older inn of the same name (*qv*). In the 19th century there was also The Swan in The Borough. See plan on page 124.

55 EAST STREET

Here was The White Hart (*qv*), a public house. It was here in 1871 and sold to Farnham United Breweries in 1903. The premises — 'late The White Hart' — were for sale in 1928. There had been two other White Harts in Farnham. This house was once owned by John Peacock (*qv*).

ST. MARY'S PLACE, EAST STREET

Terraced dwellings have been here since at least 1840, and the name St. Mary's Place was in use as a domestic address in 1836 when John Webb, an East Street grocer, lived here. A site near here was known traditionally as St. Mary's Well.

PARK SCHOOL, ST. JAMES' AVENUE, EAST STREET

Built in 1896 as a mixed school for 364 children.

ZINGARI TERRACE, EAST STREET

Four integrated houses totalling seven bays and of three full floors. The terrace is built of brick, rendered in cement (except ground floor façade) and painted. The roof is slated. The façade is symmetrical, corniced and parapeted. A verandah with decorative cast iron work runs its length at ground floor level.

Fenestration: Ground floor, front windows are square, large paned; First floor, recessed three-pane-wide and topped by a cornice. A mild string separates them from the top floor windows. All windows are architraved and sashed, those on the first floor having additional sill embellishments of cast iron.

Interior: In the west end is a helical staircase rising from a quadrangular well through all floors. Banisters are turned and connect with a slim mahogany rail. The strings have applied scroll brackets.

This terrace was built by William Birch on land acquired from George Trimmer (*qv*) in 1861. The most striking alterations were made in 1960 when the then drab cement was painted. At this time, too, the verandah was repaired, its earlier concave metal roof then being slated and ironwork tidied up. The largest house was converted into flats.

This is a striking block of a date later than generally supposed. Here is a strong feeling for Georgian proportion and detail, yet the ironwork, vigorous as it is, is Victorian in character, as are the ground floor front windows. There is a handsome staircase with the elegance of one built in the Regency, yet with modifications to details of design. Birch (*qv*) was born in Farnham at about the time 90 West Street was built. It would still have been a new house when he was an apprentice. It is not surprising, then, that Zingari should retain so much of the 18th century Farnham style. It is, in fact, Farnham's equivalent to late Regency. But thirty years late. The Georgian style had become so strongly established as Farnham vernacular that it overshot the Regency and early Victorian periods by years. This may account for the remarkable lack of typical Regency style buildings in Farnham. But perhaps it is more accurate to suggest that Farnham's Regency period is represented particularly by the brick-built, slate-roofed houses such as can be seen on the west side of Castle Street and at 34-37 West Street (*qv*).

There are other instances which strengthen this theory of over-shooting. See also 60-61 West Street, Stanley Villas in Guildford Road, 2 Downing Street and 29 East Street. There are others, too.

Birch's were well established in Farnham by the 1820s. Thomas was a carpenter the century before, and Thomas, carpenter, was at 43 The Borough (*qv*) in 1805. The Birch's lived in and owned several houses about 32 Castle Street. In 1841 Ann (*b* 1754*), Martha (*b* 1791*), Harriett (*b* 1806*) and others, including those below, were there. A lead plaque was found some years ago in Figg's Yard (Long Garden Walk) bearing the inscription 'W. Birch. Builder, Farnham, 1851'. Robert Birch was a druggist in 1824, and Robert (*b* 1793*) was upholsterer and cabinet maker trading in The Borough in the 1820s; William later. From Longbridge, Frank Copper Birch (*qv*) worked with Norman Shaw on such buildings as Pierrepont and 75 Castle Street (*qv*).

William Birch (*b* 1801*) died in February, 1862. Zingari might therefore have been his last big enterprise. Was 2 Downing Street another of his late works? It has the confident handling of Zingari, was probably built at about the same time, is of comparable brick, and window detailing is remarkably similar. Having compared architraves (straight and segmental) one thinks of 118 West Street (attributed to Harding) and the Coffee House in Downing Street (*qqv*). Two years after William's death Mrs. Birch was owner of three houses at Zingari, twelve cottages at Rookery and three more houses in Castle Street. Perhaps Birch's Yard was taken over by the Figgs. They have for many years been builders in Farnham and still occupy the same yard. Although there may be no connection, Figgs have lived in Farnham since the 16th century. John, yeoman, and Abraham, cordwinder, died in 1710; two Thomas's in 1660 and 1664. Richard, cooper and brewer, and Sarah (b 1796*), were in business in The Borough in the 1820s-1850s. Another family, probably shoemakers, lived in East Street. Charles and his wife Mary (*bb* 1795**), Ann (*b* 1822*) and William Figg (*b* 1824*) were members.

The plaque at Figg's was presumably made in celebration of Birch's jubilee.

RED CROSS HOUSE, EAST STREET

A red brick and tile building which was once Trimmer's Cottage Hospital — built shortly after plans were approved in 1894. George Trimmer (*qv*) left money for this purpose. In the 1930s a new Trimmer's Cottage Hospital was built in Waverley Lane.

BATH TERRACE (Bath House and West Meon House) EAST STREET

A four-bay three-floor pair of houses with areas, built of brick and stone with cemented façade and a slate roof.

Fenestration: Ground floor, two sash windows, four panes wide; First floor, four casements two panes wide; Second floor, four square sashes, three panes wide. All windows are shallowly recessed.

Doors: In bays one and four. Both have semicircular fanlights with radial tracery design and cement cased surrounds, finished with pilasters and cornice. Each surmounts a flight of steps.

Built almost certainly in 1847 by William Patrick (*qv*) of Farnham on what was earlier part of John Nash's New Field hop garden.

The building is of interest as it can be closely dated and shows many early symptoms of the decline in classical façade design which was to come. It still, of course, retains much that goes to make a good elevation, and has a considerable amount of Georgian character, but like a number of the earlier 19th century pairs this one tends to fall visually into two parts, although one building. Had the doorcases been together in the middle and windows been more sensitively placed, for example, this need not have been so. Worth comparing with this answer to the problem are 23 and 24, 60 and 61, 91 and 92 West Street, several pairs in upper Castle Street, 46 and 47 Downing Street. The tendency since such early semis were built, especially in recent years, has been to keep the doors apart, allowing a central stack and preventing door-step gossip.

Presumably Bath Terrace was built speculatively as Patrick was a builder who constructed it for himself. In the 1840s a William Patrick (*b* 1819*), bricklayer, lived at 83 West Street (*qv*). He was at 68 West Street (*qv*), still a bricklayer, with Esther (*qv*, *b* 1817*) his wife, and son William (*b* 1844*), ten years later. But almost certainly the builder of Bath Terrace was the William Patrick (*b* 1803*) who lived in East Street. He had a son, Henry (*b* 1833*).

62 EAST STREET

Hereabouts was The Surrey Arms. A pub of this name existed in 1871, still in 1915.

73 EAST STREET

Here was The Eagle, open by 1871 and still so at the end of the century. It was one of George Trimmer's (*qv*) houses which, with all those buildings to its east (on the north side), was not built before 1840.

75 EAST STREET

Here was the Preparatory School of Mrs. Margaret Tideman. It was in existence in 1878.

Until its conversion into a motor showroom in 1960, the building in the north-west corner displayed on its south front some very neat blind arcading in brick. It was of a quality comparable with that still to be seen at 41 West Street (*qv*).

This was probably built as The British School *c* 1833, for in that year an application was made by townspeople for such an establishment in Farnham. This would have been necessary for non-Conformists not wishing their children to attend the Church of England school yet requiring that they should receive schooling which included scriptural education. The National School (*qv*) in Castle Street was connected with the established national church. There was also an infants' school in the town at that time. It was perhaps behind 35 The Borough (*qv*) where a building — referred to as The School Room in 1839 — was situated. No definite connection has been established with it.

The cost of The British School was estimated to be £300. It abutted the east side of the Chapel here built by The Independent Congregation of Dissenters, possibly in 1792. Between the Chapel and East Street was, for some time, their burial ground, which probably included a number of brick-built vaults. Early pupils were taught by Henry Brewster and Miss Elizabeth Sharpe, and by the early '90s over 230 were on the register. For many years, in fact until its recent conversion, the old school accommodated a knitting factory — now removed to premises nearby.

There were other early Chapels. One was behind 38 Castle Street (*qv*), another, built in 1852 (Baptist) is in Bear Lane. Mid-century another was in Long Garden Walk, and a new Sunday School room was opened (Wesleyan) at the Congregational Church in 1912, T. R. Wonnacott (*qv*) being the architect responsible for this extension to his Church. The previous school here had been opened in about 1897.

When Dr. Willis made his visitation to Farnham in 1724 or 1725 he recorded that Farnham, with a population of 2,500, had no Papists, eighty Presbyterians, thirty Anabaptists and twelve Quakers. Congregationalists' struggles are written about elsewhere (See Farnham Inheritance, Bibliography, pp. 62, 63).

Thomas Beddus Mill (*qv*), by his will of 1828, left to Joseph Johnson (*qv*), his tenant, 'Minister of the Dissenting Meeting House in Farnham', a legacy and the house in which Johnson lived. It was probably 89-90 East Street (*qv*). In 1841 Joseph Johnson (b 1778*) was at this address and was once described as a Dissenting Minister.

There is nothing to distinguish these premises architecturally, but associations of the place are of interest as it was here that George Sturt established his wheelwright's business in 1810. Remains of his house (later 83 East Street) and the shop (joining on the west) are now part of the more recent building. It was mostly here that the experience which is written into Bourne's 'The Wheelwright's Shop' was gained. The site was bounded on the west, as today, by a footway, but the road itself has since been widened — to the width of two attached cottages (formerly 85 and 84) which stood to the west of the early alleyway. The chapel and its forecourt burial ground bounded the east (see 80 East Street). Sturt also owned two other cottages abutting 83 on its east. One remains. (See plan on the following page.)

Old Sturt had worked for a wheelwright, William Grover, who started a shop here in 1795. It is George Sturt (alias Bourne, grandson of the wheelwright George Sturt) who suggests that Grover built the shop and houses at about that time. However, this was not the beginning. In 1706 George Draper, wheelwright, bought part of Robert Hewitt's hop-ground and started the association of this site with the trade. The link remains today, although for many years of the 18th century a blacksmith worked here.

William Grover (*d* 1824*), wheelwright, and his wife Ann (*d* 1827), probably lived at 7 Park Row; an easy walk to work, turning off Bear Lane across uninterrupted hop fields to the back of the shop. It is unlikely that Draper was new to his trade for others of that name had worked at the same craft before him in Farnham. They include John Draper (*d* 1657) senior, and John Draper (*d* 1691). Contemporaries would have been Edward Hodger (*d* 1695) and John Shrubb (d 1701). He worked at Wrecclesham. John Draper, senior, was married to Mary. His eldest son was William; then John and Edward the youngest. Edward inherited his father's house at Ash (called Chitties?). Another son, George Draper, had predeceased his father, leaving five children, among them another John Draper. John senior's daughter, Elizabeth, married John Weekes, of Farnham.

Sturt's partnership with William Keen ended in 1826. Bourne claims it was because their wives argued over the business. Keen was Sturt's wife's brother. A condition of their parting, Bourne says, was that Keen should not practise as a wheelwright for twelve years. So Keen (*qv*) started coachbuilding almost next door.

It is generally supposed that Sturt's activities were confined to that site. George Bourne does not, to the writer's knowledge, mention it, but his grandfather's works were also to the south of East Street where, directly opposite to his two little cottages mentioned above, he had another shop. With it was some land laid out in the late 1830s as a decorative garden. Its east boundary adjoined Keen's new premises. There was another wheelwright's shop and yard, now 26, 27 and 28 (qv) East Street, which belonged to Joseph Ellis and was used by Sturt and Keen in 1818. Sturt was still there 21 years after. Keen later still.

The business passed to Bourne's father in 1865. He died in 1884 and George Sturt, alias Bourne, took over. He sold out to his partner, William Arnold, in 1920, at a time when the age of wheelwrights was rapidly dying and when Bourne's heart was more in writing than in motor cars. Through Arnold is the link with Arnold and Comben, motor engineers, now of West Street.

Sturts living in East Street in the mid-19th century included George (b 1785* at Haslemere), wheelwright, and his wife Sarah (b 1783*) and their sons, John (b 1812*) and Francis (b 1823*), both wheelwright's journeymen, and Margaret Sturt (b 1827*).

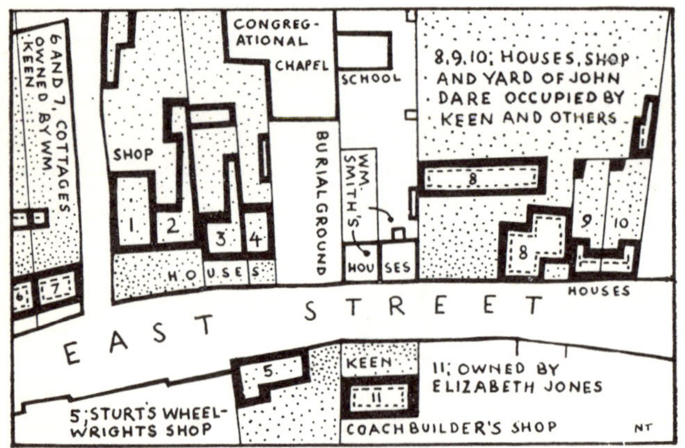

THIS MAP, based on Harding's, shows the property owned or occupied by Sturt and Keen in 1839. Sturt's 'The Wheelwright's Shop' has a photograph of 1 and 2 taken about 1916. 6 and 7 (once 85 and 84 East Street) were demolished, allowing the side-road to be widened. These cottages totalled four bays with doors in bays 2 and 3 and upper sash windows in bays 1 and 4. 5 was later given up by Sturt in favour of his premises opposite.

A brick, timber and tiled public house.

Consent for rebuilding was given in 1929 and, along with others reconstructed at about that time, e.g., The Plough, The Marlborough Head, The Jolly Farmer, Runfold, it is in a pseudo-Tudor style.

Before reconstruction the east end had a projecting wing (see illustration). Sturt writes that as a boy he used to see the Town Crier sitting in his upper room there. Sturt's workshop was very near and his aunt, speaking of the 1820's, recalled the wazegoose, or party, held at The Seven Stars after a waggon was finished at the shop.

The Seven Stars has been in existence under that name for well over two hundred years and was occupied by the Bromley family, sometime coachmakers, 124 East Street. The Bromleys (*qv*) were probably tenants of the Knights who had acquired the house by 1840. Edward Bromley (*b* 1814* at Guildford) was landlord here in 1841, by which time his son, Edward, was aged two. Edward was still landlord in 1855, his mother, Mary (*b* 1771*), having been here over thirty years before. Edward's wife was Ann (*b* 1817*). They had other sons — George (*b* 1846*), William (*b* 1848*), and two small daughters, Caroline and Celia, in 1851. Edward senior's sister was Henrietta Bromley (*b* 1802*).

In 1750 the property passed from George Chasin (*qv*) to Thomas Peace, then to James Hewett (*qv*), carpenter and brewer. Widow Hewit received the King's Bounty (*qv*) in 1757.

In 1888 J. H. Knight (*qv*) offered The Seven Stars for sale, with a carpenter's shop, at an annual rent of £35.

* 89-90 E A S T S T R E E T

Shop premises which from their present outward form suggest a development of some interest over many years (see illustration). Miss Rebecca Johnson had a boarding school for ladies here in the 1870s and possibly the '80s, too, while at number 90 Joseph Johnson traded as a manure merchant.

Joseph, senior (*b* 1778*), and Ann (*b* 1781*), were here in the 1840s when Elizabeth (*b* 1809* in Warrington) was described as governess. She and her sisters — Frances (*b* 1816*) and Mary (*b* 1819*) — were still here with their young-lady pupils in the early 1850s; their brother, Joseph junior (*b* 1817*), too. At the same time a Miss Harriett

Johnson (*b c* 1790*), schoolmistress, was in Lower Downing Street or Church Lane.

Thomas Beddus Mill (*qv*), in his will of 1828, left his house, garden and premises in East Street, then in Johnson's occupation, to Joseph Johnson and his heirs. See 80 East Street.

* 93 EAST STREET

The Mays probably lived at about 45 Downing Street, whereabouts in the later 1830s Elizabeth May ran a seminary. She was born at Petworth and had retired by 1851 when her age was stated as being 77. She had two daughters, Elizabeth and Martha, whose school was later at 93 East Street. Perhaps they took over from Miss Hannah Hopwood (*b* 1787*) who was hereabout before them.

George Sturt attended the school before going to Poppleton's (*qv*), 'Miss May, so thin, so fragile, so unoffensive, is not yet effaced from my memory. She is gentleness and kindness embodied'. She was still here in 1878 but four years later Miss Martha Moore's Boarding School for Ladies advertised from the same address.

90 EAST STREET. A detail of the south-west corner showing accumulations which suggest an interesting structure buried within. Tile hanging and buttresses presumably result from the demolition of its neighbour.

Both the May daughters were born at Odiham. In the 1850s Charles May, also born at Odiham, was a tea dealer in business at about 110 East Street.

If a document superscribed 'House in East Street now let to Miss May' refers to this property, 93 East Street was surrendered by John Tanner of Haslemere, in 1733, with other property south of the Park. John Tanner of Haslemere, gent, sold property at The Nelson Arms (*qv*) in 1729. He also owned Canterburys (probably Brightwell's, *qv*). From his only son, Thomas, the 'House in East Street now let to Miss May' (written on the deed at a quite recent date) passed to Robert Shurlock (*d* 1782) in 1773, and after his death to James Stevens (*qv*) in 1784. Shurlock (*qv*) was a tanner. He owned land at Headley and in his Farnham properties was a place in East Street called The Folly (which he had bought from Thomas Tanner). His widow, Ann, died in 1824. Their children were Robert, Ann and John. Folly Hill probably has no connection with this property, the Folly there (what form did it take?) being once situated to the west of the road.

George and Henry Botting, grocers, advertised from 93 and 94 in 1891 and 1915.

* 9 4 - 9 5   E A S T   S T R E E T

Here was The Royal Oak, a memory of which is retained in the name of the yard behind. The whole front was restored during this century. What had once been two dwellings (94 a cottage, 95 a pub) were thrown into one and a shop-front — by H. Falkner (*qv*) — inserted. The yard and its entrance were retained.

Early in the 19th century the pub was J. and J. Knight's. To the rear, alongside what is now the north-west corner of the yard, was John Wells' (*qv*) large kiln. This, and adjacent buildings on the north side, were offered for sale in 1874 after the death of Stephen Smither (*qv*) whose property it had been. It was described as a 'brick and tile kiln with 6 fireholes, two drying kilns, large store and two cottages each containing three rooms'. The Royal Oak passed from Farnham Brewery in 1877 and was again for sale in 1891. The pub was at that time described as being built of brick and tiled, with the exception of a portion over the gateway which was timber built.

* **99-100 EAST STREET** (Gordon's and The Mikado)

Two of a group of shops with varying earlier 19th century fronts and slate roofs built on to the remains of houses which included timber framing in their construction. Here, in the 19th century, was the school of Henry Poppleton. By 1890 number 99 was advertised as Farnham High School (for Gentlemen's Daughters only).

In 1855 Poppleton's School was in West Street, probably at about number 119. At the same time a Henry Poppleton was ironmonger and tin and iron plateworker, West Street. But the school was in East Street for many years. In 1878 the master could advertise himself and his establishment impressively: 'Henry Poppleton, L.C.P., F.S.E., F.S.A., College Boarding School, Certificated drawing master, department of science and art'. He was born in Wakefield, where the name is not uncommon, about 1821, and was married to Elizabeth, his senior by twelve years.

Sturt went to school here after leaving Miss May's, 93 East Street (*qv*), and he leaves an account of the old schoolmaster's end. Having left at his own request to attend the Grammar School, he wrote '. . . An unquiet conscience insisted that it was my own fault when, years later, Mr. Poppleton's school being all but gone, and his wife dead, he, lonely and poverty-stricken, had retired to a near village. For many years he would not speak to me . . . when he was growing old and shabby, and trembling at the lips. One day, word came that he had been found dead, starved and dirty and neglected, in the old schoolroom — his only home at last'.

Sturt devotes a whole chapter of 'A Small Boy in the Sixties' to Mr. Poppleton's.

* **111 EAST STREET**

One of three terraced dwellings with the outward characteristics of local mid-19th century buildings. It housed the Preparatory School run by Mrs. Mary Mason, which existed in 1878 and still in 1892.

* **118 EAST STREET** (Heath Bros.)

Here was The Green Man, 'one of Farnham's many dismal public houses', which existed early in 1823 and still in the '90s. Under the plaster skin are extensive remains of an early timber framed house on three floors. An inserted front dormer window has been removed in recent years.

The pub was owned early in the century by the Knights, and was offered for sale in 1888 by them.

* 1 1 9   E A S T   S T R E E T   (Heath Bros. Pram Shop)

A double-fronted shop with three bays above. The roof is slated, windows are sashed, recessed, four panes wide.

This 19th century front disguises a largish two-floor timber framed house, of which there are considerable remains. It was a jettied construction of two bays with tie-beam truss. In the west bay is evidence of an early passage-way between this and the neighbouring house. An awning over the fascia-board is a remnant of the Victorian shopfront of Hawgood's furniture and china shop. See 120 East Street.

* 1 2 0   E A S T   S T R E E T   (Heath Bros.)

A double-fronted shop of three bays on two floors, dormer windows above.

Before becoming a shop, these premises retained the character of a private house with central pedimented door-case. Here was The Unicorn Hotel, earlier The Unicorn. There was another Unicorn in Red Lion Lane, but as that property was described in 1857 as two cottages, it is presumed here that early references to The Unicorn concern 120 East Street, although that for a time early in the 19th century was described as a house and brew-house owned by John White, not as a pub.

Before 1779 Thomas Smither, baker, had agreed to sell to Andrew Bristow (qv), junior, brewer, the freehold house with stable, dwelling, yard and outbuilding called The Unicorn, for £250. It was occupied by William Freeharry. He left it to his son, Thomas, and daughter, Diana Brown, to complete the transaction. His other son, James, had emigrated to Philadelphia. In 1792 Freeharry, victualler, was still at 120, and Diana Brown was living in the adjoining house (119? qv) which had a barn, kiln, and three-quarters of an acre of hops. Occasional references occur throughout the century: John Dear was here in 1826, William Swinden in the 1870s to '80s, and Lennox Barber in 1891 when The Unicorn Hotel was offered for sale by Farnham United Brewery.

Not much has come to light about Thomas Smither. Two of that name died in 1783, the wife of one in 1775. There were nearly as many Smithers in Farnham as there were Knights. Stephen Smither (*b* 1801*) was later a baker at 32 West Street (*qv*). Several other Stephen Smithers were prominent. The will (dated 1752) of one left to his son, Stephen, four acres on the south side of Dogflud (East) Street (or possibly the eastern half of The Borough), with the barn he had purchased from John Mabberly (*qv*). He had two daughters, Anne and Jane. To his son, Charles, he left his own house in West Street, and the house adjoining its west side, also the house then recently converted from two dwellings, with malthouse, brewhouse, hop kilns and stable yard or gate leading to them, in West Street.

Stephen Smither was a popular name. The dates of death of six have been found — 1760, 1764, 1784, 1790, 1792, 1876; of a son, Samuel, in 1780, and of daughters, Mary and Anne, in 1773 and 1783.

In the earlier part of the 19th century John Dear was landlord at The Unicorn. John Newall and William Dear were carriers who took loads twice weekly to Guildford from The Unicorn, and in 1841 John Dear (*b* 1762), and Ann (*b* 1767*) were still living hereabout.

* 1 2 4 AND 1 2 5 EAST STREET (Babyland
and Burnett's)

Probably one cannot do better than quote a deed of 1790 for early facts. It is at least concise. Francis Bunch, eldest son of Thomas Bunch (*qqv*), deceased, woollen draper of Farnham, conveyed in consideration of £250 'all four messuages there-tofor five messuages and formerly but one messuage formerly of Matthew Dare in the occupation of John Harding late in the occupation of George Loveland William May junior and John Bigmore formerly the inheritance of Mary Woolgar then of Edward Marshall since of Thomas Bunch': which would take us back quite a long time from 1790.

In 1822 the property passed from Andrews, butcher (*qv*), to Ellis, Catherine Ellis (*qv*) being the owner in 1839. Besides 124 and 125 she owned most of the property in lower Bear Lane including five cottages, stables and a kiln. She also owned Sturt's yard on the south side of East Street. Catherine Ellis was a hop planter. With her son, Thomas, agricultural labourer, Alfred, a tailor, Mary, a draper, and three other Ellis's, her household was a very mixed one. Alfred Ellis, brewer, was here in the 1850s.

Perhaps number 125 is best remembered today as The Queen Street Tavern, or as The Fourteen Penny House. Both names were apt. The first was a result of Queen Victoria's visit to Farnham in 1857, on the occasion of which an attempt was made, it is said, to rename East Street; the second for the custom of allowing patrons to drink as much as they wished for 1s. 2d., on condition that they observed two simple rules.

Number 124 was offered for sale, but not sold, by Hazell's (*qv*) executors in 1882. Sturt tells us of his own association before that with the shop, then Charlie Ivens', corn-merchant's — 'queer oldfashioned, up two or three steps', and in the '90s Edward Bromley's (*qv*) coachbuilder's shops are said to have been to the rear as well as in South Street. Number 125, then for a long time a shop, was offered for sale by Farnham Brewery in 1928. The premises were altered in 1936 when A. W. Chennells, outfitter, now late of Downing Street, opened his business here.

Bear Lane runs north from where The Borough and East Street meet. Bear Lane was once Park Lane, and Park Row was called Park Lane too. Park Row was also known as Bear Lane (in the early 18th century), but is referred to as 'lately called Bear Lane' in 1842. Until about a hundred years ago they formed one way, with no High Park Road. Bear Lane once claimed Farnham Police Station and is said to have acquired its name as the site of a lock-up for performing bears. Was this at its foot, where East Street shelves back? There must be a good reason for such a feature, as at the top of Downing Street. At the top of Bear Lane an alley leads to Farnham Park.

The former St. Polycarp's School (now in Waverley Lane), built in 1896 for £700 to accommodate 120 children, and the Roman Catholic Church, were in Bear Lane. The school's architect was G. Bulbeck.

Among early patrons of the school were the Bishops of Southwark and Sebastopol and Sir William Rose. Managers were Father Gerin and Messrs. C. Borelli (*qv*) and G. Ward when an advertisement in the 'Farnham Herald' of October, 1899, stated that the school '. . . . provides for children (boys, girls and infants) a thorough English education, with all the advantages of a public school and special care and attention of home training'. Charges: Infants 2d. per week; Standards 3d. to 9d.

A partly conjectural view of St. Andrew's Church, showing the early tower and cupola and old Chantry School which was demolished in 1758. Edward Beaver (q.v.) bought the materials for £42. The school, seen here to the right of the north porch, is supposed later to have moved to West Street, becoming Farnham Grammar School. See 25 West Street.

WEST STREET

West Street begins at the town's western extremity where it serves as a still partly rural introduction to a grand architectural climax — a splendid group of town houses on its south side. These include as highlights Willmer House and Sandford House, then an interestingly varied procession of buildings to the street's other end, where it joins The Borough. The sunnier north side has its counterpart in a less grandiose but still magnificent group from 80 to 93.

The street's greatest secondary asset is probably its yards and alleys leading north and south. Steep Mead Lane and Church Passage lead to the river; Potter's Gate, Fox Yard, Timber Close and Hart's Yard penetrate with varying degrees of directness into The Hart. Open farmland, a minute from the centre, rises gently to the Castle and continues westward that invaluable open belt which includes Farnham Park. It is paralleled on a different plane by the grassy flood plain of the Wey.

113 WEST STREET. The Lion and Lamb Hotel as it appeared in the 19th century. Later, shopfronts were inserted.

WEST STREET (At its junction with Downing Street and The Borough) The Round House (Demolished)

At this junction West Street shelves unexpectedly southwards to Downing Street, leaving a wide space. This was once known as Snow Hill and later as Snower Hill. The space has been there for 170 years. Here stood Farnham Round House.

Perhaps its name was derived from the building's shape. It has also been suggested that the name might be a corruption of the Pound House. If the former, another problem arises. When the site was excavated some years ago the only valuable evidence discovered was square foundations. As the Pound House was demolished in 1639, there is little help there. The Round House was here over a hundred years later.

Despite the mystery which surrounds this building, of which no description is known, something of its late history can be traced, as in 1668 it passed from Thomas Hole (*qv*) to Nathaniel Cobstick. By 1775 it had become a pub known as The Star, which Robert and William Trimmer (*qqv*), brewers, held on lease for a maximum of fourteen years and fourteen years later Bristow Bradley (*qv*), another brewer, arranged to sell the land, 'where lately stood The Round House', to Andrew Collyer of 121 West Street (*qqv*). Although details do not present a complete picture, this apparently does not finally settle its life. It could not all have been demolished as in 1790 The Star was still there and in 1794 the tenement and premises known as The Round House, occupied by Peter Lambert, were bought for £150, with a further £50 for the land, by public subscription. This was in order to remove its nuisance to the turnpike and travellers by demolishing the building. In 1791 a Peter Lambert is described as a plasterer, shopkeeper and freeholder.

1   WEST   STREET   (The Alliance)

A public house, reconstructed about 1930 to the design of G. Maxwell Aylwin and H. Falkner (*qqv*). Long before rebuilding, here was a slate roofed wine store on three floors with two widely spaced bays facing north. A pilastered shopfront once ran continuously round the angle to Downing Street.

Before 1768 the property was Abraham Smithers'. It was associated with many people, including John Starr, Richard Cowdery, William Martin, John Drinkwater, John Jackson, Thomas Howell and then William Forester Portello (*qqv*) in 1836. Portello was a chemist born in Hammersmith. His wife Emma (*b* 1823*) came from Bagshot. About 20 years later the property became George Trimmer's (*qv*), soon after which, presumably, it became a pub supplied by his brewery. Robert Nichols (*qv*), cordwainer, not printer, probably had his shop here. Many of the earlier occupants were doctors, like the Drinkwaters, of whom there appear to have been several generations in medicine.

In 1793 Richard (*qv*), surgeon, died; his widow, Elizabeth, in 1808. In 1761 a Richard Drinkwater married Elizabeth Lutman at Bentley. It was probably their son Richard, surgeon, who bought 13 West Street (*qv*) in 1804 and died in 1841. Two sons of a Richard, James and Thomas, died in 1776 and 1786. In 1841 Richard Drinkwater (*b* 1776*) was at 13 West Street. John Drinkwater (*b* 1781*, *d* 1867) who inherited the house (presumably after his father Richard's death in July 1841), was also a doctor. His wife Anabella (Ridley) (*b* 1771*) predeceased him by fifty years. They had not less than two daughters, Ann, and Elizabeth who married William Paine (*b* 1813*) of the hop growing family. Their children included Elizabeth (*b* 1844*), William J. M. (*b* 1846*), Anabella (*b* 1847*) and Georgiana (*b* 1850*). A William Paine died in 1860. His sons were Alfred Richard Drinkwater Paine and William J. M. Paine.

7   WEST   STREET   (The Queen of Hearts)

Built in the early 20th century to the design of J. A. Eggar, this replaced a two-floor, two-bay, parapeted shop of brick and tile with a flat hood and bracket door. Anthony Williams (*qv*) had his ten oasts and hop-bagging room to the rear. Four of the oasts were formerly a malt kiln. Williams had occupied the property of John Hunt hereabout from about 1840 at least.

8   WEST   STREET   (Franklin and Chilcott)

A symmetrical brick built shop of four bays and three floors with deep eaves above cornice and paired brackets. A painted string course divides upper floors.

Fenestration: Ground floor, a double shopfront below a common fascia; First floor, four recessed sashes; Second floor, similar, of three-quarters height with brick aprons below sills.

A cottage and house here were owned by James Betts (*b* 1771*), butcher, who was resident in 1841. Ten years later his son Charles (*b* 1807*) was carrying on the business. His wife was Ann (*b* 1806 at Ashstead). They had daughters Ann, Mary and Jane. These Betts' had earlier been at 38 Castle Street (*qv*). William Betts of The Borough was also a butcher. He had a son William (*b* 1850*) and a brother John who had retired from butchering by 1851.

In their business the family was succeeded by Ebenezer Aylwin. Mr. Aylwin kept his sheep in the churchyard. Not an uncommon practice. Thomas Mills, another butcher, did much the same 200 years earlier. He kept his pigs there, allowing them to dig it up and cause 'grave damage'.

The churchyard served not only to absorb the dead, but to feed the quick and cure the ailing. One named Morgan, of St. John's College, left a manuscript now at the Bodleian. He recorded in 1684 '. . . they have one church in Farnham with a tower, though less, like that at Winchester. The churchyard abounds with Mallows an excellent plant for Clisters so that dead bodyes are here found to be good for something, because they breed Mallows to supple the Arses of living people. But enough of this. I proceed to the names of my friends that have been and now are in St. John's'.

10 AND 11 WEST STREET
(Elphick's Junior Shop)

Two brick buildings, united by a common shopfront and fascia, totalling six bays on three main floors under tiled roofs. Above bays four to six is a tile-faced addition with two sashes.

Fenestration: Ground floor, a plate-glass shopfront; First floor, six recessed sashes; Second floor, six similar of three-quarters height.

The cottage-style shop on the site of number 10 in the 19th century was the birthplace of Augustus Toplady, writer of 'Rock of Ages'. The building was demolished by John Knight of Bentley. He built in its place a house very similar to number 11, already there. The two, with stuccoed ground floor façades and square-hooded doorways, were converted into shops in the earlier part of this century. Their present shopfront was fitted in 1960 when the property was largely reconstructed.

J. A. Eggar (*qv*), who designed houses and was an auctioneer, lived here and occupied 9, 10 and 11. He added the top floor. He also produced a book — 'Remembrances of Life and Customs in Gilbert White's, Cobbett's and Charles Kingsley's Country'. It relates many anecdotes of local interest.

Number 10 was a home of the Fewtrells who for many years were at Farnham in tailoring and allied trades. They numbered many. Here, mid-19th century, were James (*b* 1813*), tailor, his wife Sarah (*b* 1812*) and children Sarah (*b* 1845*), Emily (*b* 1846*) and James (*b* 1848*). Earlier, Elizabeth (*b* 1791*), tailor, and Ann (*b* 1826*) were here. In the '40s John Fewtrell owned a house — probably 13 East Street. He, too, was a tailor (*b* 1766*). Another group were at about 101 West Street. They included Elizabeth, bonnet maker, and her daughters Sarah (*b* 1822*) and Emma (*b* 1824*). They were both dressmakers. The Misses Sarah and Emma were later at 94 West Street (*qv*) and dressmaking into the 1890s. James, a gardener, died in 1811. Earlier the name is so frequently encountered that only a few which may help to order confusion of like names can be included: James (*d* 1767), son of James; James (*d* 1810), son of James and Ann; Ann (*d* 1810), wife of James; Mary (*d* 1802), wife of James. John Fewtrell married Lucy Little (1783); Mary (*d* 1787), wife of John.

Number 11 was the house of Robert Page about mid-18th century (see 6 and 7 The Borough). By the 1830s John, William and Mary Knight (*qv*) owned the house, which was occupied by Edward Knowles (*qv*) and thirty years later The London and County Banking Company opened here. Shortly after, it moved to 38 The Borough (*qv*). Nelson and Goodrick, outfitters, were at number 10 at the same time as Canute and Co., clothiers, were at 11. Nelson and Goodrick were soon at 11 as well and occupied both shops until about 1960.

It is said that cellars were once a schoolroom. Williams (*qv*), a chemist, was once living hereabout.

12 WEST STREET   (The Farnham Dairy)

A brick built shop of four bays and three floors with tiled roof behind a parapet, against which there is a modillion cornice. There is an arched gateway in bay one.

Fenestration: Ground floor, a shopfront occupying approximately bays two and three. The window is divided by slender shafts supporting arched heads. The fitting is contained between two engaged and fluted half-bred shafts; First floor, three-pane-wide recessed sashes; Second floor, three-quarter windows, as below them.

Door: In bay four, contained within the window fitting.

Interior: Inside is a wooden serpentine staircase with slender rail.

'1767 R.S.' is visible on a rainwater head at the front. Although this probably does not belong here the date is about right as a reference of 1773 describes the place as a new-built dwelling. It was built, however, by William Watts. The position of the rainwater head might suggest that the top floor is an addition. However, another explanation of its appearance here is given under 13 West Street (*qv*) and it is a more convincing one.

Many alterations have taken place, although the ground floor has, for very many years, served as a shop. At the back was once (for Farnham) an extravagant dining room, the rounded back wall of which had niches outside, over-looking a pleasure garden. These recesses were presumably to contain sculptures or urns and can be traced in the dairy building which now abuts the south end. The shopfront is one of very few better Victorian ones still intact.

The *c* 1770 building replaced another which was known until shortly before that date as The White Lion alehouse. In a reference of 1737 the premises were described as a free-hold messuage, leased by Mr. Watts (*qv*), carpenter, from Edmund Chase. No mention of The White Lion is made although it was certainly there in 1727 and 1756. Chase had a son, Edmund, and a daughter, Mary who died without issue in 1771. Twenty years later an Edmund Chase was at Fren-sham, a cutler. Thomas Chase was a freeholder in 1775 and so was George Chase of Frensham. A George Chase of Frensham voted in 1727.

Watts seems to have bought the property he previously tenanted at about the time of Mary Chase's death, then to have built his new house. Watts died about 1795, Mary, his daughter, having married Thomas Knight, draper, whose shop was here by 1804. Hence William Watts Knight (*qv*) who conveyed number 12 with 23 and 24 West Street (*qv*) to Mrs. Elizabeth Knight in 1868.

There are Watts-Andrews-Knight-Merriott-Johnson cross-currents, and George Johnson (*b* 1806*), draper, opened his shop here too. It was still operating in the '90s, but by 1915 this was Carew Stockwell's dairy. Johnson's wife was Kesiah (*b* 1809*).

William Watts, carpenter, had an apprentice, George, son of William Hewitt, in 1725. A William Watts married Elizabeth Butler in 1760, and in 1845 died Elizabeth (Watts), wife of James Stevens (*qv*, *d* 1850). One William Watts was son of John Watts, carpenter, of near 25 West Street (*qv*), and brother of John, husband of Elizabeth.

A symmetrical and parapeted main block of five bays on three floors, brick built under a tiled mansard roof. A modillioned cornice separates upper floors, the lower ones being divided at sill level by a string course. This continues across a more austere block of one bay abutting the west end and gives continuity to sills of varying levels.

Fenestration: Ground floor, a modern shopfront; First floor, windows are recessed, three panes wide. The centre bay, set back, contains a Venetian window, while other windows on this floor have sashes, the halves of which are of unequal height, lower parts without glazing bars; Second floor, a small central square sash is positioned between two lunettes.

Interior: Most has now been cleared, but remains of two decorative plaster ceilings can be seen. The front one is delicate and of late 18th century style (cf fanlights at 23 and 90 West Street). The other, heavily rubbed, uses rococo motifs, not so delicately. An earlier ground floor plan can be traced.

The building can be divided into two parts: 1, The main house, 1776; 2, The westernmost part, which might be as early as the 15th century in structure.

1.   The house was intact when bought by Chilton and Scammell, drapers, in 1869. The doorcase was a good one but vanished many years ago. One can imagine how the front appeared though as the door was remarkably like the one fitted recently to 88A West Street (qv) even to the ogival fanlight. The house was of second rank locally and replaced other houses — probably four in all.

2.   This part contains behind the innocent brick façade remains of a largish timber framed building — probably the eastern half of a house which once extended through to 14 West Street. One bay of the early building has recently been revealed. As in most Farnham houses, timbers were not highly finished. In the early 19th century this part was definitely still a dwelling, being converted later to a coach house with passage separating it from the main building at ground floor level. This accounts for the brick detailing above. There was a brewhouse behind.

The history of this house, as a whole, can be traced to 1727 when it was the property of Lazarus Turner who bought it then from John Boult. But long before this the greater part had been a principal inn — The Antelope — later converted to four dwellings with a malthouse. Earlier occupiers included Richard Kelsey (*qv*) and his daughter Ann, wife of Richard Barrett and later of John Hook. Robert Kelsey, surgeon, died in 1697. An inn named The Antelope was established by 1607. The Antelope, described in 1727 as having some time formerly been here, is also referred to in a list of the chief rents of the Rectory in 1726. Perhaps another Antelope had taken its place by that time.

In 1764 the property was bought by Richard Sumner (*d* 1783), a doctor. It was presumably he who rebuilt the house three years later. Inscriptions under staircases are not usually the most reliable evidence for dating a building, but 1767 has recently been found and it might well be accurate in this case, as the rainwater head at 12 West Street (*qv*) bears that same date; and the initials R.S. As 12 was certainly rebuilt after 13 we have almost positive proof that Richard Sumner built this house in 1767, his commemorative rainwater head being later moved from the end of his new house to the front of his neighbour's on the rebuilding of the latter.

In 1802 the house is referred to as a capital messuage. It passed to Robert Trimmer (*qv*), of Alton, who soon sold to Richard Drinkwater (*qv*), another doctor. With the house went a tenement to the west which was later rebuilt to make a coach house. This is the part which contains a bay of the timber framed building noted above. It was occupied by Stephen Caesar, formerly by Charles Pink and before him by widow Lucy.

Sturt recalls the days when The Times, costing 3d., was often shared by families, changing at midday. Sometimes he did the changing. One place of call was in West Street. 'Down a dark passage was a side door, and the passage had on it the name "Drinkwater" — probably the person whose house I had to go to'.

After John Drinkwater's (*qv*) death the property was bought by Richard Chilton in 1869. It was occupied by Mrs. Elizabeth Paine, Richard Drinkwater's daughter, and the house described as 'a genteel family freehold residence with garden, two-stall stable, coach house, lofts and yards'. It went for £1,320, quadrupling its selling price within a century. Other attractions included a capital wine and beer cellar, knife house, brew house with two coppers and a dairy. Chilton, with his partner Scammell, built up the drapers and outfitters business which was bought by George Elphick (*d* 1921) in 1880. Under his family's name the business thrives today.

Lazarus Turner had been sitting tenant before buying. One of that name was baptised in 1693. He was the son of Robert and Ann. William Turner (*d* 1730*), glazier, later had tenants here. His brother was Robert (*d* 1749*), a plumber, his cousins local glovers Henry (*d* 1753*) and John Allen.

A Richard Sumner was chemist in Farnham in 1717. The family had connections with Crondall, and the Richard who bought 13 West Street left it to his sister Mrs. Maria Bennett. On her death in 1791 she, a widow, left the property to her cousin James Smither. Perhaps it was Sumner's 'medical and chirugical books' that she left to John Newham (*qv*). Her India cabinet and china in it went to Anthony Williams' wife Lucy.

The Drinkwaters and Paines who were here later are noted particularly under 1 West Street.

ST. ANDREW'S SCHOOL, CHURCH PASSAGE, OFF WEST STREET

Built mainly of stone and tile, the south block is in a mid-Victorian ecclesiastical-collegiate gothick style. It presents an often picturesque façade, with rugged chalky stonework assuming various colours and a wide range of brilliances according to its humidity and to the light. Its appeal as a building is more pictorial than architectural.

The main block was opened in 1860. In the south-west corner of the site is what was built as the master's and mistress's house. Mr. Dewdney and Miss Elsworthy were its first occupants. The opening was not without its dramatic prelude as, shortly before, the bell tower, top heavy with a great amount of lead, was blown down. The architect was Colston, of Winchester. Chinnocks built the school for £2,030, Mr. Halsey (*qv*) having given up his ground rent on the yard for the good cause. As this sum exceeds the one quoted below it probably included the dwellings and other work on the site as well. The hundred years old front will be difficult to outmatch for picturesqueness, scale and compatibility with the church when (inevitable?) expansion comes. There are few buildings about the town which do not relegate this stone to side walls. Here (as at Alton — Colston again?) it is used with considerable effect. 1876 saw some extensive additions made. The infant department, north and north-west, was added. Twenty years later the school was 'redecorated and outside undergoing great alterations', and in 1905 further extensive work was done.

The site has for very long been owned by the Church and was once the Parsonage Yard. The school itself began its life elsewhere — probably at the Freemason's Hall, Castle Street (*qv*) — as the National School, which was founded by subscriptions raised in 1813. The 'old schools were dark, without classrooms and unfit for the purpose for which they were assigned'; N.B., not for which they were built.

The State first intervened in education in 1833. Such voluntary bodies as The National Society and The British and Foreign Schools Society received grants, and the State-Church partnership was established.

The National School and The British School (which was at 80 East Street, *qv*) were the mainstays in Farnham schooling for most of the century. Private schools continued to flourish and well over thirty were established in the town during the later part of the 19th century, many in East Street, and mostly in private houses. There was also the Grammar School at 25 West Street (*qv*).

The first part of St. Andrew's school cost £1,080 to build and replaced an earlier building in the same yard. This occupied the south angle of the Parsonage Yard and has been described as a barn. L-shaped, it was nearly as large in area as the church itself. Might there have been a great tithe barn here?

16, 17, 18 WEST STREET

Until rebuilt late in the 19th century four houses fronted the street here. Two, which were once the house built by John Watts (*qv*) about 1730, where 18 now stands, were the property of Henry Gosden Gray, grocer. He had been a grocer and cheesemonger in Farnham for thirty years or more when William Kingham bought Gray's business in 1852. He acquired also the property itself twenty-four years later. Number 16 was, before the business expanded, a long and narrow building running down Church Passage. Between it and the churchyard were once two more dwellings since replaced by the warehouses of Kingham's who retailed here for over a hundred years from the time of William's original enterprise.

When the church tower was elevated about a century ago it is told that this passage served a valuable purpose. To lift new stones a pulley block, rope and horse were used. The passageway was the horse's walk each time a load of stone went up. This was made possible by the purchase for £20 of land from Mr. Trimmer in 1850 to widen the footpath.

By 1851 Henry Gray (*b* 1793* at Cranley) employed three men in his grocery here. His wife Mary was born about 1798 in Farnham.

19 WEST STREET (The Wheatsheaf)

A brick built and tiled public house reconstructed in recent years.

This pub became so named between 1756 and 1769. Before that it was known as The Spreadeagle. There is no mention of an ale house here in 1733-5 when the property (with half an acre) passed from J. Brown, husbandman, to Thomas Stanton, baker, although there is one, by name, in Stanton's will of 1749. He lived on the west side of Castle Street in a house he had lately bought from John Salter, and owned two houses in The Borough or East Street which he had bought from his brother-in-law Robert Knight (qv) and which were occupied by Thomas Cummins and Mr. Miller. The Spreadeagle was let to Thomas Westbrooke (qv) who in 1757 received his share of the King's Bounty (qv). Stanton left the property in trust for his wife and sons.

For the last quarter of the 18th century and much of the 19th the pub was Knights'. It was sold in 1888 to the Farnham Brewery. They offered it for sale three years later and Reid's Brewery bought it in 1896.

The Wheatsheaf, Farnham, is the setting of a detail in Michael Sadlier's 'Forlorn Sunset'.

19 AND 20 WEST STREET (Between, Penfold's Yard)

Here once was Penfold's Yard which now gives rear access to the Art School. Where the pottery is were stables of the Penfolds (qv). The yard was known by this name one hundred and twenty years ago. A cottage and kiln belonging to Elizabeth Penfold were in the yard. It is probable that this entrance was once under a gateroom belonging to The Wheatsheaf (qv). See also 25 West Street.

20 WEST STREET (Laurette)

One of an unpretentious pair of middle 19th century appearance, it houses a prize architectural decoration. Farnham is not remarkable for its plasterwork; unless for the lack of it. Relatively few pre-19th century houses run to cornices even in the principal rooms, although there are a few quite good ones. Some others have stock cornices but pre-19th century ceiling or wall plaster decoration is quite rare. It is therefore even more astonishing to find in this small house plasterwork unexcelled in the district. Limited to one ceiling on the ground floor, it is of full-blooded Restoration character — coffered, foliated, scrolled, wreathed, rosetted, be-cherubed and cartouched. Who was responsible is not known, but a possible clue has come to light. Before 1716 the house was owned by Samuel Thompson who conveyed to John Watts (*qqv*). Thompson was a Londoner and haberdasher by trade, admitted to the Haberdashers' Company in 1700 by servitude of John Taylor. There is then a link with this house outside Farnham at any rate not long after the ceiling was made.

Both houses were owned by Abraham Crowley in 1839. In 1836 Abraham Crowley of Alton owned a one-third share of a house in West Street called The New Inn. It was at that time occupied by John Rumbell. See also 25 West Street.

The shopfront of number 20 replaced an earlier one in about 1930 and is said to have been designed by John Kingham, like those at 84 West Street, *c* 1929.

22 WEST STREET (Georgian Cottage)

Converted to a shop from a dwelling *c* 1950, when the then new bow window was made and added. There was a flat hood and bracket doorhead and a sash window on the ground floor until then. See 25 West Street.

23 AND 24 WEST STREET

A pair of asymmetrical brick and tile houses totalling eight main bays on two main floors with dormer windows behind a parapet. Number 23 is of three main bays; 24 of five. A secondary recessed bay gives side access through an arched doorway and visually divides the houses. The cornice has a frieze with flutes and rosettes. A plain painted fascia divides floors.

Fenestration: Ground floor, six recessed three-pane-wide sashes; First floor, eight similar; Above, five flat topped dormer windows with sashes.

Door: In bays three and six; Ionic pilasters supporting open dentilled pediment and broken entablatures which contain architraved semicircular fanlights with radial metal tracery.

Dated 1790 on rainwater heads, the houses, virtually untouched, are stylistic contemporaries of numbers 41 and 90 West Street (*qqv*). They share similar frieze decoration and parapet treatment, delicate decoration and a generally very neat and precise appearance. Numbers 23 and 24 might have been the speculations of Daniel Batchelour (*qv*). He owned property here (probably this site) and speculated, building for example Factory Yard. But there is no evidence and the quality is very different from his cottages. Not long after 23 and 24 were built, the Knight family owned this pair, and later George McDonald (*qv*) was landlord. Both were conveyed by William Watts Knight (*qv*) to Mrs. Elizabeth Knight in 1868 at which time Mary Betts and Harriett Andrews were occupants — both widows (*qqv*). Earlier, Richard Andrews (*qv*), solicitor (*b* 1804*) and his wife Harriett (*b* 1809*) lived hereabout. Slomans (*qv*) were possibly here too. At number 23 lived Sidney Stapley (*qv*), architect and surveyor (and later on Inspector of Nuisances to the Local Board). He worked for George Trimmer (*qv*) and was probably responsible for some of his pubs and other buildings, for example The Albion, The Fox and Hounds, Natalie House and Send House (*qv*). But this is a guess, based on certain similarities of character, not on written evidence. See also 25 West Street.

25 WEST STREET (Farnham School of Art)

A building of two main floors and four bays, fronted grey brick and roof tiled. Bays one and four project, have gables facing north, string courses between windows, and flush stone coigns. Windows are transomed and mullioned in stone.

The school is of two main builds — the east bay 1872. The remainder (of this front block) was rebuilt *c* 1895 to the design of Paxton Watson (*qv*). Extensive alterations to this building and additions to the rear have been made since 1950.

Before the late 19th century alterations, there was, where bays two to four now stand, a house with façade of late Georgian character (see illustration). It appeared to be timber framed, at some time jettied over the street. As a result of the refronting, it had three 1-3-1 sashes in flush boxes on the ground floor, pilastered and pedimented doorcase, a tiled roof and sashed dormer windows. The front was stuccoed, and the house as a whole was more compatible with its neighbours than is the building which has replaced it.

The Art School once served as Farnham Grammar School and later as Farnham Girls' Grammar School. For the sake of compactness, the background history of 20-25 West Street inclusive is dealt with under this head, as until 150 years or so ago they were in single ownership. The block was sold to John Watts, carpenter, by Samuel Thompson (*qqv*), haberdasher, and others of his family in 1716. Watts died about 1752 and left to his son John and Elizabeth his wife two houses then in his own possession and Thomas Baker's, the houses being the eastern ones of those he bought from

Thompson. Another six houses adjoining he left to William Watts (*qv*). John Watts senior was father-in-law to Andrew Merriott (*qv*) who lived at number 26. By 1754 Watts' property here included one acre of hops tenanted by Benjamin Stevens. It was bounded on the east by the hops of Westbrooke (Thomas Westbrooke was at The Wheatsheaf, *qv*) and the rivulet on the south, the ground of John Wigmore being on its west. Wigmore was in the Church and in 1768 the Parish paid a John Watts £3 11s. 9d. for timber to repair bridges in its care.

It appears that in 1769 the eastern tenements included a bakehouse, as well as a hop kiln and sawhouse and that they were occupied by Peter Edwards, a baker, who entered contract with Richard Watts of Winchester, peruke maker, who had inherited part of the estate.

The early 19th century saw some complex transactions mainly between Samuel Locke, DD., Walter Waller and Daniel Batchelour. Locke was once master of the Grammar School, and what is part of the Art School is probably what is referred to in a description of property written in 1809, when Batchelour conveyed to Locke 'all that parcel of land then added to and made part of the garden in possession of Samuel Locke together with the farmyard belonging and adjoining'. On this land a hop kiln, stables, coach house, storerooms, cowhouse and granary had then recently been erected; probably part remains in the buildings in Penfold's Yard (*qv*), now part of the Art School pottery. Later, ten acres of land were in Dr. Locke's possession, including Whitmore at Frensham.

A guide to the time of earlier building at 25 West Street is to be found on a bracketed oak beam built into the new Grammar School in Morley Road. It came from the old school, and bears the date 1607. Some account of what is known of the school's history is in the Victoria County History. It may, however, be added here facts which have recently been found.

A petition of 1682, recently printed by the Surrey County Council, includes informative details. Local inhabitants being clearly not satisfied with the running of this institution under Edmund Parker, 'who for many years past hath bin master of the schoole hath by his frequent absenting himselfe from the schools and neglecting the schollers rendered the said Charity almost frutless few or none coming to the schoole frome abroad and the inhabitants to well knowing his Negligence and frequent absenting himselfe and how little proficiency Children have made under him and with all his continuall Imprudent Deportment therein hath beene Necessitated to there Great Inconvenience and Cost to send theire Children to other schooles whereas if an Industrious man were made schoolmaster it would Incourage strangers to send there Children to the schoole and the Inhabitants besides the conveniency of having there Children well taught at home would reape other great advantages by promoting the trade of the place'.

Forty-two years later, when Dr. Willis made his visitation, things had not looked up much despite the petition. 'The school is very low in its reputation and though there are only six boys required to be taught gratis I cannot find that there is now that number now in the school'. George Parker was by then Master. Like father, like son?

At that time the school was still attached to St. Andrew's Church and endowed by Bishop Morley's house in West Street, with three tenements and a garden, worth £20 a year.

Morley's house too was in a bad state, Willis noting that although capable of accommodating thirty boarders it would cost £100 to put right. That was in 1724-25. The filled-in arch to the right of the church porch is where the school formerly stood. The building previously here was not, as the stones suggest, an abutment running south-north, but it ran parallel to the nave's main axis. In height it was about as the nave, with a simple single-ridged roof, five stepped-buttresses along its north wall, a lancet window between each pair. In the east wall, high up, were two more windows which overlooked the porch. It seems as though this building was sold and the money put towards patching up the bishop's house in West Street, thereby transferring the establishment to 25 West Street, for in 1758 the materials of the building were sold to Edward Beaver (*qv*) for £42. But even then the place floundered for another hundred years. Under Dr. Locke it seems to have done no better. He had brought with him the sons of twelve gentlemen and would not teach others. He left in 1822. Of that year is an indenture of two parts for a West Street property, including a farmyard, between him and John Augustus Brooke of Bloomsbury. Elizabeth Hooper (*b* 1801*), governess, and some girl pupils, were hereabout twenty years later. In 1849, however, the Grammar School was reorganised, perhaps under the guidance of Richard Sankey (*b* 1803*), vicar, who probably lived here at about that time, then under the Strouds the school prospered, having about 75 scholars at 36 guineas around 1870.

The Grammar School moved to its present building in

1906. It was constructed by Crosby and Co. at a cost of £13,000 excluding fields. Its roll by then was 110 day boys and 25 boarders. The Girls' Grammar School, which is said to have had its origins in Mrs. Swayne's (*qv*) school, was established by the Rev. T. Gardiner in 1903, then moved to 25 West Street which it left on the opening of its new building in Menin Way in 1939. Farnham School of Art, previously at 17 South Street (*qv*), has since occupied the West Street building. At the time of writing, Farnham Grammar School had begun its first major expansion since 1906.

See 80-81 West Street.

25 WEST STREET, Farnham Grammar School. A partly conjectural reconstruction of the Master's House which stood before the west part was rebuilt late in the 19th century.

2 6   W E S T   S T R E E T   (G. M. Aylwin, Architects)

An asymmetrical three-bay house on two main floors, built of brick, with tiled roof behind a corniced parapet. The front is encased and detailed in cement, a moulded string course dividing floors and horizontal rustication emphasising the lower parts.

Fenestration: Ground floor, three-pane-wide sashes in bays two and three; Second floor, three similar windows. All are recessed and architraved in cement.

Door: In bay one. Flat hood over consoles, all in cement.

Much of this house, including the façade, may be dated *c* 1845, although extensions have been made at various times, particularly *c* 1930, to the east and south.

A number of Farnham houses have fronts similarly

rendered. They include 27, 59, 66, 67, 69, 118, 122 West Street, 27 Castle Street, and a group on the north side of East Street. These vary considerably in quality and date. The best in Farnham include 118 West Street (*qv*), the group in East Street, and this house — 26 West Street. They appear to be the earlier ones, and owe relative distinction to their adherence to clear cut lines and sensitive disposition of parts, guided by classical principles. There must, about mid-century, have been a good craftsman in this medium in the town. But by 1890 it was found necessary to go as far as Kent to find someone capable of doing similar work at 59 West Street (*qv*). By comparing 69 and 118 West Street degrees of success in the use of this material can be gauged.

In 1811 Richard Turner (*qv*) sold this house to the Marquis of Lothian for £1,050. It was part of his estate which once included 27 West Street (*qv*) which had been sold off separately in 1808. Their earlier ownerships were common for many years.

John Ray Merriott, musick master, bought the house for £550 after the death of Charles Beauchamp Kerr, his brother Mark Robert Kerr having inherited it. John Newnham (*qv*) had then recently bought a neighbouring part of Lothian's estate. Merriott died in 1829 and 26 West Street passed to his brother Edwin (*b* 1806*, *d* 1843) and from him to his wife Frances Ann Merriott (*b* 1820* in Southampton). It was one of her sons, the Rev. John Hepburn Merriott (*b* 1841*), who sold the 'messuage with courtyard and chaise-house' to Frederick Bolton of Lloyds, shipowner, shortly after Frances Merriott's death in 1899. The house (with number 27) became a training school for clergy and for a time the downstairs front room was annexed as a Grammar School classroom. See 25 West Street.

It is likely, therefore, that Edwin Merriott, 'professor of music', or his young widow, was responsible for most of the house that we see today. Elizabeth Ann Merriott had other children — Arthur (*b* 1842*), Frederick (*b* 1842*) and Fanny (*b* 1844*).

The name Merriott (Marriott) appears frequently in Farnham records during the 18th century and occasionally back to the 1660s, probably earlier. Andrew (*d* 1805) was a staymaker in 1791, Andrew senior having died in 1776. One of the Andrew Merriotts was father-in-law to John Watts (*qv*) who lived nearby, and Richard, of Godalming, owned a house in West Street in the 1780s. It was not this one, as a carpenter named Peter Smith (*qv*, *d c* 1780) was owner at that time.

John Merriott (who had been organist at Basingstoke) ran a music school in West Street in 1820 and with his brother Edwin, organist at St. Andrew's, provided concerts for public hearing at The Goat's Head (*qv*).

John Ray Merriott's mother and sister were both named Ann. Ann, daughter of James and Ann Merriott, was baptised in 1800. Another Ann, Andrew's daughter, died in 1773. Andrew married Ursula Mayhew in 1759 and (presumably) yet another Andrew married Mary Hodges less than a year later. John Merriott married Mary Hillyer in 1764 and Mary (née Hodges?), wife of Andrew, died in 1792.

27 WEST STREET (Newnham House)

An asymmetrical brick built parapeted house on two main floors of eight bays under a tiled roof. The front, which projects to contain bay six, has a cement casing.

Fenestration: Ground floor, three-pane-wide and recessed sashes in all but bays one and six; First floor, three-pane-wide recessed sashes except in bay six. All of these windows are contained in cement architraves. Bay six contains a 1-3-1 window above the main door; Above, three square-headed dormer windows with rectangular leaded casements.

Door: The case has panelled cement pilasters and flat cornice containing a semicircular fanlight with a lantern. Bay one is a gateroom with a secondary door also. Above it, a semicircular light with open iron grille.

A large building, generally of 18th and 19th century character, with a long walled garden leading to the canal which runs through several properties adjoining. The house is clad in typical 19th century manner with grey cement. Compared with some other examples which have received similar treatment the result is austere.

Indentures of lease and release of three parts were made for property here (which included number 26 *qv*) between George Chasin (*qv*) the elder, of Dorset, of the first part, Giles Taylor and Samuel Harper, both of Middlesex, of the second part and William Parker, of Farnham, brewer, in November 1750.

Parker died twenty years later and in the following year the property passed to Peter Smith (*qv*); in 1794 to John Hewitt, possibly as tenant. The Marquis of Lothian, who lived then at Vernon House (*qv*) bought all but number 26 and also over half an acre of Richard Turner's land (which adjoined the garden) in 1808. Number 26 followed shortly afterwards. This ultimately left the Kerrs with a solid block of property from the Art School to Willmer House as well as premises on the north side of West Street — e.g., 90 and The Plough (*qqv*).

Newnham House derives its name from a family who bought part of the Marquis' property after his death. Before December 1819 John Newnham was here, for an indenture of that date describes number 26 as being bound on the west in part by the garden wall of John Newnham belonging to the premises lately purchased by him. It is unlikely that Newnham bought as one dwelling all that is now known as Newnham House. It might well have been more than one habitation for some time afterwards, being once divided perhaps between bays five and six.

The fact that the west end has only one window (very small and near the roof) is intriguing. Here is a great area of brickwork — unopened and not new. Outbuildings of Vernon House once abutted part, but they were relatively small though penetrating deeply from the street, down the boundary wall. Was there once another house here, standing where the ornamental garden is now? If so, it had gone before 1840 and probably a long time earlier than that. Did Byworth's (*qv*) stand here? It was owned by the Vernons in the 1650s and was described then as 'being near abutting on the said [West] street on the north and on the new river on the south'. Was the canalised stream at the bottom of these gardens once called the New River? Very likely so. What is now a gateway leading from the bridge over this canal might mark the south end of 'a road or passage leading to the Bishop's [of Hereford, *qv*] Meadows' running between Newnham House and neighbouring property. The gate opened from Vernon House garden to what was once known as The Marquis of Lothian's Walk.

Farnham's recent heraldic achievement bears on its scroll the motto 'BY WORTH'. It is interesting to find that the Yorkshire industrial town of Keighley's does too. But the puns are different.

Newnham House passed from the Slomans (surgeons, like the Newnhams) in 1898, and early in the 20th century was used as a training school for clergy. It was known as the Bishop's Hostel until 1919 at which time the two houses were connected. Since the 1930s number 27 has been Newnham House Guesthouse.

John Newnham was a Farnham doctor in the 18th century. In 1791 J. Newnham was surgeon and apothecary. At the same time Charles Newnham was a doctor at Bentley, and John Newnham at Ash. The Farnham family may, of course, have been peripatetic practitioners. Edward Charles and Edward, both sons of John, died in 1794 and 1795 and by mid-19th century William Newnham (*b* 1791*), surgeon, became prominent in town affairs. He was at 27 West Street in the early '40s and the early 1820s partnership of John Newnham and Son had by the '50s become Newnham and Sloman. William Newnham, above, born in Farnham, was married to Caroline (*b* 1792*). They had a daughter Mary (*b* 1836*). Others, probably also their children, were Caroline (*b* 1826*), Catherine (*b* 1826*) and Philip (*b* 1832*). In 1785 a John Newnham married Mary Dowden (*d* 1800), the daughter of William Dowden (*qv*) junior. William Newnham's eldest daughter married John Manwaring. On her death in 1904 it was recorded that she was the widow of Kingsley's 'Saint and the Hopgrower'. Samuel Sloman (*b* 1817 at Exeter, *d* 1897), surgeon, once lived nearby, possibly at 24 West Street (*qv*). His wife, from Farnham, was Catherine (*b* 1824*, *d* 1878). Three of their sons became doctors — Samuel (*b* 1847), Herbert (*b* 1853) and Frederick (*b* 1862).

It is of value to record in some detail names and dates of Farnham doctors for more than general interest value, for they frequently signed documents as witnesses, for deeds of mortgage (for one reason or another), and as beneficiaries in wills. They can, therefore, help place otherwise undatable facts and documents. Apothecaries are also included as some, in business early in life as chemists, later became practising doctors.

Surgeons in Farnham who would have been contemporaries of the Slomans included Edward Knowles, Richard Drinkwater, Thomas Leigh, Richard Sumner, Samways Oke and Robert Clarke (*qqv*). Others, here earlier, include dates when they are known to have been doctors if evidence has been found. They were: 1634, William Bicknell (*d* 1688); 1660s, George Rogers, Richard Kelsey and Nathaniel Cole; William Mathews (d 1688) was granted his licence to practise, in Farnham, in 1662; Thomas Tamworth (*d* 1690); Robert Munk (*d* 1709); 1712, William Pratt; 1771, Richard Cowdery; 1791-1809, John Jackson; John Bradford (*d* 1802); Caleb Barker (*d* 1808); 1827, Dr de Michelé; John Randall (*b* 1787* in London) and chemist in The Borough 1845; 1841, John Ellis (*b* 1818*), an assistant to Newnham.

Chemists were Christopher Clapham (*d* 1702); 1717, Richard Sumner (*qv*); 1731, Sherman Wall, who had as apprentice Thomas Clapham; 1714, Robert Norris; 1826, Thomas Everell, William Williams and William Portello (*qqv*).

A mainly brick built house on two principal floors and of square U plan. The parapeted street front is rendered in cement, is symmetrical and of three bays in the central member.

Fenestration: Ground floor, central member, two sashes three panes wide in bays one and three; First floor, three similar. The flanking members are blind to the street front but are of two bays depth on inner return faces. Each has two similar three-pane-wide sashes on each floor.

Door: Central member, bay two, engaged fluted Doric columns supporting broken entablature and triangular pediment.

South elevation: Of yellow-grey (bays one to six) and red (bays seven and eight) brick, asymmetrical, on two main floors totalling eight bays span. Eaved roof of slate and tile. A bay window rises the height of this elevation, embracing bays one to three. It is capped in slate.

Fenestration: Ground floor, bays one to six, windows to ground level; bays seven and eight transomed and mullioned, each with four leaded lights; First floor, bays one to six, recessed sashes three panes wide; bays seven and eight, smaller, flush, wide-boxed sashes three panes wide. Above bay eight a dormer with casement and flat top.

Interior: Of asymmetrical plan it is partly panelled in oak—some apparently original. There are two staircases. One (east wing) has turned oak banisters and has wainscot through main floors. A glass dome lights the other main stairwell. In the upper north-west room is a tempera wall decoration. In simple pigments it depicts in two dimensions a three-dimensional carved chimney piece of monumental early renaissance character. Bishop (1561-1580) Horne's achievement is set among a wealth of architectural features and texts.

Other features: The front court — contained by three wings — is paved and set; the street front closed by spear-head iron railings. They contain centrally an iron gate topped by a lamp. This central feature is decorated with wrought iron arrowheads and scrolls. Rainwater heads in the angles of this court are dated 1721 and nearby in the cement casing are two plaques with the date 1881 and the initials J.K.

The house has been much altered and is of several distinct builds. The east wing is of pre-Renaissance character, its staircase dating perhaps from the first quarter of the 17th century. Other parts are early, especially in the west wing. The street façade can probably be dated from rainwater heads, viz.

1721, and the back central portion was rebuilt about a century ago. Recasing of the front in cement probably took place in the year indicated on the plaque, 1881. The blind ends result from an earlier truncating, said (for reasons unstated) to have been in 1721 also, and the possibility of Timber Hall (*qv*) joining, if not now forming part of, Vernon House, has been noted. The roof was largely restored in 1962. What made necessary the mid-19th century building in yellow brick is not clear. Perhaps it was fire or dilapidation. Before rebuilding, the garden front followed similar lines as now (even then the east wing looked like part of what had been once another building). There were two main floors of four bays and in bays two and three were deep windows the style of which was adopted when rebuilding. Bay one contained a large mullioned window four lights wide. Above was one smaller, with three. This west end was of earlier character than the central part. A large stack ran up through the roof apex of the east wing at its junction with this central portion — the roof-line lower than now — and the west end might once have been finished with a Flemish type brick gable end on the garden front. There was an entrance at about where bay four is now. Outbuildings, detached, east of the house, have been demolished recently.

The mansion has been described variously at different times, and with it went other properties. When Sir Thomas White (*qv*) left the house by his will of 1635 to Henry and Joan Vernon, it was known as Culver Hall and with it went the house adjoining (Timber Hall or Byworth's? *qqv*) where Robert Bicknell (*qv*) the younger lived; also three water mills under one roof. In 1716 an agreement was drawn up on the proposed marriage of Anna Cathrina, second daughter of George Vernon, to Charles Vernon, a London Merchant. It provided, on condition that Charles discharged heavy family mortgages, settlement for property in Kingsley and East Worldham, the Manor House of Dockenford (alias Rocks Hall) in Binstead, many widely scattered closes, hop ground called Potters and Cupgate (Cobgate, The Hart?), lands called Babbs, Posworths, North Mead, South Mead, Babbs Close Mead, Cocksbridge Mead and Sluice Mead; also a house built in Mead Hatch, four water corn mills under one roof and hop kilns and stores in Potter's Gate (*qv*). The principal West Street properties are described in some detail; 'All that capital messuage Culver Hall garden and appurtenances in the occupation of the said George Vernon and the messuage or tenement adjoining . . . now or late in the occupation of Edward Hewett and the messuage or tenement known as

Timber Hall and a garden . . . abutting on the river on the south now or late in the occupation of Bettesworth and three cottages in Farnham occupied now or late by George Bradley John Rivers (*qv*) and John Griggs'.

If, as is stated in another document, Timber Hall adjoined the west of Vernon House, then Hewett's house adjoined elsewhere. There has long been a gap between 27 and 28 West Street.

Sir Charles Vernon left the estate to his daughters Elizabeth Aislabie and Anne Vernon. His will was proved in 1762; sons Charles and Thomas, also his wife, having predeceased him. Two years later Anne married Dr. John Butler of Winchester who became Bishop of Hereford. Hence Bishop's Meadows — of Hereford, not Winchester.

In 1804, widowed and childless, Mrs. Butler died, and the property passed at last from the Vernons to be shared by Sir William Pierce Ashe a'Court, Bt. (*qv*), only child of Annabella a'Court (one of three daughters of Sir Charles Vernon's brother, Thomas), and by Charles Edward Repington, eldest son of Matilda—another of Thomas's daughters. It was they — a'Court and Repington — who sold to William John Kerr (*qv, d* 1815), Marquis of Lothian (*qv*) in 1806, "All that capital messuage or mansion house *formerly* Culver Hall now in the occupation of the said Kerr and all that messuage or tenement buildings yard and garden on the east side of the said capital messuage now in the occupation of Lord Charles Beauchamp Kerr, also that messuage or tenement *formerly* called Timber Hall on the west side of said capital messuage now in the occupation of John Johnson . . ." They sold also The Plough (*qv*) four tenements on the north side of West Street, hop kilns (probably in Potter's Gate) occupied by George Coldham Knight (*qv*), the house in Mead Hatch and also the 'water corn mill *formerly* four', with many other lands, for £14,700. Kerr disposed of most excepting, particularly, property about Vernon House (previously Culver Hall) to William Marsh (*qv*) of Knightsbridge for £11,200 eighteen months later.

The old name, Culver Hall, is probably derived from its having a dovecote. This would have been a relatively rare distinction. Culver was an alternative name for pigeons and doves, particularly in the south and east of England.

Farnham mills generally are not within the scope of this guide, but as 'four mills under one roof' in the context of Vernon properties is appetising, an exception is made; also, as remains of the mill were recently demolished a brief record of its passing may be excused.

The mills in question were lately known as Weydon Mill, formerly Weydowne or Mead Mills. Weydowne Mill stood a few hundred yards south of Vernon House, across Bishop's Meadows. The Mills are mentioned among properties which included The Swan (*qv*) in a deed of demise between the Woodroffes (*qv*) in 1624, and if Mead Mill was in fact once La Medmulle (as seems very likely) something of its early history can be found in Mediæval Farnham. Seller's map of 1680 names it Sluice Mill, which gives a connection with Sluice Mead (1716 above) and Hangars Mill is a later name connected with the same site. In the later 18th century it is referred to as West Mill (East Mill was at Hatch Mill) and Weydon Mill is named Farnham Mill on Bryant's map of 1823 (Hatch Mill then named Bishop's Mill). Richard Bishop (*d* 1705) was once at High Mill. Weydon Mill was demolished about 1920. It had been a fine brick and weatherboard tiled building astride the river with undershot wheel housed within its structure. Cottages adjoining its north end were occupied for another forty years. Downstream a short distance was at some time a 'mansion house' which stood on land once belonging to Andrew Collyer (*qv*). The site has been identified. By 1836 Weydon Mill was owned by the Simmonds family. William Smith, miller and baker, was working there late in the century.

Vernon House was sold by Charles William John Kerr to James Knight (*qqv*), banker and brewer, in 1844. He died in 1868 and had eight children, one of whom, John, solicitor, inherited and retained the house until 1886 when Capital and Counties took over Knight's business. They are presumably John Knight's initials on the plaques, suggesting that he was responsible for the cement casing, which at the time of writing, was soon possibly to be removed. Some secrets will be unveiled. Through the purchase by Duncan Norfolk Bethune, a relative, Vernon House stayed in the Knight family's possession until early in the 1930s.

Following some years of neglect, threats of conversion to a motor garage and then occupation by the Canadian Army, Vernon House became a branch of the Surrey County Library. In very recent years the original gateway lamp was removed and not put back and a good lead cistern bearing the initials CAV and date 1721 or 1727 in foliated characters has gone also. The former date seems the more likely in view of that date being on rainwater heads also. The mural, for long covered by panels, was uncovered again recently and is to be restored. Charles I's nightcap story is well known. It is on view to the public and was given by the captive King to Henry Vernon (*b* 1588*, *d* 1656) in 1648. Henry Vernon was the son of George Vernon of Harleston, Staffs, and grandson of Henry Vernon of Hodnet and Tong-castle, Shropshire.

The inhabitants of Vernon House were for centuries part of the life of Farnham, often holding positions of authority as well as their considerable local estates. Something of these occupations is recorded below, but in this context cannot be dealt with fully. Briefly, Sir Thomas White, in his will of 1635, left this house to Henry Vernon (of the cap) — 'son of the brother german of my first wife' — and to Henry's wife. They had three sons and four daughters. Sir George Vernon (*b* 1629*, *d* 1692) inherited, then George (*d* 1735). His daughter, Anna Catherina, married in 1716 Sir Charles Vernon (*d* 1762), a London merchant, and it was partly through his riches that the family prosperity — which is thought to have been sapped in the Royal cause — was restored. Despite the fact that they had already been rewarded with the nightcap, and honour, the conditions of this marriage must have been a relief to the local family. Of the seven offspring two daughters are now important. Ann married Dr. John Butler (Bishop of Hereford, above) and her younger sister, Elizabeth, married William Aislabie (*qv*). Neither left children so the estate went to rather distant relatives — William Pierce Ashe a'Court, of Heytesbury House, Wiltshire, and Charles Repington, of Armington, Warwick.

Through marriage local Vernons had close connections with the Woodroffes (Ann Vernon, daughter of Mr. George Vernon, *b* 1674*, *d* 1736, married George Woodroffe, *d* 1779, of Poyle, *qv*) and Mary Vernon married George Coldham. They had a son Peter (*d* 1732). It was probably he and his widowed mother who sold Waverley Abbey (*qv*) to John Aislabie (*qv*), Peter having inherited from his great-great-grandfather Richard Coldham, who bought the estate in 1609. It is probably through Peter Coldham's daughter Mary, who married John Knight, that the Coldham-Knight line was secured. They had a Coldham-Knight child. From that point we find ourselves involved with Weybourne House (*qv*) and with other families too — the Venables Vernons and Pleydell Bouveries; locally with the Crumps, e.g., Coldham Crump Knight. The ramifications are complex and far-reaching.

C. W. J. Kerr (*qv*) finally broke Lothian's connection with Vernon House by selling to James Knight, for it appears that his family no longer lived here at that time (1844). A sea-faring family was in occupation. They were the Bowens, who presumably rented from Kerr. William Bowen senior (*b* 1796*) was a mariner; Julia (*b* 1806*) his wife. They had a largish family with William (*b* 1826*), the eldest son, at sea by the age of 15. Only the youngest child, Charlotte, was born here (*c* 1841), the family having probably arrived about three years before. They had left by 1844 which was a little before the Victorian alterations and just after a tragic voyage for the Bowens, during which their children Frederick (*b* 1836*) and Charlotte (by then aged 2), both died, outward-bound for Bengal, on the (ex?) East India Ship Southampton.

William, the father, was probably its captain, as a William Bowen was in command of the Southampton from 1841 — the year in which this Blackwall Frigate of 971 tons was built at Wigrams — until 1854.

William Bowen, the son, appears not to have risen above Second Mate's rank. A William Henry Bowen acquired that certificate (936) in about 1848 but cannot be traced as having risen further during the next sixteen years. However, another William Bowen was commander of The Kingston from 1819-1822. This was possibly his grandfather, but proof has not been found.

The Kerr family is said to have done much for cricket in Farnham and are, by some, thought to be responsible for the ground in Farnham Park. The Marquis is said to have formed a ladies' eleven. The path leading from the church-yard to Bishop's Meadows was once called The Marquis of Lothian's Walk — thought to have become popular with him when blind. To Charles Beauchamp Kerr's will of 1816 is a Codicil: 'I give for the support of the Farnham Female School of Industry, under the head of Mr. William Newn-ham [*qv*, his neighbour] 2 guineas per year for six years', that was, if it lasted that long.

29-31 WEST STREET

Adjoining cottages built of brick and timber under a tile roof. The whole is of asymmetrical elevation, there being a gable facing north on number 29. Most windows are leaded casements. The front is colourwashed.

An innocent-looking brick façade which probably covers considerable local architectural history. Here was at least part of Timber Hall. The house is referred to in deeds as having been also on the sites of 32 and 33 West Street (*qqv*) but we can tie this evocative name fairly securely to these cottages as in another document they are referred to as 'three messuages tenements or cottages formerly one messuage once known as Timber Hall on the west side and adjoining the mansion house', ie., Vernon House. These cottages are then referred to by tithe numbers 527, 528, 529 — by which 29-31 were identified in 1840. Some internal structural members give validity to the former name.

As late as the 18th century the name Timber Hall was still in use, as there was a mansion house called Culver Hall (Vernon House, *qv*) with which went a house called Timber Hall and three cottages. It is known that 32 West Street was once three dwellings. It is difficult though to decide the limits of the old house, as the adjoining rooms of Vernon House might incorporate or have been built in place of part of it. And then, if Vernon House has been reorientated, as has been suggested, there are other possibilities. In a very small scale plan of *c* 1870 an unbroken partition wall appears to divide the west wing of Vernon House from east to west about half way back. A cottage to the rear of 29 and adjoining it has been demolished since then.

The cottages are said to contain a massive moulded wooden roof-truss in the east part. This all suggests that an open-hall type house had a floor inserted, a gable built up, was refaced in brick and subdivided into separate dwellings. Close inspection has not been possible.

In his will of 1635 Sir Thomas White (*qv*), in leaving property to Henry and Joan Vernon (*qqv*) mentions Culver Hall with '. . . the next house thereunto adjoining wherein Robert Bicknell (*qv*) the younger now dwelleth'. Another mention is made in a settlement of marriage of Charles Vernon (*qv*), of 1716. It refers to the capital messuage Culver Hall and the messuage or tenement adjoining now or late in the occupation of Edward Hewett, and all the messuage known as Timber Hall, and a garden, formerly a croft, of about one acre abutting on the river on the south, then or then recently occupied by Bettesworth. In 1806 there is a change. The house is referred to as formerly called Timber Hall. It had been converted into two houses and was occupied by John Johnson. This description again states the location as being on the west side of the capital messuage.

These cottages, during the 19th century, housed two families of carpenters and builders in business long enough to have worked on many local houses. Thomas Nash (*qv*, *b* 1791*) and another Thomas Nash (*b* 1826*), John Nash (*b* 1830*) and Beauchamp Nash (*b* 1831*) were all here by the 1840s. Ten years later there was another Thomas (*b* 1844*) and William (*b* 1823*), carpenter. William, John and Beauchamp were all carpenters and nephews of Hannah Nash (*qv*, *b* 1823* at Crondall). She was in business also as a carpenter and is later encountered at The Plough, 74 West Street (*qv*). During the same years another Hannah Nash, probably daughter of Henry and Mary (*bb* 1767**), long established as farmers in East Street, was known as a cowkeeper. See plan on page 117.

The Pearcys were in two families, probably at numbers 29 and 31. John (*b* 1781*) and Thomas (*b* 1811*) were bricklayers; Charles (*b* 1806*) a plasterer. In 1855 George, Charles and Thomas Pearcy (*qv*) advertised as builders, of Downing Street, although they retained premises in West Street for more than 35 years later. In the 1830s George Pearcy (*b* 1806*) advertised as a builder from East Street where he lived with his wife Ann Pearcy, probably not far from the Marlborough Head. Their children included George (*b* 1836*) and William (*b* 1842*). Alfred Pearcy (*b* 1828*), also a bricklayer of the family, lived in Castle Street. Thomas Pearcy and his family and Maria and Charles appear, rather surprisingly, as occupants of The Old Vicarage (*qv*) in 1851.

32 WEST STREET (P. A. G. Elsmore)

Three brick built shops on two floors and of four upper bays under a roof — slated on the north and west, tiled on the south. To the back are timber-framed and brick-filled wings. The west side and back of the main block are slate hung.

Fenestration: Ground floor, three shopfronts; First floor, four-pane-wide recessed sashes in bays one, three and four; a blind recess in bay two.

This was another property owned, as neighbouring ones, by the Kerrs (*qv*) early in the 19th century. The date of refronting appears to be near mid-19th century, and behind the house are quite extensive remains of a timber framed building. Parts of Timber Hall? The premises were once three dwellings.

Down the yard to the west side are remains of the Marquis of Lothian's stables, which were once fronted with a series of good brick arches. They are now severely defaced having been cut into. This building was once described as having four stalls, loose box, chaff house and harness room.

William and Sarah Pullinger (*bb* 1801**) were here by the late 1830s. He was a baker (Boulanger?). By mid-century William, with his wife Maria (*b* 1815*) was still here in the same trade. His children were William (*b* 1834*), Sarah (*b* 1839*), Mary (*b* 1843) and George (*b* 1850*). An Edward, son of a William, died in 1806, and Ann, a William's wife, in 1805. In 1780 Robert Pullinger married Mary Winslade, both of Farnham. William, a baker, died in 1871. Before 1850 another baker, Stephen Smither (*qv, b* 1811*), also carried on business here but the property eventually became Pullinger's. It had previously been occupied by John Nash (*qv*) and John Loveland.

In 1875 Pullinger sold to the Knights, but Frederick Pullinger was still here as a grocer in the 1880s and the property was described as a 'house and shop with extensive premises for an old established business of a baker and grocery' when put up for sale with other of the Knights' properties seventy-five years ago. It was leased to Mr. W. Coleman. At that time one of that name, a prominent town councillor, lived at 90 West Street.

There had long been a carpenter's and painter's shop in the yard. About mid-century it had been occupied by Thomas Nash and John Pearcy (*qqv*). Since Pullingers, the main shop has been occupied by William Oakly, George Mason, Ernest Folett, Craille's, and Burrows — all grocers. Shops in the west part are recent conversions.

33 AND 33A WEST STREET

A pair of houses on three floor, the fronts have been stuccoed and backs tile hung. A tiled roof of quadrangular plan contains a lantern skylight.

Fenestration: Ground floor, two four-pane-wide sashes; First floor, two similar; Second floor, two half height sashed windows.

Door: Each is contained in its own bay and is cased with reeded pilasters and a simple pediment.

Superficially this is of early 19th century appearance, but the building is older. The visible roof is built over an earlier one (mainly of two small ridges parallel with the street). Until thirty years ago this was one house. At the east end are signs of a shopfront having been removed, and this part served as Turner's drapery, shoe and furniture store from the mid-19th century. Before that it was the workshop storeroom of Elmer the painter. He also had a shopfront type window which is referred to as a north light, below, and which can be seen in Hassell's drawing of 1822 (see Farnham Inheritance, plate 35). There is, as yet, no evidence of his house having been converted to a shop between the time of his death and Hassell's visit, but there was a shop here by 1867.

The building's early 19th century appearance is immediately suspect as windows relate unhappily to the façade, the general proportions of which are suggestive more of a timber framed building than of a brick one. Windows are pinched under the eaves and generally the tight grip of the Georgian builder is not apparent. This is not necessarily because it had been weakened greatly aesthetically by this time, but probably because the rebuilder had been dictated to by the structure already there. Much of this remains inside. And from the outside too it can sometimes be seen. When atmospheric conditions are favourable the disposition of subcutaneous timbers can be seen underlying the stucco.

Stephen Elmer was here in 1769 and his name first appears in a list of freeholders of that year. He died in 1796. According to deeds, 33 and 33A with the buildings earlier abutting the west end were once known as Timber Hall — a name which suggests that a considerable house was here. The cottages abutting the west end of Vernon House are also referred to in separate deeds as once being Timber Hall. It was either a very large hall or, more likely, part was the actual hall or house and part outbuildings, all of which were referred to by one name.

Stephen Elmer the younger was a painter who combined the unusual distinctions for a Farnham man of maltster and A.R.A. and exhibited there from 1772 to 1795. He was one of a family of limners. Stephen, son of Stephen, died in 1714, and in 1707 Mr. Elmer and his brother received payment from the churchwardens for painting, and there were subsequent payments for similar work. At one time St. Andrew's church had large murals at the intersection, and an Elmer painting (The Last Supper — once altar piece) is still at the church. It was presented by Henry Halsey (qv). Mural paintings at Waverley House (qv) were also Elmer's work.

There were at least two Stephens and two Johns living in Farnham, and James continued to live in this block into the 19th century. One John Elmer died in 1767 and Elizabeth, wife of John, in 1773. Mary, wife of Samuel Elmer, died in 1804.

Stephen the younger gained a considerable reputation, being named 'the famous game painter of Farnham'. Benezit gives the date of his death as 1796; the Parish Register, two years later. In the Whitely Papers at the British Museum is a note, written in 1789, on the man: 'At Farnham, in Surrey, on the left as you leave the town from London, with a north light and a south wall, amidst sweet water grapes and a pallet, such as none but his own, to paint them — as modest as unenterprising — more ostentatious of other Masters than himself — liveth Little Elmer. . . . His fish, his fruit, his game and dogs are well known . . . he can paint with precision seldom known but by himself. The Duke of Kingston knew this, and therefore used to supply him with game;— Now the neighbourhood withhold it all, leaving it doubtful whether to refer it to poverty of spirit or taste. Lord Delawar and the Bishop of Winchester are to be excepted; the Bishop has given Elmer a Mandarine Drake and a Gold Pheasant to paint, and for Lord Delawar, he has a nigh-finished picture of Moor-game, and a Landscape'.

Elmer's own collection included a small Correggio and a Rembrandt as well as still lifes of lesser Masters.

A public sale (without reserve) of 148 of his pictures was held at the Great Room, 28 Haymarket, under the title 'Elmer's Sportsman's Exhibition' in 1799. Early in 1801 a fire in Mr. Elmer's Gerard Street (Soho) house entirely destroyed the premises and his valuable collection of paintings. He was then described as 'Mr. Elmer, the celebrated painter of dead game'. Not as 'the late Mr. Elmer'. So this Mr. Elmer was probably Stephen's son William, well known too for his similar work, some of it produced in Ireland. Benezit notes that he was the son and élève of Stephen, exhibiting at the R.A. in 1778; the Royal Academy's Archives say from 1783-1799.

Another of Stephen's contemporaries thought of him highly enough to write, 'a person of good genius in every Branch of his Profession', and he was still held in good repute locally in 1864 when an exhibition of his paintings was held in the temporary museum. They included pictures of Farnham, none of which seem to be in the greater public or local collections. The quality of his fruitier pictures can now be judged by seeing those at Willmer House — a few yards from where he lived and worked.

At the time of Stephen's death his niece, Frances Sarah Caroline Elmer, was living with him in Farnham. She inherited the property. He remembered his nephew, Samuel, painter, and his wife Frances, also their daughter Frances. His brother Richard had three sons, Richard, William and James. William, too, was a painter. Stephen left to him his utensils of painting, and he, too, lived at 33 West Street.

The Elmers' connection with Farnham probably ended when Frances sold this property to the Marquis of Lothian (*qv*) in 1815, after which it passed to James Garfath (*qv*), Robert Smith (*b* 1826*) later setting up in business here as clothier and draper. He sold to Thomas Turner (*d* 1893), after eleven years, in 1867. The house, which by then included a double fronted shop, was offered for sale by representatives of the late T. C. Turner in 1931.

Perhaps the Alexander (*qv*) sisters also lived here for a time as tenants mid-19th century. Their school was well known locally as a 'seminary for children of genteel parents'.

39 **WEST STREET**, Sandford House. A detail of the cornice and parapet, said to be dated 1757.

3-12 Castle Street presents an interesting and varied group of buildings all fronted in styles deriving from the renaissance and dating from about 1710 to the late 19th century.

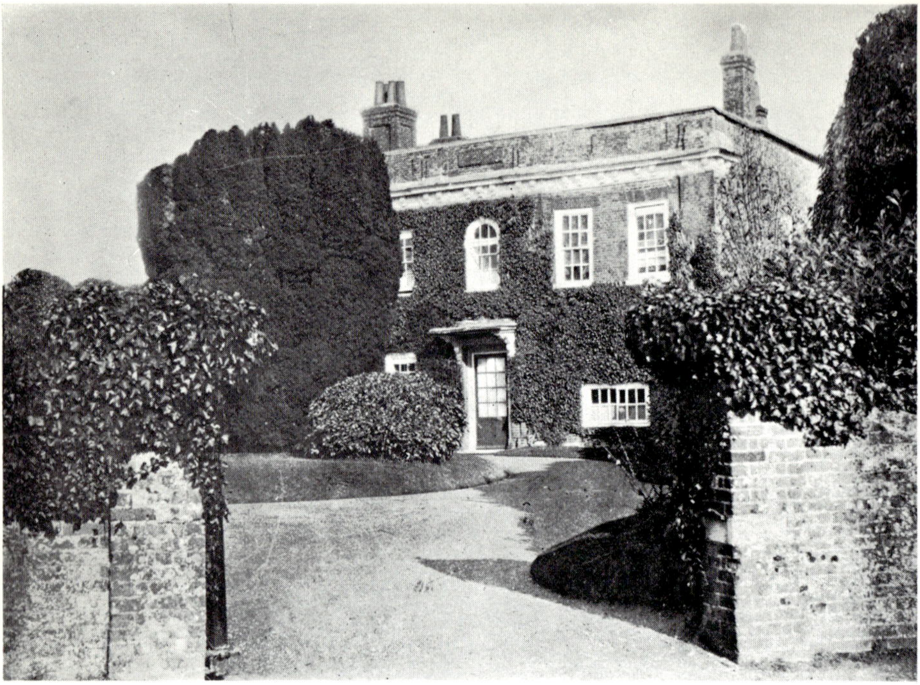

PLATE 28

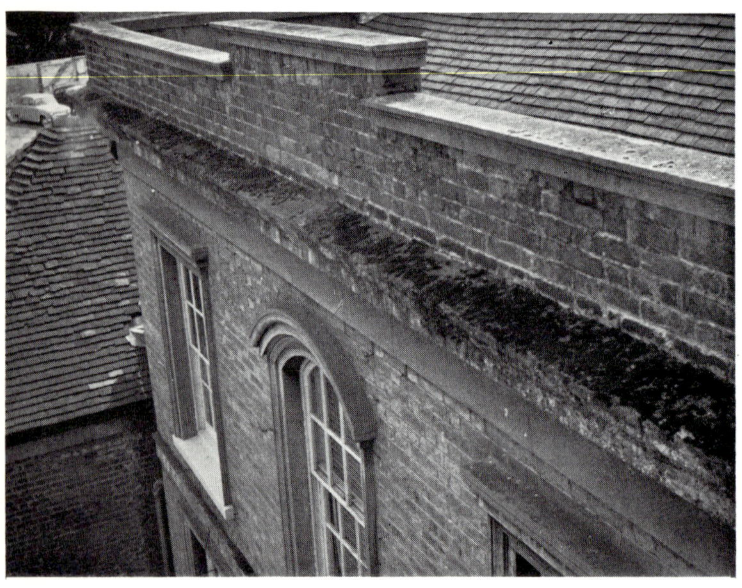

The Grange, above Castle Hill. A photograph probably taken during the first few years of the 20th century. It shows that the often supposed late 17th century east part on three floors is in fact of very recent building. Page 60.

PLATE 29

2 Downing Street. Probably a mid-19th century extension and refronting by William Birch. Page 71.

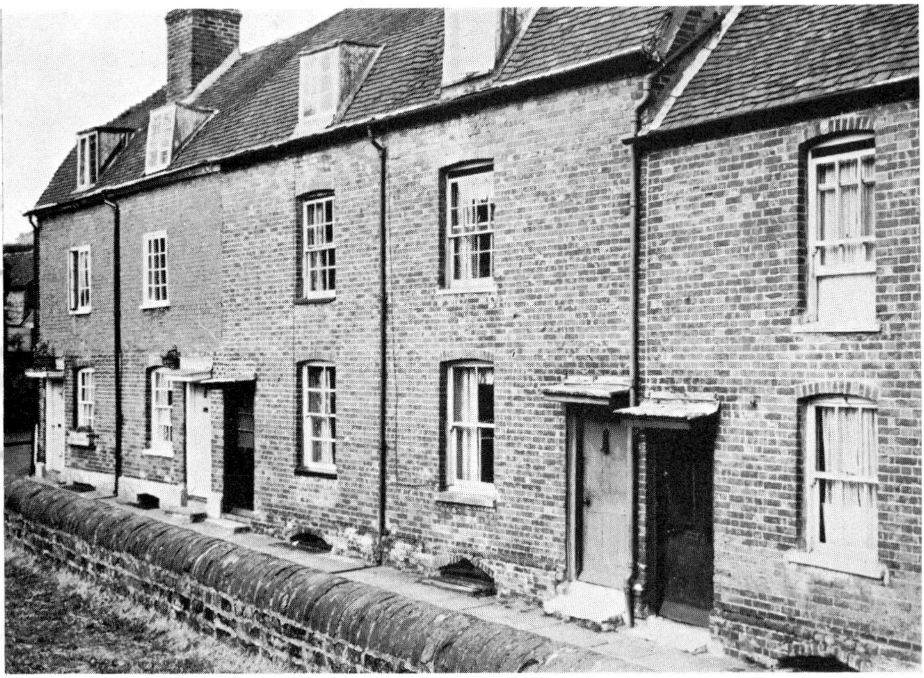

PLATE 30

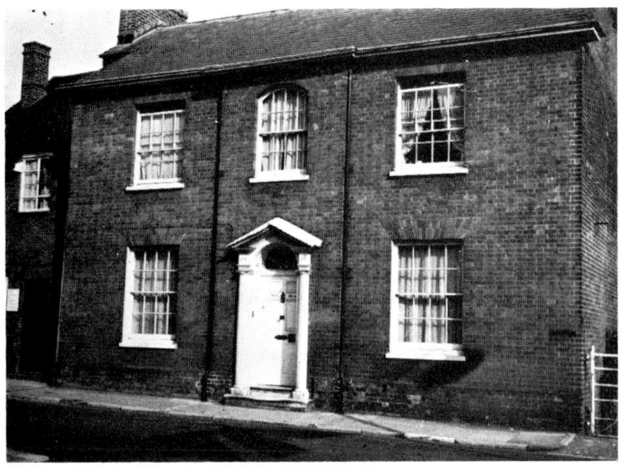

Middle Church Lane. Upper parts of the two farthest houses appear to be faced with especially designed tiles. These, hung on battens, joints mortar-filled, were sometimes used to give the appearance of brick, yet avoiding brick tax.

PLATE 31

29 East Street. A house of mainly mid-19th century origin which clings to Farnham's 18th century vernacular in its conception and some details. Page 114.

PLATE 32

Tanyard, drawn by John Hassell in 1822. The tannery existed here before Red Lion Brewery developed around this house. Page 99.

PLATE 33

Trimmer's Almshouses, West Street, 1893: one of two groups which flank the entrance to Mount Pleasant. Page 182.

Waverley House in 1822. The basic appearance is retained despite many changes. Colin Campbell built an earlier house hereabouts. Page 231.

PLATE 34

East Street. Part of an environment likely soon to change drastically. The central block is of Victorian appearance and has particularly neat brickwork and eaves treatment for its date. In the 1880s Andrew Crosby, plumber (and later contractor) advertised from here.

PLATE 35

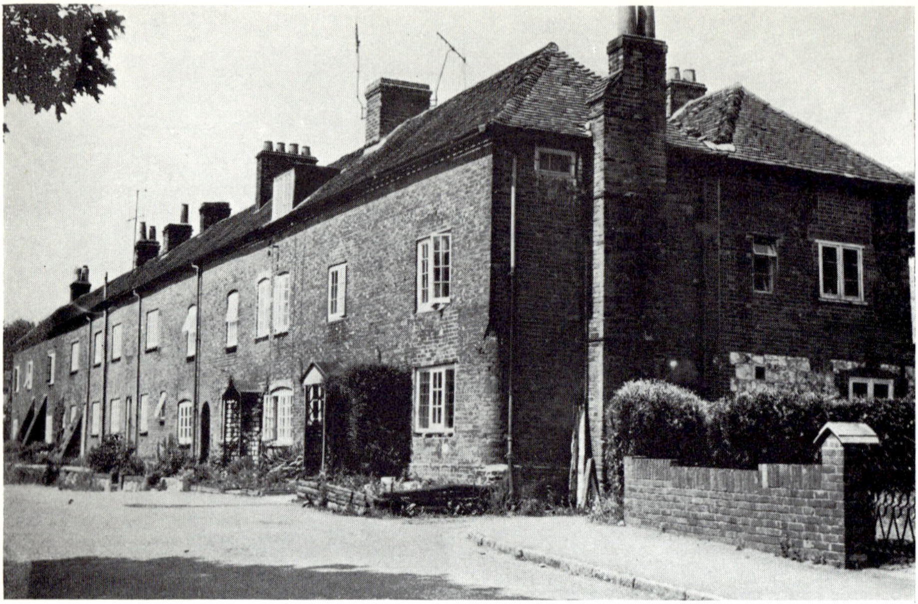

PLATE 36

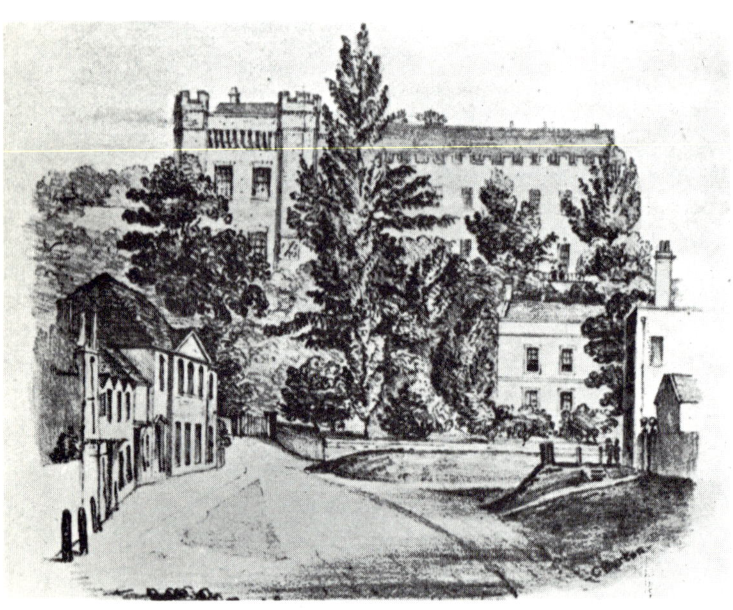

Kilns in Beaver's Road. This block, with other buildings once at its west end, were known by 1839 as Beaver's Kilns. They have long been converted to dwellings.

PLATE 37

Castle Street. A mid-19th century lithograph by C. Burton, showing the earlier Cedar Court and Castle Hill House.

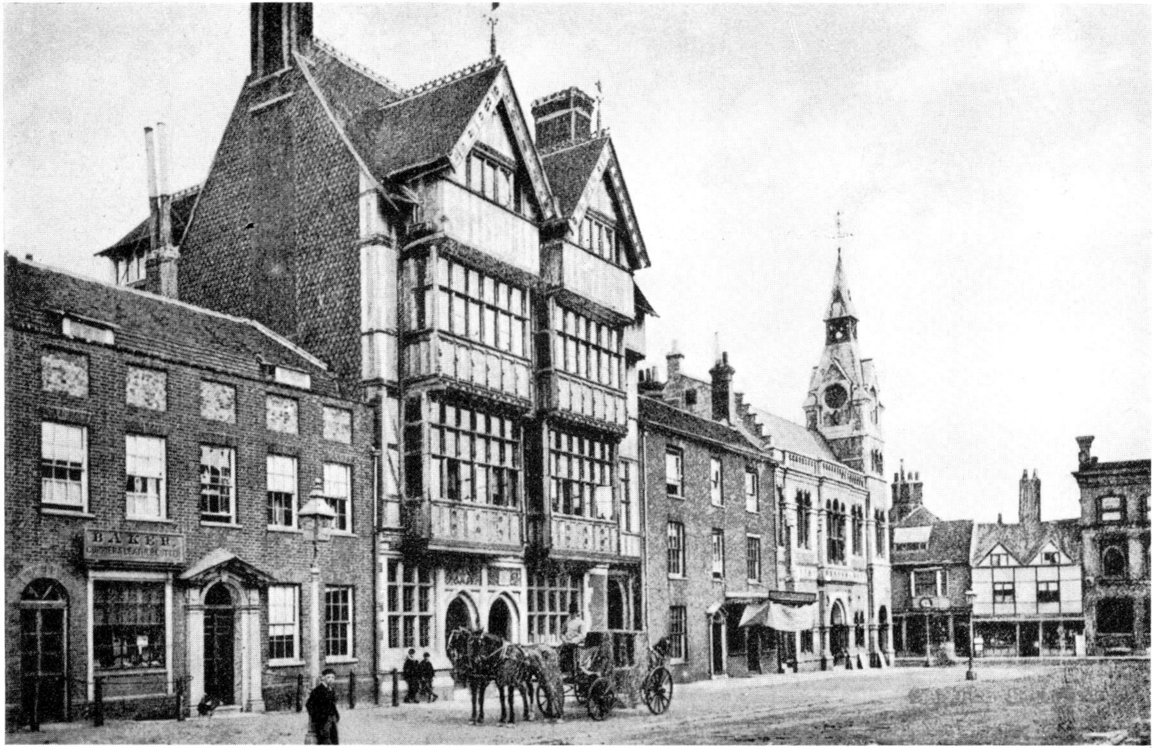

Lower Castle Street, showing Norman Shaw's giant bank building, Wyndham Tarn's Corn Exchange and the Westminster Bank before its 1904 extension, with Cheston as architect.

PLATE 38

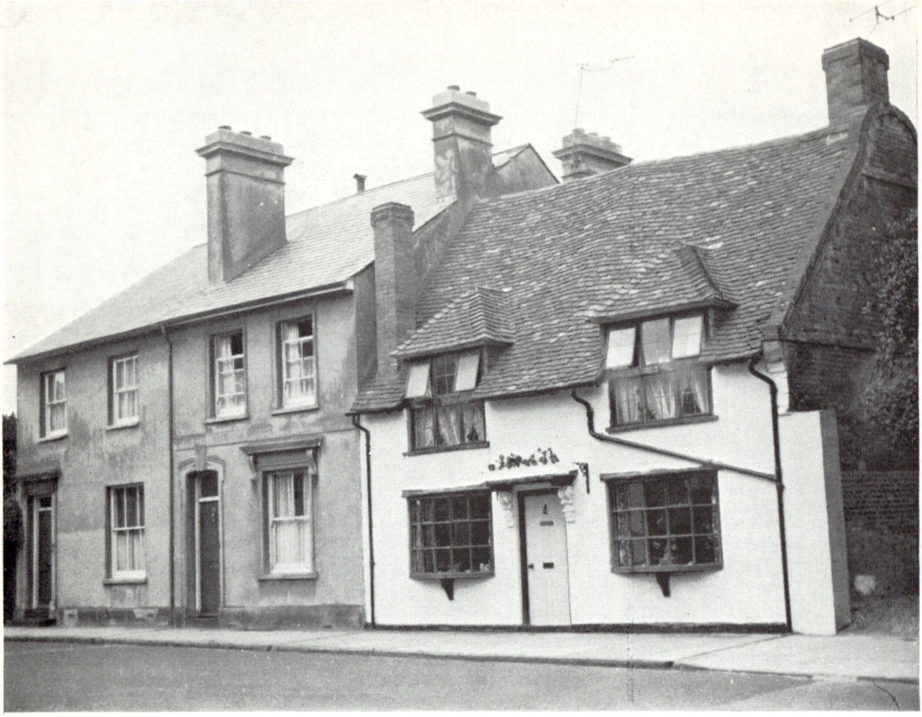

PLATE 39

66-68 West Street. Number 68 was restored and considerably altered from a humble cottage in the late 1930s. All the existing front windows were then inserted. Pages 186, 187.

PLATE 40

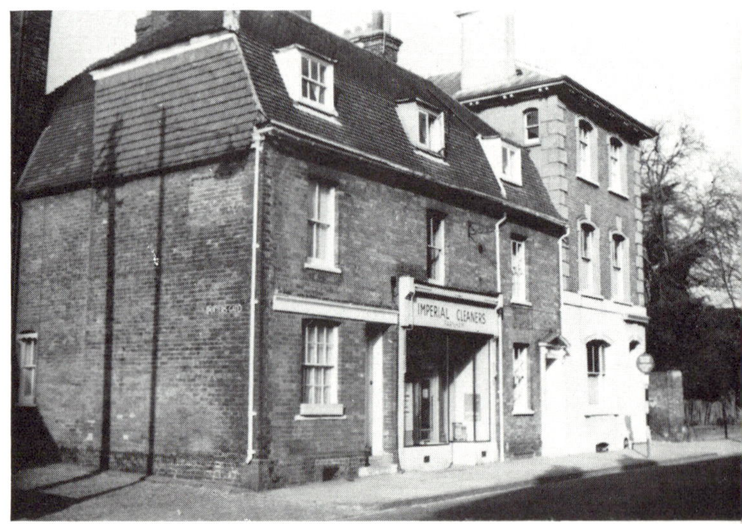

76-79 West Street. Numbers 76-78 share some outward characteristics of a Farnham house which was built in 1799. Number 79 was built about seventy years later.

Leetday House, drawn by E. Hassell in 1828. The place is better known (through its long association with local courts) as Lawday House, a name some time corrupted to Lady House. It has been much altered and added to since Hassell's day.

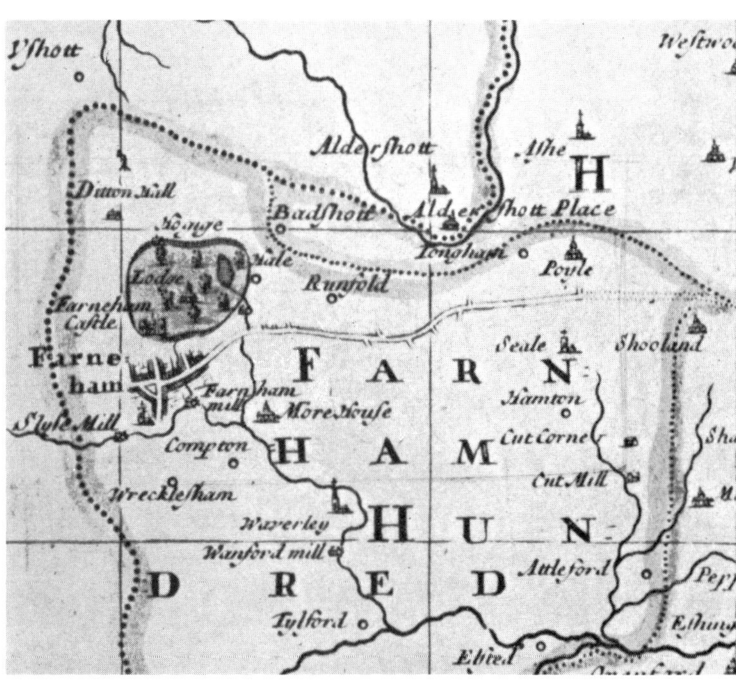

From John Seller's map of *c* 1680, (produced by John Oliver and Richard Palmer). The Park enclosure and some houses are depicted pictorially while streets and rivers are in plan. The pond is shown in Farnham Park and what appears to be The Round House (triangular) is indicated. Weydon Mill is named Sluce Mill. Bounds of the Hundreds are marked.

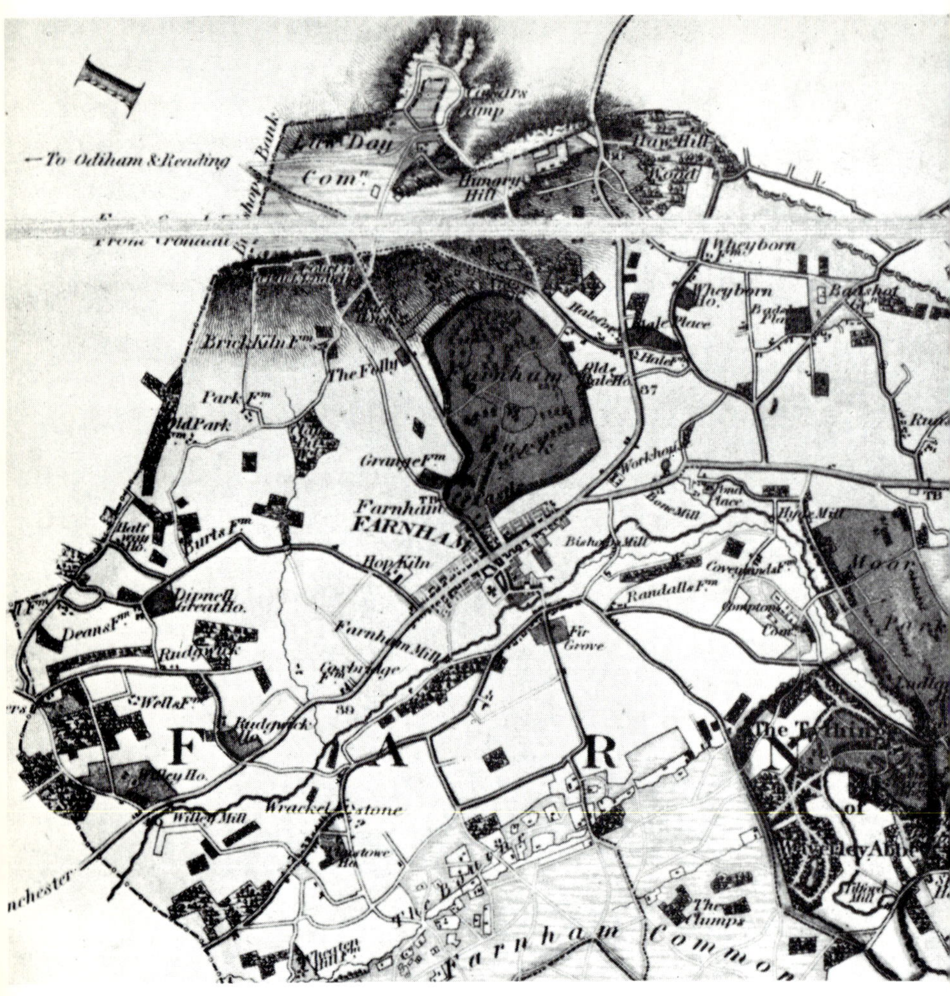

From A. Bryant's Map of Surrey made 1822-1823. Apart from showing locations of houses sin demolished (e.g. Dippenhall and Badshot) this map marks The Folly, large kilns off East Stre toll bars and parish boundaries.

College Gardens, West Street, are where the Military College
once stood. Hassell made this drawing in 1822. The title reads:
'Formerly the Military College'. This was after the move to
Camberley. Page 192.

PLATE 44

PLATE 45

Firgrove House, west front. This view indicates from the
outside some stages in the development of the house plan.
Page 100.

PLATE 46   Badshot Manor House, demolished not very long after, was drawn by Hassell in 1822 and is the only known existing depiction of it. Page 232.

PLATE 47   The School, Castle Street, drawn by J. Hassell in 1822. This might have been built as Mr. Baker's Musick House. It served for very many years as the National School and is now the Masonic Hall. Page 59.

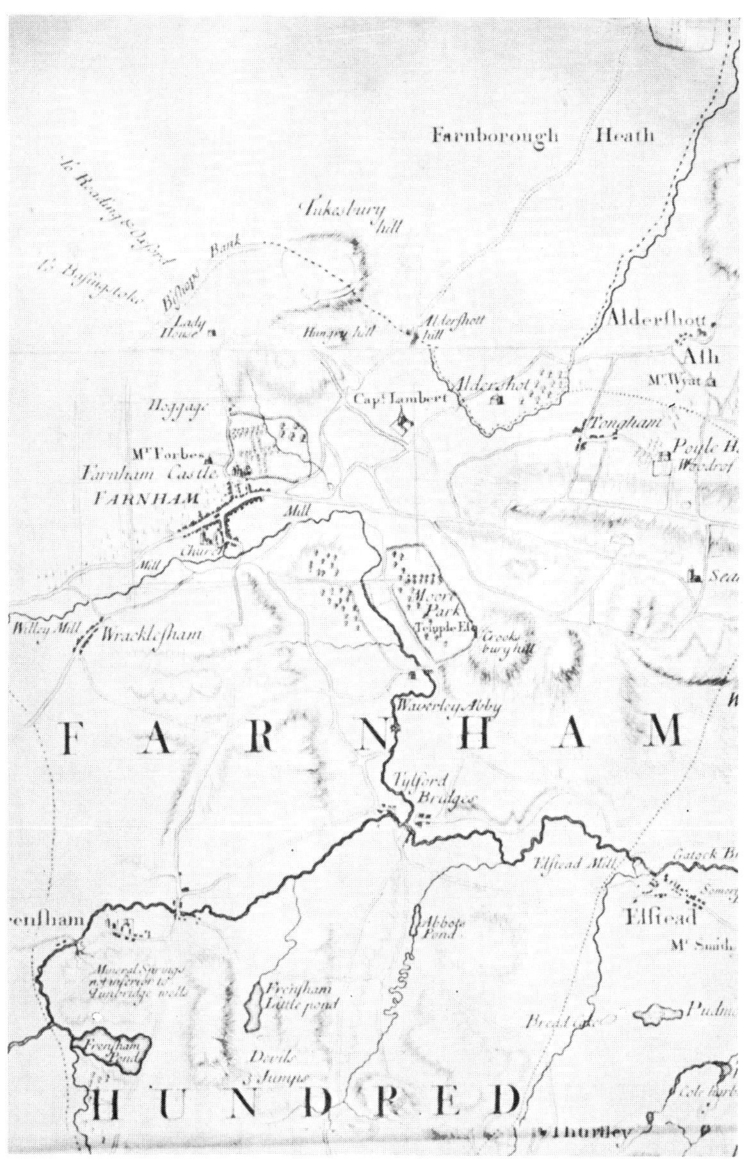

From the New Map of the County of Surrey by John Senex, 1729. Houses marked, which are mentioned in this book, include The Grange (Mr. Forbes), Moor Park (Temple, Esq.) and Lawday (Lady) House. The Round House (rectangular) is indicated at the east end of West Street.

PLATE 48

PLATE 49

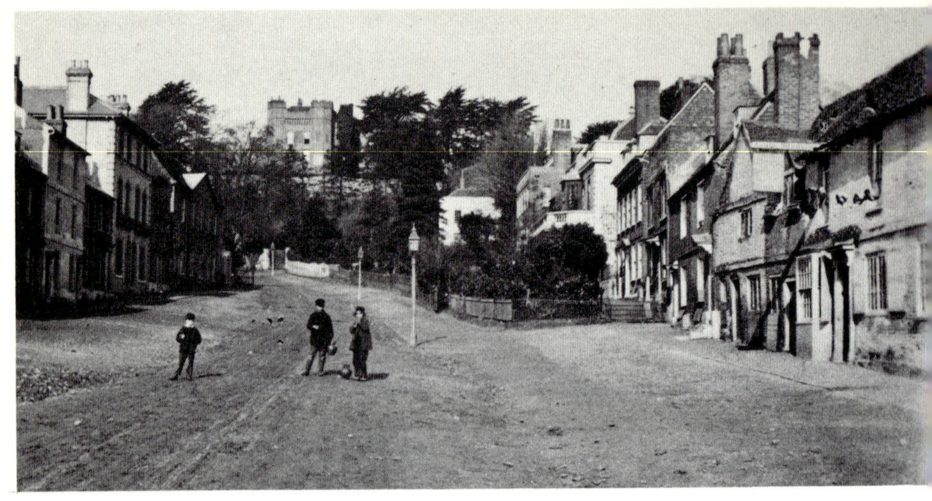

Castle Street. This view, taken c1860, shows the Nelson Arms, right. Below the Masonic Hall can be seen newly-built 39 & 40. The dwelling where 41 now stands awaits demolition. Page 44.

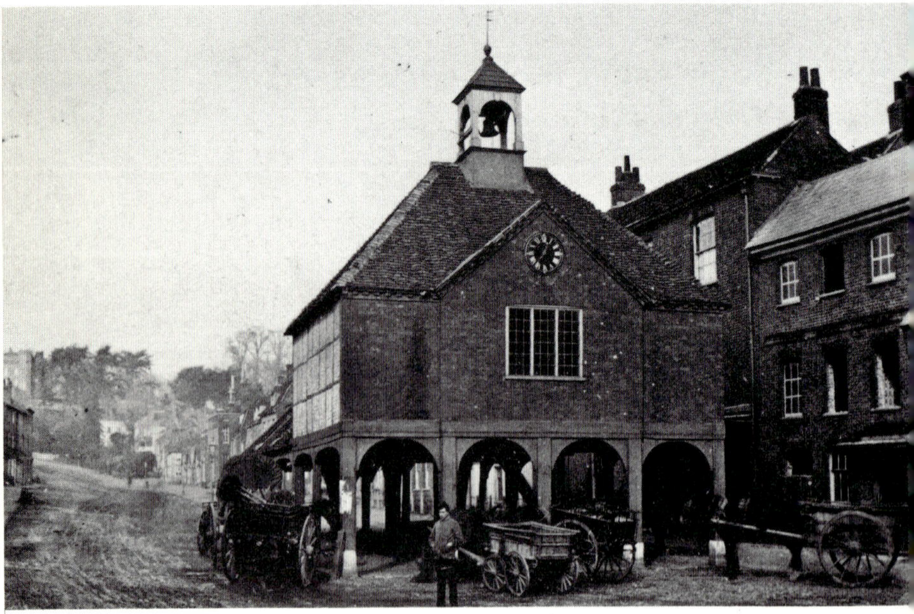

PLATE 50

Castle Street, showing the Old Market House, demolished in 1866. See Plate 23 and page 15.

PLATE 51

Vernon House, garden front. Watercolour by J. Hassell, 1822.
See also Plate 7 and page 153.

PLATE 52

East Street, late 19th century. While there have been extensive alterations and demolitions on the south side, virtually everything visible on the north was cleared for the Woolmead redevelopment. See Plates 11, 35 and Supplementary Inventory.

A block of three three-floor brick built houses with a slate roof and recessed sashed windows. Doorcases are simple, pedimented, and plain pilastered. Adjoining their west end is a fourth member, now a shop, with metal-framed windows above.

The block was built speculatively by James Garfath (*qv*) and was finished in 1834. The houses stand more less as built, except for the westernmost which has been altered greatly in appearance twice — once on its conversion to a pub (when the whole front was Tudorised with dark brown applique 'beams' and pebbledash) and again in the 1950s on conversion to a shop. It was then that the vertical windows which still gave unity of pattern and rhythm to the block were replaced by horizontal ones and the whole façade was rendered white. If Hassell's 1822 drawing of 33 West Street (*qv*) is to be trusted, a timber framed building which this block replaced was encased in brick during the 17th century.

Many superfluous pubs closed after 1900. The problem of over-provision was not only recent. In 1576 seven ale-houses in Farnham were superfluous, compared with eleven 'mete for that purpose', according to a report by Robert Aston, Thomas Chape, Thomas Barrett and others, sent to Sir William Moore. 'Mete' were houses of Richard Wild, John Jagger, Henry Avenell, Thomas Beldham, Thomas Goodyer, Thomas Parker, Thomas Quayte, John Hide, Michael Kinge, Thomas Rosier, and Henry Battell. Houses of Thomas Bristowe, William Brown, Robert Skymere, John Lawrence, George Avenell, Thomas Walker, and Nicholas Basden were not approved.

37 West Street was a beer house by the 1880s and later became known as The Holly Bush. It was conveyed to Farnham United Brewery in 1903 and had closed by the time Courages offered it for sale in 1939. But perhaps this end house had been converted to a shop only a few years after building. Thomas Loveland (*b* 1808*), brewer and grocer, lived here.

James Garfath was a prominent builder in Farnham. His yard was at 85 West Street (opposite this block). There were other Garfaths — John, son of Joseph (*d* 1784), James, carpenter, son of James and Fanny (*d* 1812); Joseph, carpenter (*d* 1800); Fanny Garfath was born in 1790*, Sarah in 1811*, Thomas in 1816*. Joseph was a carpenter in the 18th century. The signature 'James Garfath 1822' is on the back of a doorcase recently refitted to the front of 48 West Street. James the elder (builder) also owned 35, 77, 78 and 85 West Street and Pentonville Cottages in Mead Lane.

38 WEST STREET (Willmer House Museum)

A house of five bays and three full floors with symmetrical façade of cut and gauged brick. Horizontal members are a plinth, moulded string courses between windows, cornice and panelled parapet with moulded coping. Vertical emphasis is given by giant brick rusticated pilasters at outer angles and a central bay of slight projection running the height of the building. Rainwater heads bear the initials J.T. and date 1718.

Fenestration: Ground floor windows very slightly recessed; First floor, architraved and aproned in brick; Second floor, windows as below them, but less tall. All windows are sashed, three panes wide, with wide boxes.

Door: Unpedimented case with panelled Doric pilasters, and architrave mouldings breaking upwards, cusped, and topped by a fleur-de-lys in relief. No fanlight.

South elevation: Five bays on three floors, almost symmetrical and built of brick, topped by a blind parapet. The width of brickwork between bays three to four and four to five is greater on the east side than between their counterparts on the west. Sash windows all have shallow segment heads and wide wooden boxes slightly recessed. A flat-hood-and-bracket doorway occupies bay three.

Interior: Plan; The front door opens into an entrance hall-stairwell which communicates with three main ground floor rooms. The symmetrical façade masks an asymmetrical subdivision of the space behind it. Stairs; These are a major interior feature. Of oak, they are wide, wainscotted and have slender turned and carved banisters rising two from each tread. Strings are inlaid in light wood with a key pattern and terminate in carved scroll brackets. There is a secondary staircase. Woodwork; The two ground floor rooms on the east and the entrance hall are panelled and decorated in wood. An arch, flanked by Ionic pilasters and topped with a richly carved cornice, connects hall with passage leading to the back door. The arch is painted, like the panelling in which it is set. A Corinthian arch connects the two east rooms, the back one of which is panelled and has a pedimented chimney piece.

Other features: Adjoining the main building to its west is a two-floor brick and slate extension with its own door. Beneath the extension, and running under the garden for some yards, is a cellar, the southern cell of which has a simple barrel vault.

Presuming the main house to have been built in 1718, no major external alterations appear to have been made since. The extension served as a kitchen and servants' quarters.

From Hassell's very bad drawing (1823) it would appear that cottages already existed there. He was given to improvising with secondary buildings. However, there is no doubt that there was another building on this site. The cellars, at least,, suggest this, even if Hassell's drawing cannot be trusted completely. It shows a cottage-style house, with what appear to be stone mullioned windows, abutting the west end. This early house extended south some yards beyond the garden-front of Willmer House, giving it for some time an L-shaped plan. When this was demolished it is probable that some of the land it occupied was made over to Sandford House (*qv*) as it seems to have overlapped the present garden boundary line.

When the existing Willmer House was built the south-west ground floor room was probably the kitchen. It is possible that when the extension was rebuilt back ground-floor windows here were lengthened to within a few courses of the ground, new larger-paned frames — like those until recently in front rooms at 88 West Street (*qv*) — replacing earlier ones.

The staircase — one of four similar designs in Farnham (The Grange, Castle Hill House and Sandford House, *qqv*) — has an unsatisfactory termination in its top-floor panelling which suggests that it was not especially designed for the house, or at least not for this position in this house. The suspicion is strengthened by the fact that the inner sills of bays four and five of the first floor have been raised several inches. This would have minimised the awkwardness caused by the wainscot overlapping the lower part of bay four window, which overlap would also make folding shutters useless even if they had been made anew to fit the then smaller opening. These two windows have no shutters yet retain bevelled return surfaces which look bleak. One could go further, to suggest that this entire staircase was once some feet to the south, possibly with a small first floor room lit by windows in bays four and five. Then, when Willmer House was added to by building the west extension, communication for servants was necessary (kitchen, etc., having then been moved from the main part of the house), the secondary staircase (which looks 19th century) built and discreetly walled off. This new case would need light — stolen from the well by the very unGeorgian window in the dividing wall. But this is all conjecture, and more convincing explanations may be found to account for the sill and other alterations.

Architecturally this house is one of Farnham's finest

works. It displays a façade of considerable richness, its brickwork demonstrating local craftsmen's skill at its best. Yet it retains great dignity possibly to the point of near-dullness compared with other, especially Continental, baroque façades. It is not by such standards ostentatious; neither is it naïve. It was not produced by a country-craftsman's intuition alone. There are several geometrical coincidences in the placing of important horizontal stresses and major vertical sub-divisions are related to that magical renaissance formula, The Golden Section — which was well tried by Europe's classical masters and known to the Ancients who inspired them. By formula, it was considered possible to fix the point on a line which divided the line into its two aesthetically ideally related unequal parts, the parts themselves being then equally satisfying in their relationship to the whole line, e.g., take a line AB. Divide it at C. Then AC : CB as CB : AB. Alternatively make AB = 13, AC = 5, CB = 8 for a very rough division, 5 : 8 being roughly as 8 : 13.

Willmer House façade can be divided in this way into 13 equal parts (using the measured drawing reproduced in Lloyd's 'History of the English House'). The projections of the centre bay coincide with the Golden Cuts, i.e., at 5/13 and 8/13 and are produced two-dimensionally up the whole façade. But this does not work out on the exact method, by measurement in fractions of an inch. Disappointing. But the front is not, in fact, symmetrical. The east half is larger than the west, and if we make our point C come at the west edge of the projecting centre bay and make very small allowances for inaccuracies in building and physical chances since, the magical 1·618 can be easily arrived at, giving CB : AC as AC : AB. The west 'half' is not as big as the east — but the inequality is not as marked as at the back of the house. (Calculations are based on measurements kindly taken by the Curator.)

The locally unusual broken, upthrusting series of architrave mouldings over the door takes the eye up and then out (at 45 degrees on either side) to the tips of the cornice, which mark the outer limits of the building's fabric. This same feeling of diagonal expansion from the focal point is reinforced through the relationship of the doorcase pilasters to their giant thirty-foot counterparts in brick which, with rustications, also form the outer visual binding of this vigorous but perhaps too strongly controlled composition which uses a Baroque vocabulary with almost two-dimensional effect. Pevsner and Nairn say, 'This is one of the finest cut brick façades in the country considered as craftsmanship, but it remains an exasperating design: with everything emphasised the total effect stays as it would be if the façade was quite plain. The intention seems to have been to turn the whole front into one indivisible unit, but it has not succeeded and remains a bewildering and rather forbidding *tour de force'*. Even so, Willmer House is one of Farnham's outstanding possessions and is among its most ambitious known excursions into the Baroque.

Obviously much has been concentrated on outer visual and material perfection. By contrast some unhappy inner details, such as a staircase cutting diagonally across a window, seem paradoxical. The back elevation is a very weak and austere echo of the main façade. But the outdoor garden life was not of such significance to country-town folk of that time as it was, say, a hundred years later when the back windows were probably enlarged. Perhaps it was money. Whatever the reason neither visual nor material considerations were of such great importance here away from the street.

J.T.'s initials on rainwater heads are said to be John Thorpe's, owner of this property late in the 17th century and therefore said also to be the builder of Willmer House. No such name appears in the Poll Book of December, 1719, by which time one would not expect the original owner to have left, unless dead. There are four others initialled J.T., John Tanner, John Taylor, John Temple, Esq., and John Thorne. The third-named is supposed still to have been at

38 WEST STREET. Willmer House Museum. A detail which shows how the multi-ridged roof is hidden behind the parapet to give a horizontal roofline from the street.

Moor Park House. John Thorne might be a contender. It is most unfortunate that deeds, which recently existed, dating from before the late 19th century, are stated not to be in possession of Surrey County Council.

John Thorpe is said (by one who remembers the deeds) to have sold the house in 1723 for £523. It eventually passed to William Pinke Paine, a notable hop planter related to the builder of 39 West Street (*qv*). Caroline Paine sold Willmer House to Sidney Longhurst (*qv*) in 1876, the premises then having been late in the occupation of Thomas Hunter (*qv*) and since of the Misses Potter. One of the Hunter's paintings of Willmer House was recently given to the Museum by a member of the Longhurst family.

William Pinke Paine might be presumed an outcome of a Pink-Paine marriage. Thomas Pynck was charged Lay Sudsidiary Assessment on his goods in the 1590s, and various members of the family were hop planters from the 18th century, if not before. Of the many Farnham Pinks (*qv*), some had connections with 14 West Street; Charles married Ann West (*qv*) in 1757, William died in 1783 and Thomas twenty years after. Mr. William Pink's widow died in 1765, Charles' daughter Martha in 1757. Robert Pink married Jane Bolton in 1781.

Willmer House remained in the Longhursts' possession until Sidney's death in 1924. Miss Willmer's boarding school for young ladies was here by 1822 and the house had got its name fifty years later. In the '50s Thomas Hunter (*qv*) had his school here. One pupil was James Longhurst (*d* 1921), who came to own the house. He was born about 1835 at Send House (*qv*) and is said to have attended also a Miss Grover's school here. In 1841 a James Longhurst (*b* 1835*) was a pupil at Hunter's opposite, and in that same year a Miss Greaves (*b* 1801*) had a school at Willmer House, although Frances Willmer still owned the property.

How long Willmers had been in Farnham it has not been possible to establish, but they were here by 1749, Richard Willmer, a woolcomber, being resident. His son, Richard, lived at Hartley Wintney. A Richard Willmer was buried in Farnham in 1760.

In 1960 the house was acquired by Farnham Council who have made small alterations, thoroughly restored the place and established Farnham Museum.

A five-bay three-floor house of symmetrical façade, built of brick. It is divided horizontally by moulded brick string courses running over window heads, and by a cornice (said to be of stucco) with a rosette and triglyph decorated frieze. The frieze (topped by a panelled parapet with stone coping) breaks on entering the centre bay. This is bridged by an open triangular pediment. The centre bay is stepped above flanking parapet level to contain this pediment, inflection between the two parapet levels being aided by decorative scrolls.

Fenestration: Ground floor, three-pane-wide recessed sashes ; First floor, four similar to those below them. In bay three a brick architrave curves to repeat the window head shape as does the string course above; Second floor, as those below them except in bay three. Here the window is architraved. A pediment over echoes the main pediment above and the doorcase below. These windows are less tall than those below them.

Door: Fluted Doric pilasters against rustications supporting a triangular pediment. There is a rectangular metal fanlight, with keyblock and voussoirs in wood above.

South elevation: Parapeted, without a cornice, and fundamentally a weak echo of the front. There is a verandah running its length. This is supported by eight attenuated wooden Doric shafts.

Interior: Plan, roughly quartered, with a hall-passageway dividing the halves and leading to the garden door; Stairs, similar to those at Castle Hill, Willmer House and The Grange. They have turned and fluted banisters. Wainscotting is divided by carved composite pilasters; Windows, all have folding shutters, except those on the top floor; Woodwork. a carved chimney-piece in the ground floor south-east room. The first floor north-west room is fully panelled in wood, as is the entrance hall.

Other features: Adjoining, to the west, is a slate roofed block and a gateroom to the stables and garden.

Built, it is said, by John Manwaring in 1757. This is another of Farnham's first class houses. High quality bricklaying and gauging are on the front, but as in Willmer House (qv) the back is of second quality technically.

The house makes a fine partner for its neighbour which in the 19th century it began to outgrow. Extensions westwards were in two stages and apparently a new garden front was built about ten feet south of the original south façade.

But as it is likely that buildings — since demolished — once abutted the east side one must be cautious when interpreting changes in the brick pattern of the east wall. Until the mid-1950s the balcony had a delicate cast iron balustrading of interlaced ogival design running its entire length. Balcony access was by a deepened window leading from the landing. It looks as though the original window in the corresponding position (before the extension was built) has been raised to centre the floor above. Fanlight tracery in the front door is recent and replaces a 19th century type stained glass one. The garden wall plaque was made recently.

John Manwaring is said to have made two replicas of Sandford House as dolls' houses. At least one remains. It is in the museum next door. If architecturally accurate there is some explaining to do as it has an eaved roof with a balustrading running round the top, enclosing a turret, in the Coleshill manner, i.e., a typically later 17th century style.

When the Manwarings (*qv*) came to Farnham it is difficult to say, but when John built this house they were a well-established family. There are several links with Dorking. A John Manwaring had his pew at St. Andrew's in 1684, and there was a Manneringe in Farnham a hundred years before then. It seems that they came into great prominence locally only a little more than two hundred years ago. Through various marriages and other enterprises they had become leading landowners having close links with the Stevens', Pinks, Chittys, Lutmans, Newnhams, Mills and Paines (*qqv*), the families between them occupying most of Farnham town's larger houses and its richest hop growing land.

At least three successive Johns tend to confuse, but they all shared an interest in hops and much of their prosperity must have come from them, for they gradually forsook their trade as tanners to take part in the local hop gamble, although John, of Sandford House, was still a tanner in the 1720s and the family continued its active though declining interests in tanning throughout the 18th century, from at least the 1660s. More and more evidence comes to light suggesting that tanning was for very many years an important industry in Farnham.

The Manwarings' tanyards, part of 41 West Street (*qv*), were to the east of lower Mead Lane and, as elsewhere in the town, the buildings were later used for hops and malting. One was known as Tanyard Kiln. This has been demolished. In 1781 John Manwaring leased to William Mears or Meeres (*qv*), a maltster, his three-hole oast with another kiln in the yard leading from West Street into the Manwaring Tanyard. With 41 West Street, in 1723, went two tanyards, two barns, a malthouse and messuage, with pasturelands and meadows. By 1794 the balance had changed — four tanyards, two malthouses, ten messuages and thirty-six acres of pasture and hops. That was on the death of John Manwaring the younger. But the industry did not flourish so in the 19th century. The story is one of decline. See plan on page 178.

It is of interest to note some of Farnham's tanners, as no mention of the industry seems previously to have been made in articles or books on Farnham. The list, which is undoubtedly incomplete, includes names of families which were later, if not earlier, among the most prosperous in the district, e.g., Nicholas Knight, Robert Bicknell, John Manory, Robert Shurlock, James and Austin Nash, John Braborne, James Stevens and, of course, the Manwarings. The less familiar include George Taylor, two John Permans (dd 1692, 1703), William Stent (d 1693), John Hearn (d 1707), Benjamin Collet (d 1714), John Elmes, Charles May, Stanley Bolen, John Woodward (d 1729) and James Cumber (d 1812). The success of hops has so overwhelmed the Farnham scene that tanning has been forgotten completely. Not that we are without reminders, for there are references to regulations and standards of the trade in town records.

R. N. Milford, in notes printed after a lecture in 1859, has extracted from local records these instructions to Under-Bailiffs of Farnham whose duties included the inspection and sealing of leather sold locally. 'Now your office is to view and search all and every tanned hide, skin, and leather which are to be sold within this borough and town, and if you find it to be well tanned you ought to marke it with your seal. But if it be not well tanned you ought to seize the same, and so you may seize likewise any boots, shoes, bridles, or any other thing which is made of leather; then after such seizure you ought to acquaint the bailiffs with it, who will appoint six honest and expert men to try the same, which ought to be done in some market day within fifteen days next after the seizure, or else they forfeit five pounds.

'And if any tanner, shoemaker or other tradesman that works upon any sorte of leather above mentioned shall wilfully withstand or deny any search to bee made, he forfeits five pounds.

'And if you refuse to seal, if the leather be well tanned, you forfeit 40s. And if you conceal any fault in your search and view, you forfeit of money one-half to the king and the other to him that will sue for same.

An Under-Bailiff could not afford to make mistakes when their wages were only in the range of 10/- to £6.

In 1609 'a certain person being a tanner, whose name is vulgar', was fined 3/- for selling unlawful leather. Two hides were forfeited in 1614 for being unproperly tanned, and in the following year the Bailiffs paid 12d. for having the hammer to seal leather mended.

There was another tannery at Bridge Square (*qv*). Tanfield House, Tanfield Cottage, etc. (at the far end of East Street) suggest the proximity of one more. There were almost certainly at least two others. Farnham could not have been a very pleasant place to live in.

The Manwarings and their family ramifications are so many and complex that no attempt is made here to note them in detail. There are, for example, over fifty births, marriages and deaths of Johns, Roberts, Thomas', Anns, Marys and Janes alone. Many can be found in the Parish Registers. Perhaps of particular note are the following concerning sons of various John Manwarings: Baptisms, John 1695, Thomas 1698, James 1700. Deaths, Johns 1694, 1759, 1823, James 1701, Thomas 1698. Other deaths: John 1716, 1744, 1762, Robert 1732, 1759.

James' died in 1720 and 1740. The former was brother of Sarah Mill (*qv*), Elizabeth Collard, John Manwaring (whose children were John, James, Mary, Thomas, Elizabeth, Robert) and of Mary Waybird. James, the brother or uncle of all those immediately above, was the son of John (*d* 1716), tanner, he being the son of James and Mary. Marriages included John to Jane Heathfield 1723, Jane to John Stevens 1755, Jane to William Dowden 1785, John to Elizabeth Lutman 1784.

These relationships cover the mainstream of the Farnham family from the 17th-19th centuries. See also College Gardens.

40 W E S T   S T R E E T   (Wickham House)

A symmetrical three-bay house on three floors of brick and tile with brick cornice and uncoped parapet.

Fenestration: Ground floor, two almost flush three-pane-wide sashes; First floor, three similar; Second floor, three similar, three-quarters height.

Door: In bay two, panelled pilasters with flat hood supported by horizontal carved wood scroll brackets with foliations and amorini heads.

Probably an earlier 18th century house in the main. The entire front is 20th century, to the design of H. Falkner (*qv*). The parapet was added and dormers projected forward to it. An earlier roof line can be clearly seen from the sides. The house once belonged to the Manwarings and was later occupied by Sampson Sampson (*qqv*).

The name Wickham House is probably recent. There was a local family of that name. William, son of William, died in 1788; Elizabeth, William's daughter, died three years earlier.

4 1   W E S T   S T R E E T   (Elmer House)

A seven-bay two main floor house, asymmetrical as a whole but symmetrical in its main part. It is built of brick with tile roof. Five, then two, blind brick arcades divide the ground floor. An angle is formed between bays five and six. Into each arch is inserted an opening. Horizontally, a painted and brick fascia divides the floors and a cornice with a frieze separates upper windows from a parapet.

Fenestration: Ground floor, two-pane-wide recessed sashes in all but bay six which has a flush plate-glass sash; First floor, two-pane-wide recessed sashes. Flat topped dormer windows above.

Door: In bay three, fitting its brick arcade, is unpedimented. The panelled pilasters support consoles, and the assembly is topped by a semicircular arch. This contains a fanlight with radial tracery. There is a secondary door in bay seven.

This house was built in two main stages — the east part probably between 1780 and 1785 and the west part in the same style about the middle of the 19th century. This extension has been more carefully done than might have been expected at that time.

The original façade brings into the street a traditional technique of arcading in brick, usually seen in Farnham only behind houses, in stable blocks and the more utilitarian buildings. Both here, and in stables, they are of first quality. The doorcase makes a pleasant change from the normally pedimented type, and the house as a whole, and in detail, is worth comparing with 90 West Street (*qv*) which, stylistically, one might have placed earlier than this by a few years. But it is possibly not the case. There are similarities in composition too, as in the formula for basic proportions. Apart from its extension there appear to have been no alterations to the front except for a dormer window added in 1961, unless the original (probably three-pane-wide) windows have been replaced. If they have, as one would expect, it is remarkable how well the later ones fit visually into the elevation. A cottage stood where the extension was built. Some older bricks, possibly from an earlier building here have been re-used at the back. Roofing timbers, too, had been employed elsewhere. There are good Adamesque chimney pieces.

John Manwaring the elder had bought the property from Thomas Lander and Thomas Palmer by 1723. The property remained with his family until 1834 when it was sold to William Knight. He died intestate and 41 West Street passed to his eldest son, George Coldham Knight *(qv)*. The Manwaring family seem to be thought of as hop planters only, but John the elder *(qv)* was first a tanner; and with this house went two tanyards which, with various other buildings, spread from behind the garden of 41 West Street to the meadows. Although the Manwarings continued their interest in tanning (John, the younger, left four tanyards in 1794), hops got the better of them, as the name Tanyard Kiln suggests. This stood at the bottom of Mead Lane, but has gone. Other buildings of theirs remain. (See 39 West Street.) The cottage which once stood where bays six and seven are had an independent history until 1785 when John Manwaring bought it from John and Ann Hughes.

The name Elmer House by which 41 West Street is alternatively known, implies a direct connection with the Elmer *(qv)* family of painters. No direct connection of Elmer with 41 West Street has been substantiated. As a house-name it appears in documents only during the Mason *(qv)* family's ownership — about sixty years from 1869 when 41 West Street was conveyed to Richard Mason *(b 1832*, d 1910)*. He was a solicitor, sometime Clerk to the Local Board, then to Farnham Council, the Farnham Justices and Registrar of the County Court. It is now a private school, and before that was The First Church of Christ, Scientist, Farnham.

43   WEST   STREET   (Empire Stores)

Hereabouts was once The Black Horse alehouse. In 1785 it was occupied by Ann Harwood, before by Edward Miles, and earlier still by Thomas Westbrook *(qv)*.

46A   WEST   STREET   (Dean's)

Until recently there was a cottage-type dwelling here, facing
into Mead Lane, with a small shopfront and door inserted
on the north front. On the west was a simple pedimented
doorcase. See illustration.

In the 1830s John Burrows (*b* 1776*), carpenter, owned
the house. Sarah Burrows (*b* 1771*) was probably his wife.
They were here in 1841 but not ten years later. The house
was interesting for its Dutch type gable seen also at Windsor
Almshouses (*qv*) and there dated 1619.

In 1851 there were three houses in Mead Lane under
construction. Sampson's Almshouses (*qv*) had not been built
in 1840, but were there before 1854.

46A WEST STREET. North end of the Dutch House, which
stood until recently as one of Farnham's few examples
of this style of brickwork.

47   AND   48   WEST   STREET

Both probably incorporate part of an earlier house which
appears to have been partly demolished and then built on to
about mid-19th century. The earlier house stood back from
Mead Lane and from West Street and had an extensive
garden — upon which, at the estimated price of £14,500,
Vernon Court was built by Brockway's for Farnham Council
in 1956.

John Hayes owned this property in the 1830s. He was a nurseryman, born at Langley Marsh in 1796*. His wife, Harriett (*b* 1795* in Farnham), was a laundress, and their son Richard (*b* 1832* at Binfield, Berks), also a gardener. Hayes was still here in the '50s, Thomas Trusler, nurseryman and florist, being in business later in the century. In 1916 C. E. Trimmer's (*qv*) Trustees offered for sale this 'desirable house and highly productive well stocked market garden' with conservatories and a shop. It was sold to James Burchett for £560. C. E. Trimmer inherited from his father in 1893. In 1924 the Executors of James Burchett offered for sale the property 'carried on as a nursery for many years'.

The house has twice been greatly altered. First, about mid-19th century, after which expansion it appears to have been sub-divided, the east part later (certainly by 1878) becoming The Rose and Thistle. This pub closed during the 1930s. The second big change came in 1955 when the nursery half was developed. A clue to the date of the early house was then found on the back of the doorcase. It was inscribed with the name James Garfath (*qv*) and date, 1822.

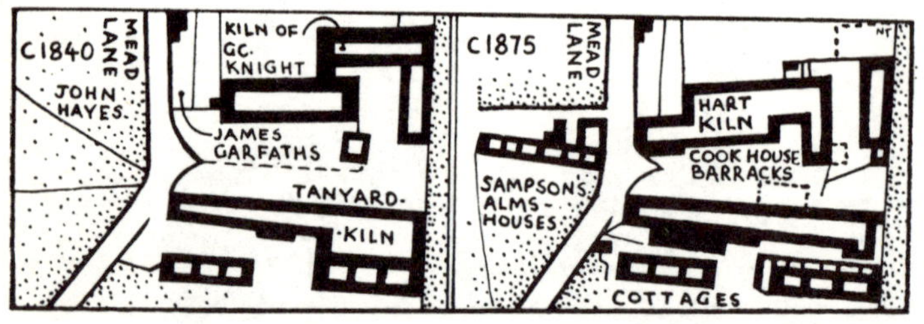

TANYARD KILN was described as containing fourteen holes and three oasts in 1875. The Hart Kiln was John Manwaring's in 1821. After enlargement, the kiln comprised fifteen holes and three oasts. By late in the 19th century other additions (hatched contours) had been made. Sampson's Almshouses and Tanyard Kiln have been demolished.

49 AND 50 WEST STREET (Heath and Wiltshire, Reliance Cottages, St. John Ambulance Station, F. C. Hardingham)

Until quite recently these premises formed a single property, most frequently associated with The White Horse and Elliott's engineering shop — once The Reliance Iron Works.

By 1842 a shop and beer house belonging to John and James Knight were where the motor garage and eastern cottages are now. The nature of the shop is suggested by the fact that when Isaac Holloway (*qv*) sold the property to

G. C. Knight (*qv*) of Coxbridge in 1809, it had been converted
to a workshop. Holloway was a wheelwright. The house
had been divided into two tenements. To their west was a
kiln of some size. So The White Horse presumably opened
after 1809 when this came into the possession of J. and J.
Knight. It closed about 90 years later having been destroyed
by fire. The cottages which replaced it were described as
newly built in 1913 and are those now awaiting demolition.
There was a White Horse in Farnham in the 1720s, but this
was at 12 West Street (*qv*). By 1876 the hop kiln had fallen
down, and 1891 saw the pub, 'large blacksmith's shop' and
cottage offered for sale by Farnham Brewery. After the fire
George Elliott bought the (late) pub, and part of the property
adjoining its west. Elliotts had, though, been here long before.

The George Elliotts enjoyed considerable local reputa-
tions as engineers; one also as Farnham fire chief. One's name
is incised in stone on the ambulance station. They built J. H.
Knight's important early motor car, made agricultural
implements (including the hand drills and seed machines
designed by Bennett, *qv*), hop bagging machines (a model of
one was exhibited at the Crystal Palace in 1851, although it
is thought that a man from Kingsley may have invented
it), and made gas, oil, steam and hot air engines, carts, vans
and wagons — not all in West Street but also behind 44
Downing Street where was a shoeing forge and smithy.

As so many Elliotts were employed making things which
last, some attempt is made here to simplify and to record
groups of the family working in Farnham in the 18th-19th
centuries. It is unlikely that these later Georges were the
first Elliotts in local engineering. Robert and Robert junior
were blacksmiths during the 1790s and 1820s; John (*b* 1816*)
in East Street, Charles (*b* 1792*) in Downing Street, and
Edward (*b* 1806) in Castle Street, were all smiths in the mid
1850s. A George, son of Robert Elliott, was baptised in 1799,
and George (*b* 1800*), blacksmith, was working at about 49
West Street in 1851. His wife was Elizabeth (*b* 1800*), and
also hereabout was George Elliott (*b* 1829*) junior, his wife
Ellen (*b* 1830*), and his son George (*b* 1850). Edward, son of
Robert, died in 1804. Another Edward was born in 1839. It
seems, though, that one George Elliott senior was working on
the Reliance site by the early 1840s as coachsmith. Perhaps
he carried on where Holloway the wheelwright (who came
from Thursley) left off. He had been here as early as at least
1779 and before him the property — then a cottage, barn
and garden—had been occupied by John Moth. Richard Moth
(*d* 1786) was a Farnham wheelwright. Sturt, writing of his

childhood, recalls that he was annoyed 'one day to see, over an old smithy, the name of some man unknown to me, a "Wheelwright". But was not my father a wheelwright? What right had anyone else to practise his trade?'

Elliotts once living in Downing Street included Charles (*b* 1821*) and his wife Elizabeth (*b* 1820*), and another Charles, both blacksmiths; Mary (*b* 1801*), Emma (*b* 1826*) and Walter (*b* 1828*). The East Street smithing Elliotts included John (above) and his wife Elizabeth (*b* 1821*), their children John (*b* 1842*) and Robert (*b* 1845*). Also a formidable 83-year-old blacksmith, Sarah Elliott (*b* 1768*), and her son William (*b* 1797*). Edward, of Castle Street (above), was married to Charlotte (*b* 1804*). Their son Edward was born in 1839*. Robert and Sarah's son Robert was baptised in 1802, their son Charles died in 1812.

A few months before the first World War The Reliance Engineering Works was offered for sale by Elliott's trustees with 49, 50 and 50A West Street, 44 Downing Street, Tavistock Cottages in Abbey Street, and land in Crondall Lane, now part of Barnett and Small's premises. A number of these lots was not sold at all; others made heavy going; for example 44 Downing Street, a sizeable house with smithy, took twenty-one bids to rise from £250 to £405.

* LION WORKS, WEST STREET
(Crosby & Co.)

A large site on which for the greater part of a century was The Lion Brewery — of which we are reminded still by gate-pier sculptures. Since the 1930s the buildings have changed greatly. Tall chimneys have been felled, storeys added to brewery buildings, others demolished or built. But one can still trace much of the earlier work. Alterations have not completely stamped out its bold functional character. For over twenty years now Crosby and Co. have occupied the premises, manufacturing timber products.

As a brewery, it was a latecomer to Farnham. There was nothing but fields here in 1839. Elsewhere, Peacock (*qv*) was carrying on Elliott's brewery, Knight's Farnham Brewery was operating in Castle Street, Barrett and Beldham were in Church Lane (*qqv*) and many others had been brewing in Farnham in the 18th century. Slater, Hewitt (*qv*), Thomas Findens and the Andrew Bristows (*qv*) were among them. Thomas Gates and John Edmunds had done so very many years before.

It is said that George Trimmer (*qv*), who founded The

Lion Brewery, started with nothing, married well, and died worth three-quarters of a million. He was born in Farnham; his wife at Dorking.

The 18th to early 19th century Trimmers were not, as far as can be found, particularly distinguished locally. Henry and William were drapers somewhere in the town, Frederic, likewise, in Downing Street. Various Johns were a cobbler, surveyor and yeoman, while a George Trimmer traded as cheesemonger in the 1820s. One John Trimmer came to Farnham as an apprentice from Morlin, in Kent, during 1724, and there was a Trimmer family at Badshot in the 1660s.

There may be no significant connection, but Trimmer and Beer went together long before The Lion Brewery started. In the 1770s Robert and William, common brewers, leased The Star (*qv*) and some time later Robert was not only carrier, hop planter, brandy merchant and maltster, but the only brewer listed in a trade directory for Farnham. In 1749 Robert was connected with The Wheatsheaf (*qv*). Ninety years later a Robert Trimmer was at Bury Court (*qv*), Bentley.

However it started, George Trimmer's success was apocryphal. Building first in the north-west corner and then down Babb's Mead, he established the new brewery. It flourished. He bought land, built pubs, developed his house and stables at 69 West Street (*qv*) and snapped up corner sites all over the district, including Aldershot. By 1851, at the age of 27, he was married to Ellen (*b* 1824*), occupied 100 acres, employed eleven men, had two servants and a groom, and was described as a farmer, auctioneer and surveyor. All this time Barrett's (*qv*), by then at Bridge Square, were prospering. But in 1890 he bought them as well for, it is said, nearly half a million. Farnham United Brewery (late Trimmer's and Barrett's), at the time of George Trimmer's death in 1892, was a big concern.

As far as it has been possible to establish the total of land owned in Farnham by all named Trimmer in 1839 was 4 acres. They belonged to Anne and Frederick. In the 1890s Trimmers — George, 'one of the principal landowners of Farnham' — owned land at Runfold, Sheephouse, Manley Bridge, Stockhams, Runwick, Dean's Farm, the east end of Farnham, Old Park and Brambletons, for a start. Farnham got something back. The recasting of a church bell, £15,000 to found Trimmer's Cottage Hospital, and Trimmer's alms-houses (*qqv*) are examples.

Trimmer's size in the terms of big brewers today was almost insignificant. But for Farnham, in the 19th century, his was a staggering success.

McDONALD'S ALMSHOUSES,
WEST STREET

Rather less cottagey than its neighbours, this group was built in 1906, endowed by George McDonald and built by Mardon's (*qqv*) who tendered for £2,709. The highest was £3,914. Arthur J. Stedman (*qv*) was architect. He opened his practice in Farnham about 1886, having served previously with Goddard's, builders. He planned a number of private houses in residential areas and was responsible for some reconstructions in the town which are noted elsewhere.

McDonald owned the nearby kiln in Chantry.

TRIMMER'S ALMSHOUSES,
WEST STREET

George Trimmer (*qv*) died on November 11th, 1892, and left money for various local charitable causes. The almshouses are in two blocks of four, one either side of the entrance to (the promising-sounding enough) Mount Pleasant. They make quite a pretty group in their picturesque cottage Tudor style of early 1893. George Trimmer's endowment was augmented by £4,000 from R. G. and C. E. Trimmer (*qqv*).

Until late-century the Mount Pleasant site was entirely undeveloped. By the mid '90s a cul-de-sac road had been indicated and over a dozen houses had been built flanking it.

SAMPSON'S ALMSHOUSES,
WEST STREET

This group of five brick, tile and stone built almshouses was erected in 1933-34 by Mills and Sons with H. Falkner (*qv*) as architect. Their predecessors, in Mead Lane, then became obsolete, fell into disrepair and were later demolished.

Eighty years before their evacuation Robert Sampson (*qv*) granted to trustees part of Rickard's Mead with the cottages on it for use as almshouses. He left investments to ensure their repair, the cottages having not been long built. They had not been built in 1840. The Memorial Sports Ground which they overlooked was once known as Sampson's Meadow.

Robert Sampson (*b* 1791 in Dorset) was brewer and maltster in Bridge Square for the first part of the 19th century. He seems to have retired to take up hop planting when a little over fifty. His son Sampson Sampson (*qv b* 1826) took over the maltings which were later bought by Barrett's

Breweries (*qv*). Sampson Sampson, who, at the age of fifteen was at Robert Sampson's house in Bridge Square, later lived at 40 West Street (*qv*). The family owned land off Crondall Lane, Lower Green Lane, and elsewhere.

A hundred years after the Mead Lane cottages became almshouses, they were demolished. For their last ten years they were reinforced block-houses — part of the defence line of ditches, pill-boxes, concrete barriers and road blocks which ran from above The Hart, down Potters Gate, across to Mead Lane and over the meadows. Firgrove Lodge was similarly pressed to service. Those picturesque, low-lying, many faceted and slate-roofed early Victorian bungalows were ideal for a quick conversion and cunning camouflage.

Inhabitants of the new almshouses must be not only 'good and deserving members of the Church of England', but also healthy ones. The nearest shop (apart from an off-licence) is at least half a mile away. See plan on page 178.

* 5 9   W E S T   S T R E E T   (Send House)

A brick built house on two floors under a slate roof with eaves supported by brackets in pairs. The street fronts are cement clad. The main front has four bays. Corners are coigned and similar decoration runs between bays two and three.

Fenestration: Ground floor, in bays one, two and four, recessed plate-glass windows with architraves. That in bay four has also a keyblock and flat hood with consoles; First floor, four similar, with architraves.

Door: In bay three, segmental head with keyblock and flat hood with console brackets.

Numbers 58 and 59, comprising two houses with gardens and a yard, were owned about 1840 by James Harding (*qv*) junior, surveyor. Where the Crondall Lane wall is now was a house which had gone in 1871. By then Send House had developed from a smaller building to approximately its present extent. The gateroom adjoining it to the west (and now a shop window) had also been built by then, and on what had been an empty plot thirty years before (now the lower part of Barnett and Small's garage) were hop buildings. Land adjoining the immediate north has also been developed since. It was George Parfitt's workshop. He worked for Elliott (*qv*) of West Street. About 1930 it became part of Barnett and Small's garage, linked with their premises at 58 West Street.

The Hardings were a building family who were active

in the period which spans the transition from Farnham Renaissance to Victorian. Their families and living-places in the town are therefore dealt with here in some detail, although few houses can yet be ascribed to them confidently. Probably 60 and 61 West Street and The Duke of Cambridge are theirs; possibly Stanley Villas too. James Harding designed and probably built the nave of Froyle Church (1812), the north aisle at Frensham (1826), Liphook Church (1836), Wrecclesham Church (1840) and, according to an advertisement in the Reading Mercury, Crookham Church (1840-1841).

Probably at Send House, lived in the early '40s, James Harding (*b* 1771*) senior, stonemason, and Mary (*b* 1771*); also James Harding (*b* 1806*) junior, surveyor, with Harriett (*b* 1811*) and children Sidney, Hector, Nelson and Agnes. Thomas Harding (*b* 1800*), carpenter, lived nearby, at about 65 West Street. His wife was Elizabeth (*b* 1800*). Richard (*b* 1838*) was his son, Emily his daughter; Thomas (*b* 1827*), William (*b* 1829*) and James Harding (*b* 1831*) were probably his children also.

William Harding (*b* 1815* in Farnham), surveyor, probably lived, shortly after marrying Caroline Wilkins (*b* 1819*) in Lower Downing Street, moving about 1850 to not far from 76 West Street. She was the daughter of William Wilkins (*qv*). Their children were William (*b* 1841*) and Anna (*b* 1843*). A William Harding of West Street advertised as auctioneer, surveyor and estate agent in 1845.

Harding and Stewart was a local building firm in the 1820s. Men of those names owned jointly property now known as 51-56 West Street. A George Harding owned Lowndes Buildings (*qv*) in the 1830s and a James Harding, son of James and Mary, was baptised in 1802. A James Harding died in 1810; Ann, wife of James in 1801.

By the 1870s Send House was a tea merchant's shop, Mr. Garraway being the proprietor. Ten years later the trustees of the late Mr. Longhurst (see Willmer House) offered 59 West Street for sale as an 'excellent shop in which a high-class grocery establishment has been carried on for many years'. About 1890 extensive alterations were made and the former business premises were redomesticated. The fronts of the house were, it is said, then encased in cement, but not by a local craftsman. Was Sidney Stapley (*qv*) the architect? The reconstruction meant practically rebuilding the south front. Before this rebuilding here was one of Farnham's most extravagant, if small, domestic gothick essays — perhaps the church-building Harding's homework. It stood as an

ornate view-stopper looking down West Street by 1870.
Bays one and two were by then much as now, with the
exception that a shopfront with door to the left of central
coigns was fitted. But the east half was a little fantasy of
gothick windows, finials, high-pitched roof, balcony and
decorative work. The central coigns mark the division. They
would be difficult to account for otherwise. The late-century
remodelling, which meant almost certain total demolition of
the east part, must have meant also that anything of the early
house here went even if it survived the gothick reconstruction.

60 AND 61 WEST STREET

A semi-detached pair of brick built houses totalling six bays
on two main floors under slate roofs. A brick string course
separates floors.

Fenestration: Ground floor, four-pane-wide recessed
sashes in bays three, four and six. In bay one a four-light bay
window; First floor, six three-pane-wide recessed sashes.

Doors: Similar, in bays two and five, they are pilastered
and have triangular pediments.

Other features: All front window heads are cast. The
one in bay two has a keyblock with bearded and coroneted
head in high relief.

A pair which helps to show how long the Georgian
tradition survived in Farnham. The houses were not here in
1839 and probably not in 1846. A likely date of building is
1847. Even in 1879 number 60 was still described as 'a modern
residence'. These houses are comparable with roughly contemporary pairs at Bath Terrace and Stanley Villas (qqv), but
are far from the last to be built in the Georgian tradition —
tradition, not revival — as dated cottages at Hale demonstrate
as late as the 1880s. A guess would put Stanley Villas after
mid-19th century. By that time the revival had started, in the
hands of professional architects.

The bay window of 60 West Street is an addition and
the roof, it has been said, has been lowered. It has certainly
been altered. Does the decorative keyblock suggest that the
roof was originally at this level? Eaves resting on window
heads are seen elsewhere on buildings of this period in Farnham. For style of building 86-87 West Street and 34-35 Castle
Street have a marked outer resemblance. There was a building here in the 18th century. Foundations remain. Number 60
appears to have been first-built of the pair.

It is not claimed that these were built by the Hardings,
but that seems probable. James lived at 59 West Street (qv)

and other members at about number 65. In 1846 the site was bought by Henry Harding from Henry Nichols (*qqv*). Later, the property was Thomas Burningham's (*qv, d c* 1879). 60 West Street was bought by his son James Winkworth Burningham (*d* 1915), accountant and Parish Clerk, for £750 in that year. Number 60 was known since the 19th century as Clifford House. Why? Perhaps there is a clue in the decorative key stone.

The site is in the corner of an old plantation, once growing hops and firs, known as Braziers, once Brasures and later Brazers. In 1889 J. W. Burningham added a large garden to 60 West Street by buying more land from M. O. Stevens for £180. It had once belonged to the Marquis of Lothian and the Vernons (*qqv*).

62-65 WEST STREET

A brick and stone built group on two floors under a part slate and part tile roof.

The terrace is typical of many smaller Farnham speculative developments that look as though they took place early in the 19th century.

The first found connection with a pub is in 1839, when Richard Mason owned a beer house here. By 1842 Joseph Brown, victualler, lived in the group and nine years later Frances Searle (*b* 1792* at Crondall), victualler and widow, lived at The Jolly Sailor, as it was by then known. William Searle (*b* 1796*), labourer and beer retailer, was living hereabout in the early '40s.

Richard Mason, carpenter, was taxed on these four dwellings in 1833. They were then occupied by Thomas Harding and John Stokes (*qqv*), Elizabeth Vanner and William Searle. On Mason's death in 1844 his son William inherited. R. and T. Barrett (*qv*), brewers, bought 62 and 63 West Street in 1854 and, eleven years later, the yard and stables alongside.

In 1916 trustees of the late C. E. Trimmer (*qv*) offered 64 and 65 for sale. They were again on the market in 1925, with 53-56 West Street and 1 and 2 Grove Cottages, Guildford Road.

66 AND 67 WEST STREET

Two cement-clad and slated attached houses on two floors, totalling four bays. A string divides floors of bays three and four. All openings in bays three and four are architraved.

Both of these houses are older than the fronts suggest. They were probably cut back, re-fronted in cement and re-roofed with slate to give them an 1865-ish appearance and better alignment with the street — into which they once projected slightly. Number 66 was offered for sale in 1916 by the executors of C. E. Trimmer (*qv*) on condition that a door-way leading to the garden of 69 (*qv*) was bricked up within one month of purchase. Combined rents of both houses were then £41 12s. per annum. 67 was again on the market in 1920; rent then £15 per annum.

Charles Vince, grocer, owned 67 in the later 1830s. He had a small shop alongside 66, which was owned by James Andrews. James Stokes (*qv*), coachmaker, probably lived at 67. James Stokes senior (*b c* 1803) and Charlotte (*b* 1801*) had a son James (*b* 1832?) and daughter Ellen (*b* 1834*). The son was also in the coachmaking trade. John Stokes (*qv*) had been a coachmaker in West Street before them. A James Stokes was landlord at The Fox and Hounds in the 1870s.

68   WEST   STREET

A symmetrical two-floor, three-bay cottage of brick with tile roof.

Fenestration: Ground floor, in bays one and three a bow window; First floor, in bays one and three casements breaking the eaves and capped with tile roofs.

Door: In bay three, with flat hood and consoles.

This property was reconstructed in the mid 1930s. The windows were then inserted and the character it now possesses formed.

The small cottage and garden (once behind) were owned by Jane Patrick in the 1830s and were occupied by Daniel Patrick (*b* 1816*), shoemaker. In 1841 arises a problem. In the same house as Daniel Patrick was Ester, Hannah, Sarah, Elizabeth Hewitt (nurse) and *nineteen* others, including a hawker, butcher and mariner — none born locally. Sighting the cottage, the thought of sleeping twenty-four people is an entertaining one.

It seems that hereabouts was The Travellers' Rest House for a number of years. Could it really have been this cottage? The Patrick's (*qv*) had connections with The Fox (*qv*).

The house was offered for sale with other properties of William Trimmer (*qv*) in 1920, at which time the rent was 8/- per week.

A symmetrical cement-clad house of five bays on three floors with slate roof and flat eaves. Cemented strings separate floors.

Fenestration: Ground floor, four recessed two-pane-wide sashes; First floor, five similar; Second floor, five similar, smaller.

Door: In bay three, cement case with panelled pilasters and entablature, mounted above stone steps.

Not, as it stands, an exciting architectural adventure, but it asserts a considerable if solemn presence, and projects the range of big scale domestic building a hundred yards or more from the town centre. It is in the Willmer House idiom but an idiom so well (or badly) worn that here its resources appear rather exhausted. Those many elements which combine to make Willmer House so outstanding are here, a hundred years or more later, stripped bare. But before the rendering acquired its subtle-coloured patina, this must have been a very bold and whitish façade, contrasting forcefully with little cottage-style neighbours the sharpness of its uncompromising lines, its scale and fine texture.

This is a rebuilding and extension of an earlier house which very likely was something like the Rectory in Church Lane, with three peaked dormer windows above two main floors of five bays. Extensive secondary buildings are of various dates. The main house was converted into flats by Farnham Council c 1947 and ten years later it was extensively restored and altered privately after conveyance. With it went the four adjacent cottages. There were once hop kilns here as well.

The early occupants of this house have not yet been traced, but they must for many years have been people of substance. It was owned in the late 1830s by William Cobbett. But not *the* William Cobbett (*qv*) for he died in 1835. He had four sons, one of whom was John (1800-1877), another William (1798-1878), a barrister, who wrote 'Law of the Turnpikes'. One of *the* William Cobbett's three daughters — Anne (1795-1877) — wrote 'The English Housekeeper'. The owner of 69 West Street might have been William the son.

In 1759 George Cobbett of Farnham married Ann Vincent and in 1836 Thomas Cobbett of City Road, London, owned freehold a house in West Street. There is a reference to an owner of number 69 as William Thomas Cobbett. It was in any case occupied in 1839 by Cyrus Blandford (*b* 1816*), a schoolmaster, who had a school here. George Gregg

(*b* 1821*) was an assistant and these two young men, neither
of them natives of the town, had among their pupils representatives of the Eyre, Wells and Varndill families — all boys,
some of whom were boarders. A Thomas Cobbett had run a
gentleman's boarding school in Farnham during the 1820s.
It appears then that Blandford took it over from him. Mary
Cobbett and John Rivers, both local, were married in Farnham
in 1767.

The property was owned mid-19th century by George
Trimmer (*qv*); conveniently close to the brewery. The house
again served as a school, this time for girls, under the Penn
family in the earlier 20th century. In 1889 Mr. and Mrs.
William Penn and daughters advertised their kindergarten
and school of music as Farnham High School for Girls, and
in 1910 as Cambridge House Private School for Girls, by then
under Mrs. William and Miss Clara Mabel Penn, who later
advertised on her own account from 69 West Street.

It is not claimed here that the Manory family (*qv*) lived
at 69 West Street, but it is possible. They were tanners, and
held houses and land on both sides of West Street hereabouts in 1648; also a close called Hop Garden and a house
then newly built abutting on to West Street and on to
Broadmead in the south which they bought from Thomas
Palmer (*qv*). James Manory was a trustee of Farnham Rectory
and Manor in 1634 and in 1648 James Manory, tanner, occupied the West Street properties. John Manory (*d c* 1664),
tanner, was married to Mary whom he predeceased. His sons
were William and John; his daughters Sarah, Elizabeth, Ann
and Mary. The exact nature of his alleged offences has not
come to light, but the Bailiffs paid to Mr. Child considerable
money 'for Mr. Manorie's tryall' in 1665. Possibly Manory
was concerned in trouble over paying market tolls. Robert
Manorye was charged Lay Subsidiary Assessment on his goods
in 1593-4.

74 W E S T   S T R E E T   (The Plough)

A timber, brick and tile public house of three bays on two
floors.

Reconstructed in 1933-4, to the design of John Howard
(*qv*) for Crowley and Co. in a pseudo half-timbered style.
Parts of an earlier building remain.

A pub named The Plough existed here in 1806 and probably for some time, but not a great many years, before.
Adjacent property went with it, including four cottages (perhaps those once in Potter's Gate), hop kilns, three acres of

hops called Potter's, and next to it two acres called Cobgate.
Part of The Hart was once known as Cobgate. These, and
the site of The Plough, were part of the Vernon estate in
1719.

In 1806 Sir William Pierce Ashe a'Court, of Haytesbury
House, Wilts, and Charles Repington (*qqv*), who had in-
herited, sold to William John Kerr, Marquis of Lothian (*qv*).
He sold to William Marsh of Knightsbridge in the following
year and it returned to Charles Beauchamp Kerr in 1815.
Mark Robert Kerr and others sold to John Cole in 1817 to
prevent dower. He probably died *c* 1837, after which Mary
Cole (*b* 1781*), victualler, was here with William Cole, a
carpenter, and Henry (*bb* 1819**), a tailor, for 30 years in all.
Then, a succession of Nashs, Lamports and others until
Crowleys bought in 1908.

In 1884 the premises were advertised for sale as a public
house with brewhouse, stabling, cowstalls and garden, with
a remunerative milk business which had been carried on for
many years on the premises.

POTTER'S GATE AND CASTLE SCHOOL, WEST STREET

Built in 1896 for 275 boys. It was until recently known as
West Street School. The road has been so named for over
200 years and 250 years ago here was part of a hop garden
called Potters. It is said that the name evolved not by way of
a person named Potter, but owing to the fact that by way
of this lane the potters travelled to Old Park to dig their clay.

On the lower west side of Potters Gate were four cottages
and adjoining them to the north was the large kiln, once of
Samuel Andrews (*qv*). The house now standing there was
built after planning permission had been granted to R. Mason
in 1909. Hop kilns in Potters Gate belonged to the Vernons
in 1719 and G. C. Knight (*qqv*) in 1806. Cottages higher up,
on the east, really belong to Factory Yard (*qv*). In 1851 three
houses in Potters Gate were under construction.

77 WEST STREET

Here was The Rainbow, which appears to have been licensed
about 1880 from off-licence premises established earlier and
of Richard Curtis in 1878. The house was once owned by
James Garfath (*qv*) and was still a pub in 1895.

A two-bay, three-floor house of asymmetrical façade, built in brick and part cemented, below a slate roof. Coigns extend above ground floor level. Eaves supported by paired brackets.

Fenestration: Ground floor, bay one, a recessed large-paned window, with architrave and keyblock; First floor, two similar; Second floor, two similar of three-quarters height.

Door: In bay one, with architrave, keyblock and slight flat hood.

The house was built for Charles Attfield (*qv*) about 1870 and appears virtually untouched outside. It is not a building of architectural importance but is interesting for some details (see illustration) and its name — Beaver House — which it had acquired by 1873. Attfield's Victorian house stands at the corner of Beaver's Yard. There is presumably a connection with the Beaver family, although they did not live here — on this site — but at College Garden (*qv*). Perhaps they owned these sites earlier or even what were later Charles Attfield's kilns which stood here before this house did.

Today Beaver's House, Yard, Road and Hill perpetuate the name of a family which seems not to have stayed very long in Farnham, considering that during the second half of the 18th century they were prominent hop planters. Although the Beavers (*qv*) were in Farnham by the 1750s (as an advertisement of Edward Beaver's in an Irish paper tells

78 and 79 WEST STREET. A detail of eaves treatment dated about 1870 compared with an earlier counterpart next door.

us), Edward appears as a freeholder only from 1764. There must have been at least two of the same name, as Edward's widow, Susanna (daughter of Alexander Lee), was buried in Farnham in 1767, and Rhoda, Edward's wife, in 1778. Peter Esq. died in the same year, having occupied the house in Farnham of Edward Beaver of Godalming.

It was one of the Edwards who bought the remains of the Chantry school for £42 in 1758 (see 25 West Street). Mrs. Mary Beaver, widow, died in Farnham in 1786. No Beaver was charged in the 1660s Hearth Tax. Land called Birds was in their occupation a hundred years later.

Beaver House served as a preparatory school under the Misses Stroud later in the 19th century. On his death in 1892 the property belonged to George Trimmer (*qv*) and it passed, as part of his moiety, to Charles Edwin Trimmer who sold it in 1905.

*   COLLEGE   GARDENS,   WEST   STREET

The site is of interest for two particular reasons. One is the potential value of such a place as an amenity as well as an incident in townscape. The other is for its associations. For here was once what later became The Staff College, Camberley. The Senior Department of the Royal Military College was established after proclamation of a Royal Warrant in 1801. The Department moved here in 1814 two years after James Moore Molyneux (*qv*) had sold the land to H.R.H. Frederick, Duke of York, The Right Hon. Henry John, Viscount Palmerston and the Right Hon. Henry, Earl Mulgrave — three R.M.C. Commissioners.

The College ran in West Street for about seven years, then moved to Sandhurst where, in 1857, it became the Staff College. The building was demolished and its site sold to William Pink Paine, for £300 in 1835. Four years later the site was named College Yard, which suggests that the garden had not by then been made by the Paine (*qv*) family.

Like the Manwarings and Pinks, the Paines are too numerous to note here in detail. Most important were probably William Pink Paine (*d* 1847) and John Manwaring Paine (*d* 1858), Elizabeth, wife of W. P. Paine, died in 1841. In West Street in that year were William (*b* 1786*), hop planter, Elizabeth (*b* 1791*), probably husband and wife (above) with their children John (*b* 1808*), Mary and William (*bb* 1816**). They lived at Sandford House (*qv*), opposite College Gardens. John Paine (*b* 1808*) was there, with his wife Caroline

(*b* 1822*) and daughters Alice (*b* 1847*) and Caroline (*b* 1844*)
in 1851. It was written by a contemporary that J. M. Paine
was the principal hop grower in Farnham and that he
employed 2,000 pickers. He occupied 600 acres shortly before
his death. He and his wife helped much to restore St.
Andrew's church. A memorial window was erected to their
memory by townsmen. Other windows commemorated
various members of the family. In 1851 John Paine occupied
550 acres and was one of Farnham's largest employers of
labour. George Paine of Downing Street occupied 200 acres
more.

Hassell left a drawing of the College building — of ten
bays on one floor — which probably ran parallel with the
street. (See Farnham Inheritance p 26.) Within a few feet
of the pavement the ground has been disturbed for a considerable depth. Brick and tile rubble is plentiful.

These buried remains might be of Edward Beaver's
mansion house. It stood somewhere on the site. Beaver (*qv*)
was another prominent hop planter. After he left, his house
was occupied for a time by Elizabeth Shepheard before passing to Molyneux. The Army also bought 'that hop kiln with
storeroom adjoining . . . late in the occupation of Bristow
Bradley (*qv*) . . . and also the east wall of a certain stable and
barn situate in the yard belonging to Nathaniel Attfield (*qv*)
at the north end of the hop kiln and adjoining the garden
behind the mansion'.

When the Army left, Charles Attfield (*qv*) occupied most
of Beaver's Yard premises, many of which are said to have
served as Army quarters. Since, most had been converted to
cottages, but in 1839 Attfield used them as stores and sheds
rather than as living accommodation. To the north of the
site, in 1812, was hopland of Benjamin Nichols (*qv*) which
was called The Bowling Green — Beaver's pleasure ground?

The entire property was bought by Farnham Council
in 1957 for development under the Ewart Bequest, and at the
time of writing was being built on — facing away from
the street.

80-81   WEST   STREET

An asymmetrical attached pair of brick and timber built
cottages under a continuous tile roof. The dwellings are each
of two bays on two floors.

Fenestration: Ground floor, in bays two and three wood
framed casements; First floor, similar two-thirds height.

Door: In bays one and four. Flat hoods with cut brackets.
80, 81 and 82 are here considered under a single head.

Their roofs run continuously. A painted board states that here are Abbott's Cottages, 1400. If one looked little further it might be concluded that this date was about 400 years out as the cottages are fronted in brick and detailed more in a later 18th to earlier 19th century style. Number 82, similarly, appears to be about late 18th century with 19th century shopfronts. But the chimney indicates otherwise, and a quick glance at the west end wall confirms that the facts are not quite so simple, even if one had not stepped down into 82 or noticed the expanse of roof surface to front wall of the cottages.

The history of the group is at present obscure, but from inside it is clear that this is a timber framed range probably once several houses. There is a good moulded frame to a blocked communicating door between the cottages, and possibly evidence of two roofs — the one we see on top of remains of an earlier one. This would account in part for low upper windows and probably too for the front wall being now about two feet forward from an earlier one. The scarred and unfenestrated west wall suggests that another building — perhaps the Beavers' (*qv*) mansion house — once stood very close, if not adjoining.

At the time of the Dissolution various chantries were granted to John White (*qv*) and Stephen Kyrton. Property included a 'corner house late in the occupation of Peter Stempe'. It was in The Borough of Farnham on the east side of the market place, and with it went a Castle Street granary. There was a lot of other property including another granary in Longbridge, land at Wrecclesham and Compton, Binsted, Bentley and a messuage 'called Chauntrye prestes mansion house', as well as property in London. This was in Somerset's day. It has been thought that 80-82 West Street might have been that Chantry House. That might be, although place names may associate it more with the extreme west end of West Street, near Mount Pleasant.

The earlier period of great domestic building activity in Farnham coincided with corn market days — when 'Farnham, except Hempstead and London [was] the greatest corn market in England, particularly for wheat, of which so vast a quantity is brought hither . . .' (Defoe, 1722). Something of the circumstances of the market's growth is noted in Farnham Inheritance, pp. 19 - 21, and Aubrey's observation·that 'It is the greatest market in England for wheat' has often been quoted. Not so Mr. Morgan's notes written in 1684 and recently found in the Bodleian Library's Department of Western Manuscripts, which confirms the other reports. He wrote, 'As to Farnham I was told by some there, for I went thither purposely to see the Town, There is usually sold on their market day which is Thursday 400 loads of wheat, and of other sorts of Grain 400 Loads more. But a great deal of this Corn is brought into store houses on the weeke dayes for the Town will not hold so many carts togeither at one time, so that I think with allowance this may pass for the greatest market in England. And this yeelds a great Income to the Bishop for he has the tole of all (the?) Corne. From thence they carry the greatest part in wagons to Guildford and Cherse and thence by water towards and to London.

'Here is also a great market for all sorts of Fruit especially Wallnuts usually sold for 2d. a hundred and sent to London . . .' Number 10 Castle Street appears first to have had a very direct link with the corn market (the capital initials of 'The Corn Rooms' does suggest something more than one of many temporary storehouses) and then to have been a product itself of the prosperity that the corn trade brought with it to the town.

Bishop Eddington established a charity with monies from properties in Southwark and a house and land in Farnham. Malden had suggested that this might have been used to endow the school which was attached to St. Andrew's church. Aubrey says that the school was probably an ancient chapel or chantry. This school has become closely associated with the Grammar School's history. (See 25 West Street).

Malden adds that when the building was demolished the school was transferred to the schoolmaster's house which was possibly the house with which the chantry had been endowed, and which was restored to the school by Bishop Morley. He left several properties to the use of the schoolmaster in 1680. They are said to have included Byworths (*qv*).

Numbers 80 to 82 West Street may have become wrongly associated with the Chantry House. There was a school here too. There also existed a very bad drawing of the old Grammar School in West Street which (in the drawing) looked rather like 80-82 West Street (which shows how bad it was). There are a lot of mights and possibilities needed to associate 80-82 West Street with the Chantry on evidence at present revealed.

The block in question was owned by Thomas Hunter (*qv*) and Ann Savage in 1839, and was occupied in part by him. It was then described as a cottage yard and garden. There was a conveyance in that year. In 1876 Hunter was named as the late occupier of Willmer House (*qv*) at which there had also been a school. An Ann Savage was assistant at The Old Vicarage (*qv*) school in 1839. Thomas Hunter was 68 in that year and Maria Hunter 53. A second Thomas (their son and later occupier of Willmer House?) was 18 and born in Farnham. Among the pupils at the Hunter-Savage school were James (*qv*), Henry (*bb* 1834**) and William Longhurst (*b* 1835*). Sidney Longhurst (*qv*) later owned Willmer House. Hunter's school was established by the mid 1820s at which time it was for day and boarding boys. George Elliott (*qv*) advertised from number 82 in 1882 as agricultural implement maker and in 1850 the address of William May (*b* 1821*), blacksmith, was Fox Yard. There was a grocery and bakery business here (1878 Elizabeth Stewart, grocer; 1891 William Stewart, baker; 1915 Richard Stewart, baker and grocer) before 82 became the Mecca Café. The block was offered for sale in 1879 when it was described as containing a large shop, two cottages and a large yard. They were let to Mrs. Stewart for £36 p.a.

During the later 18th to late 19th century there were many private schools, such as Willmer's and Hunter's, in Farnham and most of those which have been located have been noted elsewhere in this book. There were, of course, even more teachers all of whom it is not possible to list here. Those teaching locally earlier in the period included Henry Daniel (*d* 1778), Robert Morley (*d* 1807) and his wife (*d* 1780), and William Wheeler (*d* 1811). Here, it must suffice to list only those who appear to have run their own establishments and after whom schools might well have been named. Henry Austin, Gents Boarding (1826); Mrs. Charlsey, Academy (1823-4); James Fenton, Academy (1823-4); John Harrington, Boarding, Borough (1839); Miss Ann Lawrence, Infants, Borough (1855); John Lee, Independent (1855); William Smith (*b* 1808* at Epsom), Academy, Castle Street (1845); Thomas Thompson, Academy, West Street (1845); and Miss Sarah Wills, Downing Street (1845). Probably with their own schools were Mary Cook (1791-6), Miss Jenkins, Boarding (1791-6), Miss Elizabeth Baker (*b* 1824* at Cheltenham) and Mary Baker (*b* 1801*). Henry Allen was teaching locally in the 1730s and Thomas Russell (*b* 1707*) between 1732 and 1758. Others were Hannah Hopwood (*b* 1787*), Jane Knight (*b* 1806*), Mrs. Miller (1790s) and Rosa Winch (*c* 1850).

The yard to the east and rear was once known as Hunter's Yard, but now as Fox Yard, after the pub once at 83 West Street.

82 WEST STREET

Premises built of timber and brick on two floors with three main bays, under a tile roof. The front has a corniced parapet.

Fenestration: Ground floor, two double shopfronts; First floor, in bays one and three, 1-3-1 wide-boxed sashes; in bay two a wide-boxed sash three panes wide, but blind.

The premises adjoin number 82 to the west and are under one roof which runs through from 81. See 80 and 81 West Street.

83 WEST STREET (Pearson's)

A shop of three bays and two main floors, built of brick and timber under a tile roof running continuously with 84. The west wall is part tile-hung.

Fenestration: Ground floor, two plate-glass shop windows with a door between; First floor, three recessed plate-glass sashes.

A timber framed house, reconstructed, then fitted with a shopfront. This is one of a once delightful group of Farnham vernacular buildings, which although much altered offers a variety of detail and style with vigorous skyline and strong patterns of fenestration. They really did group. However some insensitive (but remediable) repainting and the loss by decay of the corniced eaves (with flute and paterae frieze) of 85 have detracted considerably from its interest.

Number 83 was The Fox. Hence Fox Yard — the lane alongside. As a pub it existed by 1823 and in 1839 was owned by J. and J. Knight. For many years early in the 19th century it was held by Patricks — Joseph, then Jane (*b* 1791*), and then Daniel (*b* 1812*). William Patrick (*b* 1819*) and James Patrick (*b* 1822*), bricklayers and builders and probably James' sons, were also here. Daniel Patrick's wife was Esther (*qv, b* 1813*) and one of their children Daniel (*b* 1844*). He was described in 1851 as victualler and lodging-house keeper. A William Patrick built Bath Terrace (*qv*).

The Fox was left, on death, by John Knight in 1856, then offered for sale by J. H. Knight in 1888. The rent, a selling point, was £25 per annum. By the 1900s the property was described as 'The Lodging House' and was again offered for sale, by Farnham United Brewery, in 1928. Its life as a pub probably ended in the earlier 1890s.

An old hop kiln once abutted the house to its north-east. It was destroyed by fire in 1907, the premises being used until that time for bottling by Mr. Bishop of The Jolly Farmer (qv). Much of this and another kiln which adjoined it to the north had probably been converted also to dwellings during the 19th century. William Crump (qv) once owned and used one of them.

Some Patricks lived at 68 West Street (qv), where they appear to have run a lodging house.

84 WEST STREET (The Mitre)

A symmetrical brick, timber and tile building of three bays on two floors.

Fenestration: Ground floor, bay windows in bays one and three; First floor, 1-3-1 sashes in bays one and three; Above, two tile capped dormers with casements.

Door: Pilastered, with triangular pediment, alone in bay three.

Owned early in the 19th century by Charles Waterman (b 1801*), the property was then described as being a house and yard. He was a tailor; was still here in 1841, ten years after which the building was stated to be unoccupied. Waterman advertised as a tailor in 1826; Charles, senior and junior, from West Street, in 1839, but there is no trace by 1855. Alfred White, cooper, was here during the last quarter of the 19th century. In 1899 the house was sold with number 83. It was again offered for sale by Farnham United Breweries in 1928. Within a year the premises, lately occupied by the British Legion, were being restored. 'A Tudor fireplace in excellent condition' was revealed and made good. The front was altered and bay windows fitted, it is said to the design of John Kingham (qv), or an assistant. Since then this has been The Old Mitre tea rooms. See 83 West Street.

88 WEST STREET (Bethune House)

A symmetrical façade of five bays and three floors, built of brick and roofed with tile. A cornice with paired modillions separates top windows from the parapet. The east half of the main block projects northwards. To the west is an extension now known as 88A (qv).

Fenestration: Ground floor, four windows, recessed, three panes wide and sashed; First floor, five windows similar to those below them; Second floor, similar, with blind glazed windows in bays two and four.

Door: Of wood and has plain radial and festooned tracery in a semicircular architraved fanlight contained by Doric fluted pilasters. The case has a triangular pediment and is set above a scroll-ended stone step.

Interior: The plan can be quartered, an entrance hall dividing the house into two — west and east. Front west room: Simple acanthus cornice and elaborately carved chimney-piece with a centre panel containing high relief amorini heads and wings. Front east: Acanthus cornice, architraved windows and a simple wood bolection chimney-piece. The back north-west quarter contains an helical staircase with serpentine rail, simple square banisters rising one or two to a tread. It opens direct from the entrance hall, the oval well being lit by a glass cone above. An acanthus cornice and low relief of acorns and oak leaves circumscribes the upper landing.

The greater part of this house might be dated *c* 1780 by general appearance. On an extension is a rainwater-head dated 1807. The downstairs chimney-pieces are also doubtful guides as they do not appear to be of the original house. The back north-east corner of the building is its oldest part and there are indications of a timber framed structure there. Ground floor front windows have recently had their two-pane-wide frames replaced by three-pane-wide ones.

Pevsner and Nairn say of 88-94, '. . . the best formal group in Farnham, all plain houses of 1760-1780 (except No. 94, typically clever Farnham *c* 20 keeping-in-keeping), plain except for doorcases and thin cornices but with splendidly urbane smooth brickwork. This is English *c* 18 town housing at its very best — not a regimented best either . . .' This is indeed high praise from judges who have seen so much.

James Shotter (*b* 1776*), solicitor, was here in the 1830s and probably still was at the time of his death in 1852. One of that name bought the house in 1818. He also owned 86 and 87 West Street and cottages adjoining their north end. William Shotter (*d* 1795) was the last Bailiff of Farnham. He resigned in 1789. His wife Elizabeth died in 1804. A William Shotter married Elizabeth Trimmer in 1767. Shotter and Evans practised in West Street as solicitors in the 19th century.

88A WEST STREET (The Little House)

A house of two bays and two floors, of brick under a tiled roof.

Fenestration: Ground floor, bay two, a three-pane-wide recessed sash; First floor, two similar.

Door: In bay one. It has a triangular dentilled pediment and semicircular fanlight with architrave and keyblock. Pilasters are panelled, topped by foliated consoles. The tracery pattern is of ogees interlaced.

This has been a separate house for about twelve years. Before, it was part of number 88 (*qv*) and was probably built as an extension to the main house in the earlier 19th century.

Before conversion to a house the ground floor of 88A contained one window only — offset to the east. This was of 1-3-1 multi-sashed type.

89 WEST STREET

A three-bay house on three floors of asymmetrical façade, built of yellow-grey brick with red brick dressings. The front is parapeted and corniced. A wooden fascia separates lower floors. The roof is tiled, with twin ridges from back to front. There is an extension to the east.

Fenestration: Ground floor, three-pane-wide recessed sashes in bays one and two; First floor, three similar windows, slightly taller; Second floor, three similar windows of three-quarters height.

Door: In bay three. Fluted coupled Doric columns supporting a triangular pediment. The semicircular fanlight has radial tracery.

North elevation: Red brick, it has no parapet but includes an area kitchen. Venetian windows light two rooms and a giant window of nine panes height with semicircular top, lights the stairwell. There is a simple pedimented back doorcase.

This is a good town house in the London style and is an important member of this distinguished group, all with façades of late 18th century character. A fascia board has been removed from between upper floors, but otherwise the façade appears virtually as built. General appearance — influenced by tall first floor windows, steps and rather slender doorcase — is of a tall, narrow house. But this impression would be modified if the fascia were replaced. The horizontal accent which this provided would have been important to its own façade and would also have helped to integrate number 89 with number 90 (*qv*). The garage and venetian-windowed room above are recent additions.

The back elevation is very different from the front. It lacks the latter's light formality and has been altered in its details.

In November 1775 number 90 West Street was bounded on its west side by a house then unoccupied, but owned by James Trimmer. Six years later it was Robert Trimmer's. A possible clue is here to the date of rebuilding of number 89. Robert was still in occupation in 1784 but by 1796 Mrs. Harrison, a widow, was occupant.

This house served during the last half of the 19th century as a school run by the Alexander family. Miss Julia (*b* 1841*) was responsible for the young ladies, and her sister, Miss Ellen (*b* 1843*), for the young gentlemen. Emma (*b* 1829*), another sister, was a schoolmistress in Farnham in the 1850s. Maria (*b* 1839*) was also a sister. The Alexander family was a large one. William (*b* 1791*) and Sarah (*b* 1793*) had sons, William (*b* 1834*) and Evan (*b* 1836*). A William Alexander owned 94 West Street (*qv*).

William Alexander (*qv*), a hop planter, born at Long-parish, occupied this house — the property of George Bury — in 1840. Amelia (*b* 1806*), Caroline (*b* 1838*) and George Bury (*b* 1836*) were here, or very near, in 1841.

9 0   W E S T   S T R E E T

A five-bay two-floor house of symmetrical parapeted façade built of brick under a tiled roof. The cornice is decorated by a frieze with alternating rosettes and flutes. To the east is a bay containing side-access door.

Fenestration: Ground floor, sashed, three panes wide, recessed; First floor, similar, but in bay three a semicircular head with fluted keyblock and radial glazing bars with festoons.

Door: In bay three, Ionic order, pilastered, with a semi-circular architraved fanlight containing lead tracery of radial design with festoons. Two stone steps, the lower terminating in scrolls, support decorative iron rails.

Other features: Folding wooden panelled shutters close from inside front windows. A carved wooden chimney piece with dentils, classical figures, lion masks, and a low-relief frieze with honeysuckle and foliated festoons combines with an ornamented wall cornice to decorate the front east room.

A less intricate scheme is used in the west front room. Here the cornice is plain and the chimney piece simply treated with dentils and a floral motif on either pilaster. A semi-circular arch with radial fanlight supported by pilasters divides front from back of the entrance hall. A similar, but unfanlighted arch spans the landing, which is lit from the north by a window similar to the one in bay three, but with squarer panes.

At one time there were two houses here with a gateway to their east and hop land on the north. They were held in trust for John Hearn in 1721. Later, these two houses were made into one, and over the cartway was a gateroom which did not actually belong to that house. The conversion had been made by mid-century, and the gateway itself blocked between 1721 and 1740 to give extra accommodation. This meant that another entrance had to be made from the north side. Hearn was a grocer. His wife, Elizabeth (*qv*) appears to have given up her interest in the property by 1775 when John Knight (*qv*) gave a mortgage. He sold to Daniel Bristow (*qv*) the elder, mercer, in 1781, very shortly after which the property was rebuilt. In 1796 it was written that Bristow 'about twelve years ago built a messuage between the messuage now of Elizabeth Godwin then of John Jolly and the messuage occupied by Robert Trimmer . . . In order to render the said messuage so built by Daniel Bristow the elder uniform compact and more commodious', Bristow bought the chamber belonging to John Jolly which was over the gateway and built it into his new house. The width of the part he bought was only four feet, for which he paid £30. So it can be fairly safely presumed that this important façade is dated 1784. Pevsner and Nairn go as far as to say that this house and 61 Castle Street (*qv*) were built by the same hand. There are similarities, too, with 23-24 and 41 West Street (*qqv*).

Few alterations have been made since the major reconstruction, although back windows look as though they have been increased to four panes wide from smaller ones. Since 1956 the large-voluted original decayed Ionic capitals have been replaced by locally carved copies. The iron railings were also added and steps rebuilt. A new fanlight has been fitted to the hall archway and the house restored to good condition after a long period of slow deterioration.

This is among the very best local small Georgian façades. It is a building of honest countenance, combining dignity with human scale, and sophistication with neighbourliness. Good craftsmanship and materials are brought together under the control of a sure hand guided by a sensitive eye. Inside and out the square and semicircle — multiplied, echoed and varied — give unity to basic areas, proportions and decorations. A module and rule of proportion may have been used. A touch of delicacy is added by the Adamesque fanlight tracery; a lightness prophetic of the Regency. To compare this front with, say, 45 Castle Street's, gives a good idea of Farnham's modifying of the Georgian style over about 70 years. Look forward from 1800 for another 70 years to 8 Castle Street (*qv*) to see the process nearing completion.

The Bristows (*qv*) have a long connection with Farnham. One Brystow lived at Dippenhall in 1480, but the name does not appear very frequently in Farnham until the 18th century, when Daniel the elder was a banker and draper, Andrew a burgher and most men of the family had a direct interest in hops. The Daniel Bristow who rebuilt this house was father of Daniel the younger who occupied number 91 (*qv*), and of Elizabeth Bristow.

When John William Kerr, the Marquis of Lothian (*b* 1737*, *d* 1815, *qv*), of Vernon House, bought 90 West Street in 1810 for £687 it was still described as newly built. 90 West Street passed to J. W. Kerr's second son (Lord) Charles Beauchamp Kerr (*d* 1816*) and then to his brother Mark. He sold it quickly to John Townsend (*qv*, *d* 1825), of Crown Court, Cheapside, Gent, who also owned property in Castle Street by 1823. John Adam Townsend, then Martha Townsend (*d* 1867) owned by 1839, at which time William Hollest (*qv*) was occupant. William Coleman (*qv*) was here by 1891.

91 AND 92 WEST STREET

A symmetrical brick pair totalling four bays on three floors under a hipped tiled roof.

Fenestration: Ground floor, in bays two and three, four-pane-wide recessed sashes; First floor, three-pane-wide recessed sashes; Second floor, similar, half height. All glazing bars removed from windows of number 92.

Door: In bays one and four, similar, pilastered, with triangular pediments. Number 91 has a semicircular architraved fanlight with radial tracery.

A neat pair of 18th to early 19th century character. They were both owned by William West (*qv*) in the 1830s. In 1878 James Nash (*qv*) lived at 91, John Nichols (*qv*) at 92, which was sold as 'the residence of the late John Nichols' in

1911 for £450 to A. G. Mardon, according to a press report. Ernest Heath, corn dealer, was at 91 in 1915. Traces of a shopfront having been here can be seen. The front is said to have been restored by Robert Kingham by 1932. At least the upper floor was built after 90 West Street (*qv*), and numbers 91-92 were almost certainly once one house, converted into two before 1818.

Number 90 West Street was described in 1775 as being bounded on its east by the house of Little and William Holdaway; in 1781 as 'sometime since of William Little and Henry Holdaway and now of Richard Moth and Samuel Elmer (*qqv*); in 1782 of William Godwin and Samuel Elmer; in *c* 1784 as occupied by Godwin but the property of John Jolly; and in 1796 as in the occupation of Widow Godwin and the property of Daniel Bristow the younger (*qv*). See also 93-95 West Street.

In 1771, property is the subject of an unidentified deed (referred to under 93-95 West Street) relating a transaction concerning Elizabeth Hearn (*qv*) and describing what appear to be 91 and 92 as two houses in the tenure of James Rivers and William Godwin. Thomas Buddle, probable builder, sold property here, or very near, to Daniel Bristow.

93 (to 95) WEST STREET
(Hollest, Mason and Nash)

A symmetrical brick built and tiled house of five bays and two floors, with eaves supported by paired brackets.

Fenestration: Ground floor, four two-pane-wide recessed sashes; First floor, five similar, in bay three, three panes wide.

Door: In bay three, pilastered, triangular pediment supported by scrolled brackets, above rectangular fanlight with curved tracery.

Other features: To the east a modern extension — number 94. Number 95 stood where The Hart road now is.

Number 94 bears a facial resemblance to 104 West Street (*qv*) especially in its door. The Ministry of Housing's list dates 94 late 18th century. Pevsner and Nairn do not disagree. Where 94 stands was, until about sixty years ago, a small house with its door on the east side, and where the road is now was a good pair, appearing to be two houses totalling five bays on two floors. They were finished in stucco, with a low parapet, contained no fewer than seven 1-3-1 sash windows, and had gone by 1895. They had been owned earlier by William Alexander (*qv*). From at least 1878 until 1891 this was the address of Frederick Tobias Robinson. It was in 1904 that Mason and Stevens submitted, and the Council approved, plans for the new road here. 94 was badly damaged by fire in the mid-1940s. Hence change in roofing tiles. The east end of the existing building is modern.

From this point some speculation is needed to establish more of 93. A single deed, without address or tithe number but dated 1818, is in the Surrey Archaeological Collection, Guildford. It would appear to relate directly to 91-93 West Street, although no definite claim is made here to that effect. For the purpose of this article it is tentatively taken to do so, reasons being stated below.

In 1818 property in Farnham was described in the deed as 'All that freehold messuage [93?] erected by the late Thomas Buddle where formerly stood the messuage then occupied by James Rivers and twelve-hole kiln and store . . . now in the occupation of William West also that freehold messuage converted into two separate messuages [91 and 92?] adjoining the first formerly occupied by William Godwin now of John Eggar, surveyor, and Ann Goodeve, widow'. All these premises were bound on the south by West Street, the house of the late George Alexander being on the east, the house and garden of John Townsend on the west. It appears that Buddle demolished and rebuilt the house and kilns in about 1781, and that in 1818 William West was in occupation.

In 1817 number 90 West Street (*qv*) was bought by John Townsend. He died in 1825 (which period covers the date of the above deed). In 1839 William West owned 91, 92, 93 West Street and William Alexander (*qv*) owned 94 and 95. See also 91 and 92 West Street for evidence allocating the deed to this group.

Thomas Buddle (*d* 1808) owned property in Farnham, farms and Halimote Manor, Aldershot. He left his real estate to Elizabeth Hill (a child), the daughter of Charlotte Wheeler (late single woman), wife of John Wheeler, a carpenter, of Badshot. Property in West Street of an Elizabeth Hill was sold in 1818. Thomas Buddle's name appeared in a list of Gentry of 1791-6.

A symmetrical brick built and tile shop on three floors with gable facing the street.

Fenestration: Ground floor, a shopfront contained between doors, with marbled fascia overall; First floor, two recessed sashes; Second floor, two casements.

At the time of writing this building and its neighbour were unoccupied pending demolition. 96 was built as a house after fire had consumed part of the former building in 1893. Before alteration to serve as a shop, the ground floor was of two bays — a door on the west, a square, architraved window on the right. The whole lower front was cement-cased to within three brick courses of first floor sills. Stapley (*qv*) is said to have been responsible. See illustration of the house previously here. This house and its neighbour were owned by Miss Lucy Ward (*b* 1796*) *c* 1840. Both were then described as houses. For many years before the fire Richard King was occupant. See 97 West Street.

96 and 97 WEST STREET. A partly conjectural reconstruction of their appearance before 96 was rebuilt.

An asymmetrical three-bay shop on two floors, a dormer above. The front is plastered; construction basically timber with tiled roof. Eaves are supported by a moulded and modillioned cornice.

Fenestration: Ground floor, in bay one a square window. In bay three a multipaned shop window with cornice above containing also the door in bay three; First floor, two wide-boxed casements; Above, a flat topped dormer with casements.

Once part of 96 West Street (*qv*). See also illustration. This house appears once to have been jettied and to have received a thoroughgoing face-lift early in the 18th century. The eaves cornice, delicate and rich, is a rarity in Farnham, but very similar to another at 6 East Street.

In the last two decades of the 19th century James Smith, carrier, corn, hay and straw dealer, advertised from this address. The property is known as part of Timberclose.

1 0 1   A N D   1 0 2   W E S T   S T R E E T
(Between, Factory Yard)

This backwater, so near the town centre, has not lost all its early 19th century light industrial air. Background history is noted under 102 and 103 West Street, as are some details concerning Arundell Place, built by Daniel Batchelour (*qv*) in 1812.

Beyond these cottages is a later development which took place largely in what was left of the half acre of hop land which John Lidbitter (*b* 1782*), haircloth factor, bought with the cottages in 1831. By the later '30s, the whole site had been developed and the north enclosed with a range of industrial buildings. The north end had been reopened, as now, by 1870.

It was in these premises that Lidbitter (*qv*) developed his sailcloth, wagon and rick cloth and hop bag factory. He transferred from premises in Castle Street and lived at 5 Castle Street (*qv*). The family seems not to have been in Farnham very long. He was not born here (Elizabeth, *b*1821* and Mary, *qv*, *b* 1826*, were). Anne, wife of a John Lidbitter, died in 1834, and John, husband of an Anne Lidbitter, died in 1843; not necessarily the same pair, nor John, the haircloth factor, but no trace of him has been found after that date.

After what we gather to have been a prosperous venture, which sold most of its ware in London, the factory had closed well before the end of the century. A number of the buildings were then converted to cottages, some possibly as early as the 1860s.

The property was offered for sale in 1899 when part was described as comprising a brick built and slated twelve-hole hop kiln and large oast and store for dried hops, with another store for green hops and large warehouse. The purchaser was to pay £12 extra for a haircloth and bagging machine.

102 AND 103 WEST STREET
(Ranger's Drapery Store)

A pair of shops totalling three bays on three floors, built of brick and stone, tile and slate, the front stuccoed and painted.

These once matched the pair 100 and 101 on the west side of Factory Yard entrance. They were built in 1812 and formed part of a speculative building scheme which included Factory Yard (qv). Front doors were in a single central opening, with a common segmental fanlight; in effect rather like the one still at 46-47 Downing Street (qv). Mixed building materials are characteristic of the period. The age of brick for specuative building was passing. Mid-19th century examples of building with chalk, flint and ironstone can be found, especially in East Street, on back and side walls.

In 1690 the property — a house, barn, malthouse, stable and hop ground — is mentioned in an indenture concerning John Forder and Richard Solme. A John Forder had been Bailiff of Farnham, and one of that name once owned the land in East Street, later the site of Sturt's wheelwright's shop. The John Forder, gentleman, who died in 1657 held copyhold lands at Runwick and Wrecclesham and was buried near his wife Judith in the South Chancel of St. Andrew's. Their children were Judith, Elizabeth and Petronel. His mother was also an Elizabeth Forder, his brothers-in-law William Terry and Edmund Fauchin, gentleman. Shortly before his death John Forder bought lands from John Yalden and Mrs. Petronel Brabant.

By 1811 development was taking place in what is now Factory Yard as six messuages and a blacksmith's shop were behind the house. Between February 1811 and December 1812 Daniel Batchelour, carpenter, had pulled down the malthouse, barn and stable and had built in their place four messuages with wash-house and brew-house behind, and at the south end of the half-acre of hop land eight cottages as well. These twelve buildings were 100-103 West Street and the cottages named Arundell Place (dated 1812). Like so many speculations of that time, Batchelour's failed. He was soon declared bankrupt.

In 1816 details of sale were published for 102 and 103 — 'two newly erected dwelling houses suitable for the reception of genteel families. Handsome stucco and sashed front, slated, at short distance from The Royal Military College' (qv). Later John Lidbitter (qv) bought the back premises, and Mary Dudman bought the two houses for £660. She occupied one and John Nichols (qv, b 1803*) the other.

Mary Dudman (b 1798* in London) was principal of a Ladies' Seminary in West Street by 1826. That was ten years before she bought these houses. She died in 1867. By 1878 Miss Caroline Biddick had her Ladies' School at 102. In 1909 the houses were still private dwellings, being very soon afterwards converted to shops. 102 became Ernest Ranger's, pawnbroker, and 103 Lionel H. Smith's hairdressing saloon. Four cottages 'known as Arundell Place', late of Thomas Burningham (qv), were sold to a Kingham in 1879 for £200. They then produced a gross rent of £24 10s. p.a.

104A WEST STREET (Surrey and Hants News)

A two-bay building on three floors, symmetrical and built of red brick, with a slate roof.

Fenestration: Ground floor, windows behind two brick arches (with a square free-standing central shaft) are integrated with doorways in a wooden façade; First floor, windows are immediately above, also behind the pillar; Second floor, single recessed sashed window centred near the top of the arches, on the outer main wall surface. It retains a valance shield.

Other features: The most striking part of the building is its shopfront with four arches. Those at either end contain doors, and the others sash windows with half-round heads. Below windows is shallow panelling, and above, a decorative cornice. Spandrels and architraves are mounted with delicate low reliefs of urns, cables and ribbonlike foliations.

Built as a malthouse by Charles Attfield (qv), this building was converted to business premises and part of a flat in 1951. Before alteration it had been the store of 104 West Street, with which it should really be considered historically if not altogether structurally. At a guess the front of 104A is of about 1840 origin. The 'new' shopfront must be placed about 1800. Before opening during reconstruction the blind brick arcades were recessed four inches, and two small, wide-framed, squarish windows were contained by each arch. Opening these arches has altered appearances greatly, giving the present giraffe-house-like proportions. It has also provided the town with a unique architectural feature. Outbuildings adjoining the back of 104A were demolished in the late 1950s.

History and associations of the shopfront are complicated and not completely explained. When many coats of paint had been removed from the soffit of the east door-frame (the west door section was added in Farnham to match the other) the name Birch was found. There is, then, no doubt that the front is an old one and that it once came from Birch's premises.

In Room 48 of the Victoria and Albert Museum is a similar shopfront. It has been there since 1926, and came from 15 Cornhill, the pastry shop of Samuel Birch (*b* 1757, *d* 1841). He sold the business to Ring and Brymer in 1836. 'Birch Birch and Co.' was painted on the fascia.

Birch's premises were demolished by Lloyds Bank in 1926, the front at the Victoria and Albert being presented to the museum by Lord Kenyon. A decorative iron grille fills the under-window portion.

The Farnham shopfront was bought in about 1951 from a well-known Isleworth dealer, who for many years had used it as part of his office.

The question now arises, which front is the genuine Birch one? We have knowledge that the Farnham edition bore Birch's name, and it is certain that the Victoria and Albert Museum front came from Cornhill (it is fully documented). So we can presume either that at one time Birch had two such fittings on the same premises (say, one at the front and another at the back or side), or that Birch had other premises in his name elsewhere and used a standard shopfront as people do today. But there is no evidence of the latter. So for want of a better explanation we must accept the former. Pevsner and Nairn presume it to be a 19th century copy.

The recent reconstruction work of 104A was under the supervision of Harold Falkner.

As this building has been so closely associated with 104, comments of a general nature appear under that head. It did, though, have a separate existence in that at various times in the 19th century it was used as a warehouse for rick cloths, hop bags, army tents and tarpaulins.

Remote though the association is, it is of interest to note
that Samuel Birch combined the work of pastry cook and
playwright. 'The Adopted Child', 1791, is one of his works.
He was also Lord Mayor of London (1814-15) and his son,
Samuel, was keeper of the Department of Oriental Antiquities
at the British Museum.

104   WEST   STREET

A symmetrical five-bay house on two main floors, built of
brick heading bond at the front. It is parapeted, with panels.
The roof is tiled and has a double east-west ridge.

Fenestration: Ground floor, four sashes, recessed, three
panes wide; First floor, as below them; Above, there are flat-
topped dormer windows.

Door: In bay three. Plain consoles support a triangular
pediment. There is a rectangular fanlight with curvilinear
tracery in wood.

North elevation: Partly rendered with cement on the
ground floor. Cement is also used for doorcase pilasters.
These are topped by a simple, bracketed, flat wooden
canopy. There is no parapet, but a bay window east of the
door.

Interior: Inside, the ground floor is roughly symmetrical
in plan. Front west ground-floor room: Panelled, and finished
with a cornice of plain modillions alternating with rosettes,
all of wood. Front east ground floor: Between the windows
is part of the capital of a cast-iron shaft embedded in the wall.
Throughout the house there is a considerable amount of
timber framing, particularly towards the back, both floors.
A semicircular wooden arch divides the hall and passage.
Soffits are panelled and have wooden flowers applied. Above
is a deep entablature with keyblock.

The house is of two main builds — one in timber and one
in brick. The later encases the earlier which is exposed only
in some secondary inside walls. The conversion probably took
place in the first part of the 18th century, if one can judge
by details. For example, the back porch, heaviness of some
glazing bars, the general character of panelling, doors and
hinges. Late 17th century has been suggested, but the façade
is certainly of 18th century design.

A second, less important, alteration was made in 1947-8
when the house was converted into three flats. Dormer
windows were added, an upper staircase inserted, and the
top floor was connected with 104A (*qv*). A cottage at the
back was reconditioned and its shopfront fitted.

It is not known if part of the house itself was ever a shop, but the cast-iron column referred to above is now in the thickness of the front wall. In that room a rectangle containing both windows is recessed and it is within this recess that the shaft-head and capital can be seen. From inside a closed-up shopfront is suggested. Outside, the corresponding brickwork does not immediately corroborate this evidence. However, around these two windows the bricks are very slightly browner, and windowheads are of a different coloured brick from their partners. These two east windows are headed by seventeen larger bricks with relatively complex jointing in places. Their opposite numbers are of nineteen bricks, of different shape. It would seem that the room was used as a shop during the third quarter of the 19th century by Charles Attfield and then carefully restored to its earlier condition by George McDonald. (See 20 Castle Street, which he also owned and may have been similarly restored.) The north side bay window is pre-1874.

At 104 the under surfaces of sills to ground floor windows in bays four and five are different from all others on this front, both floors.

The first-known owner of this house was Robert Bicknell (*qv*), whose place of abode in 1719 was given as The Temple, but the property changed hands several times by 1800, when William Dowden (*qv*), wine merchant and grocer, sold to the Attfields (*qv*). Charles Attfield (*b* 1811*), maltster and corn-dealer, had kilns at Beaver's Yard (*qv*). His family at 104 West Street included Henrietta (*b* 1811*), his wife, and a son, Ernest (*b* 1848*). Other Attfields not mentioned elsewhere in this guide include Francis (*b* 1793*), carpenter, of East Street, and his son Francis (*b* 1831*), and Robert (*b* 1791*), butcher, of about 73 West Street. His children included Charles and Robert, also butchers, and a carpenter, Frederick Attfield. Nathaniel Attfield (*b* 1803*) and his son Nathaniel (*b* 1840) lived about 26 Castle Street. He was described in 1851 as gamekeeper.

In 1838 Robert Lamport (*qv*), hop planter, sold the adjoining hop kiln and store (104A) to Sarah Attfield, who, with her son Charles (*qv*) and his children, occupied it until 1875, when it was sold by Ernest Attfield to George Mc-Donald (*qv*). Sarah Attfield was a corn dealer and hop planter. Charles built the malting which replaced the kiln and store. McDonald used the malthouse as part of his tarpaulin and rick cloth factory (see 104A). In 1885 he was the manager of Metcalf and Sons, sack manufacturers, of West Street. (Did they take over when Lidbitter *qv* died?) His father, John

McDonald, a gardener, owned 20 Castle Street, and George was landlord of 23 West Street (qv) as well as 104. He was born in 1834, died in 1904, and was responsible for Mc-Donald's Almshouses (qv). After his death the house passed to the Hart family (cousins), who owned it until 1946.

The Bicknells were a prominent local family. One is even responsible, indirectly, for the many houses we admire today, for it is recorded that he introduced hops (and thereby fortunes) to Farnham in about 1597. A Mr. Bicknell told Aubrey in about 1670 that the first grower in Farnham was his father. The family had much to do with running the town and as their names appear so frequently as bailiffs or jurors, in accounts, on documents and in public records some are noted here. Robert junior occupied 104 West Street in 1695, his father living at the same time probably at 99. One Robert was a tanner. Robert, son of Robert, was Christened in 1701; Susan, wife of Robert, died in 1693, and a Mr. Robert three years later. Robert senior was taxed on four, and Robert Bicknell junior on seven hearths in 1664. William Bicknell of Badshot had at least two sons (John and Josiah). A William Bicknell died in 1696. One of this name was a 17th century surgeon. The will of John Bicknell, written in 1633, made provision for teaching 'six poor and mean men's children'.

In 1783 Martha Bicknell married John Baker. George Bicknell was Christened in 1698. It was Joan, the daughter of Robert Bicknell, who married Christopher Gary (qv) in 1711. They had a daughter, Jane.

105 AND 106 WEST STREET
(Lombard House and Rangers Furnishing Stores)

A pair of brick and tile houses of three main bays and three floors each. 106 is converted to a shop. Both have blind windows in central upper bays with four-pane-wide fenestration above ground floor level.

Once substantial town dwellings, they both have much in common with The Queen's Head (qv) façade, and the five-centre arched door of 105 is closely related to one at 5 Castle Street (qv). These West Street fronts date perhaps about the 1830s. Number 106 appears to have had all windows altered. The present shopfront was fitted in 1906 and other alterations were made for Ernest Ranger by architect Alfred Guyer (qqv). At the east end was a gateroom leading to the stable yard behind.

In 1813 number 105 was described as being late of Mrs. Mary Manwaring and now of George Trimmer (*qv*). Later, if not then, he owned both. By 1840 they were Ann Trimmer's (*b* 1796*). She lived at 106. Another Ann Trimmer, daughter of John, died in 1761, and John, son of William and Mary Trimmer, died in 1782. Other Trimmer deaths not mentioned elsewhere in this guide include Thomas, 1763; Elizabeth (widow), 1775; Susanna (widow), 1790; James, 1789. Trimmer marriages include Robert to Elizabeth Scott (1766); Elizabeth to William Shotter (1767); William to Sarah Gardener (1768); and Lydia to Richard Paine (1781). An Elizabeth Trimmer, wife of Robert, died in 1803. Harry Lovelace, pawnbroker and furniture dealer, was in business here for many years later in the 19th century. He was succeeded in 1894 by Ernest Ranger whose business still thrives here. Henry Hayes (*b* 1809* in Lambeth), also a pawnbroker, was here about mid-century.

*   1 0 7   W E S T   S T R E E T   (G.P.O.)

A two-floor building of three bays with sashed dormer windows above, plate-glass windows below, and a slate roof.

Once a house of early 19th century outward character with symmetrical façade. Upper windows were 1-3-1 sashes in bays one and three, and a recessed three-pane-wide sash in bay two. The 1-3-1s were repeated below, with a wide doorway between them. Its case was recessed and topped by a wide-radius fanlight with radial tracery. The façade had been encased in grey cement before the Post Office conversion.

Behind was a large pleasure garden, now built upon. Access to this, the stables and carriage house, was under the gateroom of 110 (*qv*).

Property occupied in the 18th century by John Hollest and Robert Trimmer (*qv*) was described as '. . . . all that capital messuage and tenement formerly into two tenements divided on the north side of West Street'. As yet not positively identified, this changed hands together with 108-110 West Street, and the estate included half an acre of garden '. . . long since walled in'. Trimmers certainly owned adjoining property. Number 107 was, in 1840, occupied by John Hollest (b 1791*) and in 1839 was described as being in the ownership of William Hollest. John Hollest was a friend sufficiently close to Thomas Beddus Mill (*qv*) for Mill to leave Hollest's children a considerable remembrance. The children were George Edward, Charles William, John Leigh, William and Mary Hollest.

William Hollest (*b* 1811*), solicitor, lived at 90 West Street (*qv*) in about 1840. His wife was Catrina (*b* 1811*), his children Catrina (*b* 1841*) and Jane (*b* 1846*). In 1841 John and Mary Hollest (*b* 1796*) were at 107 and in their time the large garden ran behind it and 108, through to 110 West Street. So it seems probable that 107 was in fact the 'capital messuage'. Later William and Catrina were at 107.

The Post Office was once called Leigh House. Thomas Leigh, of 9 Castle Street (*qv*), had a daughter Mary (*b* 1719*, *d* 1789) who married William Willis. Thomas' grand-daughter was Mary Leigh Willis. In 1783 she married a John Hollest. This would account for the house name and also help the case for 107 having been the 'capital messuage' above. In John Leigh Hollest is another clue.

A John Hollest the elder died in 1818 aged 86. His daughter married James Webb of Wickham who died in 1852 aged 85. Jane Webb, a widow and annuitant, born at Chichester in 1767, lived in Castle Street at the same house as her unmarried niece and great-niece, both named Mary Hollest (*b* 1793*, *b* 1821*). The Hollests were solicitors in Farnham for many years. The name is retained in Hollest, Mason and Nash. W. Hollest, solicitor, died in 1880.

Leigh House has been the G.P.O. for about 50 years. This was previously at 115 West Street (*qv*) and before that at two locations in The Borough. The conversion of 107 West Street is said to have been carried out by Cox, assistant to Paxton Watson (*qv*), and later an architect of Thames House.

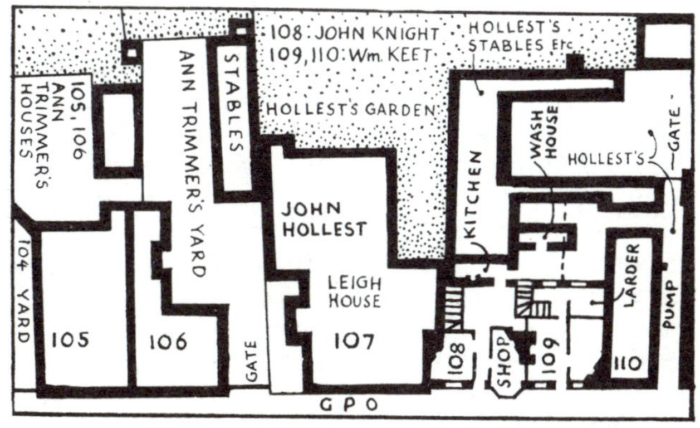

1840. Properties, which include what was once The Swan Inn, as they were at that time. 108-110 were bound by Leigh House (G.P.O.) and its premises on three sides. As the east front room of 109 was described as a parlour and its west front room as a sitting room, 110 was presumably Keet's shop. Internal doors once connected all three of these shops.

108 WEST STREET (The Furniture Mart)

On two main floors, with cement-clad upper façade containing three-pane-wide recessed sash windows with architraves. The roof is slated.

This was at one time part of 109 and 110 (*qqv*), having been subdivided before 1687. A new shopfront was fitted and internal alterations were made in 1960-1961.

Until recently here was Andrews' music shop, Farnham branch of a business established in Guildford in 1857 by Thomas Andrews, who died in 1895. The business was sold to employees and it carried on in Farnham for another 65 years.

109 WEST STREET (Pullinger's)

A shop on two main floors with brick front under a tiled roof. A dormer window is contained by the south-facing centrally placed gable — at right angles to the main ridge.

Fenestration: Ground floor, a double shopfront; First floor, three recessed three-pane-wide sash windows; a casement with lozenge leading above.

The main ridge suggests continuity with 110, but the building is not so obviously a part of 108, which it once was. Inside — upstairs and in the roof — there are still visible signs of their direct connection which is borne out conclusively by documentary evidence.

These three once formed The Swan Inn. It was a house of considerable antiquity, for it had already closed and had been divided into three separate houses by the 1680s, though operating in 1604. An account of that year, giving sources and amounts of Farnham Corporation Income, records ' . . . Dewes which hath been acostomly payed to the baylleffs of the borough and towne of ffaernham, beyond the memory of any man that now liveth, as aniall rents always retained, as ffolloweth . . . For the 4 Inns . . . 28s. 0d. That is to saye, of the George 7s. 0d. Of the Swan 7s. 0d.' The other two were The White Hart and The Antelope (*qqv*).

In 1652 The Swan is still mentioned by name in a deed of demise between (1) Thomas Woodroffe of Poyle and Lettice Woodroffe, of Poyle, widow, and (2) George Woodroffe of Pepperharrow, Thomas' brother. Real estate included the manors of Wicke, Claygate, Fermans, the rectory and parsonage of Chobham, the capital messuage of Badshott (*qv*) and the Warren, and The Swan, with all barns, buildings, stables, ' . . . and the croft of land now a hop garden to the said messuage belonging', and Waydowne Mills, alias Mead Mill (Weydon Mill, *qv*) together with 23 acres at Dorking and other land in Hampshire and Camarthen. A considerable estate. By an agrement of 1647 all this had been leased to Lettice by Thomas. It passed to Richard White, from Sir George Woodroffe, in 1687. The property probably included 107 West Street (*qv*) as well.

By 1840 two shops were already here. 108 was still a dwelling, owned and occupied by John Knight (*b* 1766*) and Maria (*b* 1796*), with its east room converted to a shop by fitting a bay window there. Maria Knight (*b* 1789), spinster, was at this house eleven years later. At the same time William Keet had his barber's shop, presumably at 110, as he lived at 109 which had not been converted to a shop in 1840. There were other Swan Inns (*qv*) and pubs in Farnham after this one had closed.

In 1795 the west part of the divided property was occupied by James Harding and William Watts (*qqv*) as tenants. William Keet , hairdresser, was under-tenant. It was probably this William Keet's son (*b* 1791*) who died in 1841 leaving his wife Ellen to carry on the business. William (*b* 1821*) and James (*b* 1826*) were hairdressers, too. Ann Keet (*b* 1761*) died in 1843 leaving the property to her son William. There were plenty of other Keets including Henry (*b* 1831*) and Ann (*b* 1825*), George Keet, Thomas and Charles.

Ellen Keet was described by about 1850 as stationer and perfumer; not a complete change as William had also been a stationer in the '20s, and it is this side of the business which continues one hundred and forty years later, in the same family, as William Keet junior (*d* 1887*) had a daughter, Emily, who married George Pullinger (*qv*), grocer. The property passed to her. This would appear, then, to be Farnham's longest-established business still at its original premises. Williams' and Borelli's (*qqv*), both late 18th century, moved since their beginning. William Keet was in business as a hairdresser by 1790.

Ann Pullinger, widow, died in 1843; Ann, daughter of William and Ann, in 1801. William Keet was partner-publisher of Milford's 'Farnham and its Borough' and he gave 5 guineas towards building South Street ten years later. Some time before 1798 a William Keet lived at a house adjoining the east of 29 East Street (*qv*). He had acquired the prefix 'late' by 1819, so it was presumably a descendant William Keet who still owned and occupied the cottage twenty years later.

217

110 WEST STREET (Farnham Dairy)

A brick built and tiled shop on two floors. The front is parapeted. There is one principal bay and a gateroom adjoining the east.

At one time a part of 108 and 109 (*qqv*) from which it was subdivided before 1687. It was probably reconnected with 109 during the earlier part of the 19th century. Number 110 is a timber framed house of which a substantial part remains embedded in later fabric. It is unusual for Farnham in having a complex-chamferred arched tie-beam and for retaining curved wind-braces. Principal posts remain. Something of its construction can be seen from under the gateroom. It is a building which, with 108 and 109, is worth thorough investigation.

111 WEST STREET (German, Addy & Co.)

A brick built house on three floors with slate roof. On the ground floor, two bays; above, one bay.

Fenestration: Ground floor, bay one, a bow shopfront; First floor, a 1-3-1 sash; Second floor, a recessed two-pane-wide sash with stone architrave and arched head.

Door: In bay two, pilastered, with scrolled brackets supporting a flat hood.

Built c 1803 for Richard Attfield (*qv*) on the site of a house which was one of three on the sites of which he rebuilt. Where the other two were is now 112 West Street (*qv*). All were demolished early in 1799 and seem to have been completely rebuilt by him.

Number 111 appears to have had a floor added in the later 19th century and a shopfront has been fitted for many years, the present one quite recently.

19th century window fashions (see 112) may have here another variation if the first floor window is original. It indicates the sash box slimming trend very well, only three or four years separating the date of this from those next door. Yet there is quite a difference in the detailing and area of woodwork to glass. The result is more like 112's when they had received their special treatment.

Clement Borelli (*qv*), silversmith, was here by 1840 and five years later he and Donato (*qv*) advertised as silversmiths of West Street. By the early '50s Clement, unmarried, probably lived at about 117 East Street, while Donato was still here with his wife, two daughters and daughter-in-law Charlotte Edwards (*b* 1831*). The house appears to have belonged to the family until 1860, having been sold by James Longhurst (*qv*), cheesemonger, in 1853.

As a shop, it served longest as a jeweller's and a watch seller's, first of Harrington's (who took on a seven-year lease from George Pullinger *qv* in 1885 at £30 p.a.), then for many years as James Dann's. The continuity was interrupted at the turn of the century when A. S. Crow, Ladies' Outfitter, was here.

1 1 2   W E S T   S T R E E T   (Biggs Ltd.)

A symmetrical brick built shop on two main floors with tiled mansard roof and eaves with paired modillions.

Fenestration: Ground floor, a triple bow window below an entablature supported by six scrolled brackets; First floor, bays one and three a flush 1-3-1 sash, bay two a three-pane-wide flush wide-boxed sash; Above, two flat-topped dormer windows with sashes.

Door: One at either side of the shopfront, under a common entablature.

Built between March and August 1799 for Richard Attfield (*qv*). It replaces the eastern two of three houses which he bought in the February from John Manwaring (*qv*). Earlier, all three had been part of the Manwaring estate and were handed on with The Lion and Lamb (*qv*) and The Hart hopground. The third house was where 111 West Street (*qv*) now stands, and was rebuilt by Attfield a little later.

The front of 112 has seen two major changes: First, *c* 1925, when the premises became Chilcott's millinery shop. A plate-glass double shopfront was inserted. It was replaced in about 1950 by the present more respectful one, to the design of G. M. Aylwin.

This is an interesting building. It is one of a scattered group of smaller houses, most of which are now shops. To be able to date a house so accurately is a rare experience. There is another similar (114-115 East Street, *qv*), 'newly built' in 1792. Another of the type is in The Borough and some more houses are similar but retain a parapet. The type is extremely neat, with tightly fitting eaves and flat-roofed dormer windows just below the roof angle. Windows are generous in size (1-3-1 or four panes wide usually) and often have wide sash boxes, sometimes recessed. Eaves are usually modillioned. We have three different modillion treatments in 112 West Street, 15 and 16 The Borough, with paired, regular, and alternating twins and triplets respectively.

At 112 the door, with simple flat hood supported by

upright consoles, was symmetrically placed; similar to the one at number 111. Windows of the house indicated a fashion trend towards a lighter touch. Earlier, the west ground-floor window was like the ones now above. On the east was one of similar pattern, but with thinner box, recessed quite deeply and apparently fitted later. When the 1950s restoration was being carried out it was found that the first floor window boxes were actually just as they are now, although some time after building, carefully fitted brick slices had been used to cover all of the wide-boxed sides except for a narrow reveal.

It is a fashion recapitulating what had been a national development a century before, although the wide, flush box seems never completely to have lost favour in Farnham during the 18th century. There was, after all, no law, as there was in London, against its use. And even there, it appears that they were often used where not very conspicuous.

Richard Attfield was a saddler and harness maker. He occupied this house for about 20 years and had a shop next door, at 113. The Attfields contributed quite a lot between them to Farnham business life in the 18th and 19th centuries. Sarah, Charles and Nathaniel were corn dealers and seedsmen, William a hop planter. James was a collar maker (and there was a collar maker's over Richard's harness shop). Charles and Sarah owned 104 and 104A West Street (*qqv*), where he built his malthouse. James and Elizabeth were maltsters, too. A Francis Attfield was landlord of The Marlborough Head (*qv*); Robert, a butcher in West Street. The whole of Beaver's Yard (*qv*), with its kiln, cottages, barns, malthouses and stores, was Charles Attfield's after the army had left. In 1841 a Francis Attfield (b 1790s) was a carpenter living in East Street. Probably his wife was Jane (*b* 1796*). His children were Ann (*b* 1821*), Jane (*b* 1826*), Caroline (*b* 1829*) and Francis.

From Richard Attfield 112 West Street passed to John Wells (*qv*), in whose family it remained for 99 years. Wells at that time was a cordwainer. His and Attfield's affinity of trades may help to account for their occupying the same house. For a short time in the mid-19th century a family of Hampshire saddlers lived here. They included John Whorord (*b* 1777*) and his son John (*b* 1813*). There was a William Wells (*qv*) in the same trade over a century before John Wells moved to 112 West Street in 1826, and a John and Richard Wells were leather dressing in Farnham well into the 19th century. Charles Stroud (*b* 1831* at Lymington) had lodgings here when he was a young teacher, unmarried.

Extensive commercial premises built of brick, timber and tile. A central archway gives access to the courtyard — flanked by other business premises.

1537 is cut in a brick plaque, now in the archway wall. This has been claimed to be the date of building. Although not in situ, not an unlikely date. But this alone is flimsy evidence. The present building was nearly all the result of a reconstruction (on the original lines) by John Kingham, about 1921.

Before rebuilding here was a stuccoed façade of Regency character (see page 133), two Doric half-columns flanking the arch, a Venetian window above and miniature iron balcony on to which it opened. There were two floors, eight bays, low-pitched roof and eaves supported by widely spaced pairs of brackets.

An inn holding this position through the 16th, 17th and 18th centuries must have a rich history, seeing the coming and going of both the corn and the hop booms. Little was written and documentary evidence is scarce. However, a number of new facts have come to light recently which tell something of the architectural changes but little of the life of this place which was once called The White Hart. One has to be especially careful in allocating data as there was another White Hart (qv) in Castle Street, also The Hart elsewhere, and what is now The Lion and Lamb was also often referred to just as The Hart — like the fields behind it.

This White Hart changed its name to The Lion and Lamb between 1692 and 1720. In 1668 Nathaniel Wroth, a London grocer, was party to a transaction with his brother George, a Farnham linen draper, concerning The White Hart in West Street. Although an inn, it had been divided into several tenements also. Shortly afterwards Nathaniel Wroth was living here with his brother. George Wroth then bought the property, together with a barn and two acres of hops. A widow, Jane Wroth, had been charged tax on eight hearths in 1664, and Mary Wroth died in 1704. She was, like Dionisius and Elizabeth, a child of John Wroth. A Mary Wroth, spinster, was married to Thomas Holford, Esq. of Newbrough, in Cheshire, at Elstead in 1683, and in 1593 or 1594 George Wroth was charged Lay Subsidiary Assessment on his goods in Farnham.

The Manwarings were not far behind. Like most of Farnham's choice properties, this was once of their possession. John Manwaring (qv), tanner, bought from Elizabeth Wroth

(widow) about 1692, the inn, the hop ground and what is now
111 and 112 West Street (*qqv*). He occupied also another five
acres of hops previously in the tenure of Elizabeth Wroth, the
land of Martha Smith marking the northern boundary of his
newly acquired estate. From James Manwaring (*qv*) it passed
to John Manwaring, his nephew, in 1720 and was still 'a
principal inn' in 1791 — the year in which a Friendly Society
was instituted here.

William Cootes, landlord, received a share of the King's
Bounty (*qv*) in 1757. After the close of the 18th century
Richard Attfield (*qv*) had his saddler's shop at the west end
of the premises.

In the 1830s The Independent, The Tally Ho, and The
New Times made regular calls and departures, at a time when
Thomas Matthews was landlord and the owners were women-
folk of three leading and connected families. They were
Elizabeth Paine, Mary Chitty and Jane Manwaring. The
Matthews', who seem to have established, and ran, the West
Street Brewery here, were in occupation and then ownership
for most of what remained of the century. A lot of new
building was done in their time. In 1907 it was offered for
sale; then again in 1910, as the freehold of Harriett Matthews.
It was bought by Kingham's (*qv*) who reconstructed what had
rapidly become a very shabby and ill-treated building.

The Wroths had been in Farnham for some time before
the first-mentioned indenture, James having been a mercer
here. There were at least two Thomas Matthews', one born
1786 to 1788, the other in 1833. Sarah (*b* 1792*) was
Thomas the elder's wife, Ann (*b* 1837*) his daughter, and
Thomas, junior, his son. Thomas Mathews senior and junior
bought The Duke of Cambridge (*qv*) in 1855. Thomas
(*b* 1833*?) and Harriett, his wife, sold The Spinning Wheel
(*qv*) in 1865. The family probably came to Farnham from
Bromley.

114 AND 115 WEST STREET
(E. W. Langham)

Shop premises of four bays on three floors, built of brick
under a tiled roof. The whole front, including eaves and
roof, of 115 is set back some inches from the façade of 114.
Eaves are supported by a moulded modillion cornice.

Fenestration: Ground floor, bays one and two contain
a double shopfront with central fanlighted doorway, while
in bay four is a recessed sash four panes wide with segmental

head and decorative upper glazing bars; First floor, four recessed sashes three panes wide; Second floor, four similar of three-quarters height.

Door: Also in bay three, with coupled Doric columns, a triangular pediment and semicircular fanlight.

This property was once two houses, but since at least 1744 both have been conveyed together. The shopfront replaced a plate-glass one in about 1952. It was designed by H. Falkner.

In the 1630s houses here were owned by the Hill family who let, among others, to Thomas Budd, Abraham Knight and George Butler.

In 1744 '. . . All those messuages or tenements with the barn stable hopkiln and all other buildings . . . gates gateway gaterooms court next to the [*White*] Hart now called Lion and Lamb later or now in occupation of John Longman and James Monger' formed part of an estate which included also '. . . all that messuage or tenement (now in five tenements) with the barn stable workhouses hopground near to the churchyard on the south side of the street or land there called Church Street leading to the river now or late in the occupation of Richard Crump' (*qv*), and land at Wrecclesham. The whole was held by Thomas Logg (late of Farnham), a tallow chandler, William Harding, staymaker, and others who lived in Alton. From them the property was bought by William Crump (*qv*), fellmonger and glover, for £300.

In 1761 Henry Bradley (*qv*) bought these two houses, malthouse and stables, from Anthony Baker (or Baber), clothier, of Alton. Thirty-five years later this Bradley had moved to Brighton. His namesakes had figured prominently in Farnham life for generations, handling considerable property in the town. Notable is Bristow Bradley (*qv*). George Bradley married Mary Grover in 1756. Another George died in 1706 and his wife, Margaret, the year after.

Having passed through various hands, and been the home of George Knight (*b* 1792*, *d* 1856), the property passed to Thomas Matthews (*qv*), brewer, of the Lion and Lamb, next door. Knight had let part of the pair to James Brockhurst, cabinet maker, but at the time of this transaction those premises had been empty for some time past. Matthews did not hold the property for long after it had been leased to Robert Nichols (*qv*), for 21 years from 1884. Here was the new Post Office, under his mastership. Almost opposite had been another Robert Nichols (*b* 1802*), cordwainer.

Knight, of Downing Street, had married Eleanor Lamport (*b* 1791*, *d* 1859), widow of Thomas Lamport, in about 1834.

Knight probably inherited through his marriage, as not long before T. Lamport had been an occupant of the premises.

Since 1906 E. W. Langham, printers of the Farnham Herald, have been at number 114, having moved in that year from Cambridge Place. They built to the rear in 1924 and expanded to 115 in 1949. The first edition of this newspaper — then called The Weekly Herald — was published on July 2nd, 1892.

1 1 8   W E S T   S T R E E T   (Currys)

A shop of two bays on three floors. Of symmetrical façade, it is brick built and roofed with tile. There are paired modillions under the eaves. Above shopfront level the building is encased in colour-washed cement, with coigns. Sills are supported by brackets.

Fenestration: Ground floor, a plate-glass double shopfront; First floor, three-pane-wide architraved sashes with segmental pediments supported by consoles; Second floor, three-pane wide three-quarter height sashes with architraves.

Built probably about 1850. Until demolition of all but the two upper floors in 1960, here was an almost untouched good 19th century façade with shopfront. This, the ground floor, and additions at the back, have now gone and the cement casing has been colourwashed. Upper parts are still of interest, though. The crisp and confident handling of architraves and pediments is refreshing to find when the embellishments of most buildings of the time tend to be heavy-handed. It is another of the buildings in Farnham which indicate that the grip which Georgian architectural manners had on local builders was only slowly loosening. This manner of handling cement has been used to good effect elsewhere, for example, at 26 West Street (qv). The Victorian shopfront — a central door with a bay window either side, each having six largish panes — although a minor one was an unfortunate loss. No equivalent remains. In 1960 H. Falkner (qv) wrote, 'This is a very important front . . .' 'Of no value,' wrote Pevsner and Nairn a couple of years later.

Sometime before conversion to this shop, the west half contained an arch leading to the rear.

In 1839 the house was owned by John Nichols (qv). Since then it has been a wool shop, servants' registry office, a saddler's, a dentist's, a fancy repository and is now a bicycle shop.

121   WEST   STREET   (International Stores)

A shop of six bays on two main floors, asymmetrical, built
of brick in heading bond, roofed with slate and tile. It has
a recessed panel on the parapet corresponding with each
window below the modillioned cornice. This runs the front's
length. An opening giving rear access is contained in the
westernmost bay.

Fenestration: Ground floor, three shop windows separated by doors; First floor, three-pane-wide sashes having wide
frames flush with the wall surface. There is a blind unglazed
window in bay four.

Other features: Behind the shop is a courtyard (entered
by the side opening) surrounded by outbuildings mainly on
two floors, built of brick and timber, and tiled.

121 and 122 were formerly, as one property, The George
Inn. Behind was a coaching yard, the remains of which
survive. The front is mid-18th century. The property was
divided in 1865.

It is said that on conversion to a shop in the later 1920s,
121 (previously still a house, but used as solicitors'
chambers) contained good plaster ceilings. On the ground
floor, bays two, three, five and six contained windows as
those above. In bay four was the doorcase — pilastered,
pedimented and with semicircular fanlight in the manner of
one now at 88 West Street (*qv*).

Number 122 successfully camouflages its identity as a
pre-Victorian house, at first glance. However, the asymmetry
of 121, and its brickwork running beyond the boundary line
suggest what is confirmed by the inter-relationship of
ground plans — that these were one building.

The George was long-established. In 1604 it had existed
for many years and, with eleven taxable hearths in 1664, it
was one of Farnham's most abundantly fired buildings.
William Clifton, the owner, had to pay tax also on eight
hearths at The Bull. The George Inn is referred to as late as
1763, and in 1757 its holder, Alexander Martin, was one of
38 landlords to receive a share in the King's Bounty (£40 10s.
for Farnham) for quartering troops between September, 1755
and March, 1756.

Andrew Collyer (*qv*) occupied the property in 1788. It
had been the Bradleys' (*qv*). In the same year he bought The
Round House (*qv*) opposite. He was one of at least three
Andrew Collyers and was proprietor of Collyer's Coaches.
This was his house and the family owned it until well into
the 19th century, after which it served as solicitors' chambers

for a century. Andrew (*b* 1796*) and Mary Collyer (*b* 1801) were here in the early 1840s, although the house appears to have been unoccupied in 1851.

The family and its immediate connections illustrate well the custom of naming children with the surnames of others — often Godparents. Within a few decades we come across Andrew Collyer, Henry Bradley, Andrew Bristow, Collyer Bristow, Bristow Bradley, Bristow Collyer, Andrew Collyer Bristow, and then Andrew Alfred Collyer Bristow. Some of these had sons of the same name. Links in the chain were no doubt the result, too, of such marriages as that of John Collyer of Winchester to Martha Bristow of Farnham, in 1756, and of Elizabeth Collyer to William Bristow of Beddington, thirty-three years later. The custom is not, of course, dead. But in Farnham during the 18th-19th centuries it was very common. Other middle-class families complied; particularly the Paines, Manwarings and Chittys.

In 1857 (by which time Collyer was described as 'of Beddington'), a plot of land opposite Weydon Mill (*qv*) was surrendered by Andrew Collyer. On this once stood 'a mansion house', though almost certainly not in his time.

No Collyer was entitled to vote in 1836 and none was a freeholder for many years before 1780. An earlier Andrew, son of Andrew and Priestley Collyer, died in 1780; Priestley, their daughter, in 1791. Thomas, carpenter, died in 1810; Mary, wife of Thomas, in 1790. In that same year Thomas Collyer, widower, married Mary Wells, widow, both of Farnham. Of the earlier Collyers, John was a freeholder in Farnham at the opening of the 18th century, and a Richard Collyer was taxed on three hearths in 1664. Others were living in these times in the Elstead district. Robert Collyer, a Farnham maltster, died *c*. 1657.

Another Farnham 18th century coachmaster was Robert Clinch. Clark and Clinch's Gosport coach used to stop at The Bush. There are several local road accidents recorded, one through the Parish Burial Register entry for James Godfrey, sailor, who was killed in a fall from the Gosport stage in 1797. Travelling outside cost about half the inside fare.

By the late 1830s many coaches served Farnham daily. A précis of the 1839 timetable gives some idea of mobility about a small country town which found itself on an important route. First, The Royal Mail called daily at the Post Office (Mr. Nichols') at 3.15 a.m.; The Independent at The Lion and Lamb (*qv*) at noon; and The New Times and Tally Ho at 3 p.m. (Sunday excepted). The Hampshire Hunt from Southampton called at The Bush (*qv*) at 3.30 p.m., and

The Railway Coach arrived from Alton mid-morning. All of these went on to Farnborough, passengers going then by train to London. Early risers could catch the local coach to Farnborough Station at 7.30 every morning. There were still more — The Red Rover from Southampton to London, The Hero from Oxford to Brighton, The Yeoman from London to Gosport. Coaches and horses were taken aboard the train for Vauxhall at Basingstoke six times daily, if you arrived fifteen minutes before the train.

Carriers went to London: George Lamport (*qv*) from The Borough, William Edwards and Joseph Tolfrew from East Street, several times a week. William Dear carried to Alton; he and Thomas Rogers to Farnborough Station, while a superior sounding van of James Faulkner took both parcels and passengers to Guildford twice a week, and Richard Stewart ran a service betwen Farnham and Reading.

Tennyson is said to have met Emily Sellwood at 121. After an engagement of seventeen years they married and eventually settled near Haslemere in 1868. In 1853 Tennyson wrote, 'The Park here is delicious. . . . What an air after Twickenham! I walked over to Hale and looked into the old premises' — probably the house of Henry Sellwood, his father-in-law.

122 West Street was conveyed by James Shiers to William Wells in 1865. At that time it included the shop tenanted by Daniel Edwards (*qv*, *b* 1794*), plumber and glazier. 121 had been sold shortly before to Robert Nichols (*qv*). Shiers sold to Anthony Williams (*qv*), wine merchant, in 1872. He also occupied kilns and hop buildings at the back of 7 West Street (*qv*).

1 2 2   W E S T   S T R E E T   (Ellis's)

Of two bays on three floors but mainly of brick cement faced, and roofed with slate. A moulding separates upper floors, and the roof is eaved with paired modillions. Corners of the façade are coigned above shop level.

Fenestration: Ground floor, a shopfront; First floor, two bay windows with sloping leaded roofs; Second floor, two recessed sashes with architraves.

Probably refronted and heightened by one floor shortly after 1865, although the ground floor already served as a shop at that time. See 121 West Street, of which it was once a part.

Extensive ground-floor alterations were made in 1962. These included removal of the Victorian shopfront and fitting a new one, together with other facial improvements above. The shop itself was also completely refitted.

Until their sale in 1962 these were the premises of W. W. Williams, wine merchants, said to have been a family business since 1780. Anthony Williams died in 1802. It is probably through him that we have a link with Peckham Williams of Badshot Place (*qv*), for Anthony gave £50, with which to buy a ring, to Elizabeth Jane Penfold (wife of Miles Penfold, *qv*), and to John Williams of Badshot Place. He was a Blissimere hop proprietor. Elizabeth Penfold was also the daughter of the renowned Peckham Williams. Anthony may have been connected with William Marsh (*qv*) as well. Christiana (Yate?) and Elizabeth (Love?), were Anthony's sisters.

The wine business may or may not have been his, but Joseph Richard Williams inherited all Anthony's real estate and he was a wine merchant, like his son, Joseph Thomas Williams. They both inherited from Thomas Beddus Mill (*qv*): Joseph Richard, hop grounds near the Castle, known as The Dell, and meadows in North Mead; Joseph Thomas, Mill's two houses in Castle Street, occupied in 1828 by Thomas Clark and Henry Brooks. Joseph Richard Williams was otherwise known as Witherell or Withall, the son of Ann Witherell, later of Tilford. Mill had an interest in Guildford House as had, later, the Penfolds and the Williams'; the latter also in 45 (*qv*) and 46 Castle Street.

A later Anthony Williams (*b* 1813*) was also a wine merchant, living at 6 West Street until about 1872, when he bought 122 West Street. His wife was Fanny (*b* 1817*), and their children included Eva (*b* 1846*), Anthony (*b* 1848*), William (*b* 1849) and Fanny (*b* 1850). William Williams (*d* 1932) succeeded to the business in 1889. One of the Anthony's, wine merchant, was married to Lucy (*qv*) by 1791, and in 1826 one of the Josephs occupied land in Farnham, the freehold of James Edwards (*qv*). An Anthony Williams later owned property — once Daniel Edward's — to the west of 10 Castle Street.

There were other Farnham Williams' (*qv*). One family was William Williams' (b 1823*), a West Street chemist mid-century. Fanny (b 1822*) was his wife. More, related to the wine merchants, lived in Castle Street.

OUTLYING HOUSES

These have been added to this guide to Farnham houses, although not in the town itself. This has been done for three main reasons — the houses are of architectural interest, have been demolished without previous known published record, or are directly associated with families encountered in the general guide. Badshot House and Dippen Hall went over a century ago, leaving few traces. Knights, Vernons, Coldhams, Mills and Trimmers are associated with others noted. Weybourne House and Waverley, particularly, are of some architectural importance.

THE RANGER'S HOUSE, FARNHAM PARK

A square brick built and tiled house on two floors of five bays. It is plain, has no gutters, a hipped roof, massive oak staircase and is enriched on the back upper floor with five ogee-headed windows with leaded glazing.

The Ministry list dates the place early 18th century. Pevsner and Nairn say 18th century with later 18th century ogival windows. These are probably the most remarkable features, as they appear to be part of the original façade, not inserts. If so, they are even more interesting if one thinks that the house is pre-18th century. In ecclesiastical and collegiate circles the gothic in building is with us even now; more so in the late 17th century. As this house was once the Bishops' Park Keeper's Lodge the presence of these details might be explained. The (upper only) windows would also have given a pretty touch to the landscape from the avenue ridge. Yet the original doors were very austere and would not be mistaken for entrances to the country house of a local man of high social standing.

During the late war the house served as a communications centre. After years of neglect the Council urged demolition which was only prevented by the efforts of others. Sympathetic occupants were found, David Nye and Partners were engaged as architects and the Ranger's House was restored and modernised. The roof has been renewed, chimney pieces fitted and 17th century doors imported from Lincolnshire. 'It is unbelievable,' said the Council chairman. Farnham had been fortunate. It now has an example of one answer to what will be a recurring problem.

MOOR PARK HOUSE

A substantial house with extensive outbuildings, once called Compton Hall, standing in Moor Park. It is on three main floors, of later 18th century character, and is stuccoed. Outbuildings and clock tower are principally in 19th century revival styles. The house contains a notable stairwell and staircase, also, as its core, the remains of a Jacobean brick built house.

History and associations of the building are dealt with elsewhere, but even in the briefest account mention should be made of Sir William Temple who lived here in retirement, and of his garden; of Jonathan Swift, his secretary, and Stella; and of Darwin who found the place so pleasant that (he said) he could not care a penny how many of the beasts were formed. There are still hints of a once romantic setting; the grotto known as Mother Ludlam's Cave and of canals, terraces, parterres, avenues and a banqueting hall.

In 1948 the house was about to be demolished, so great was the damage caused directly by and as a result of military occupation during the war. Since then thorough repair and reconstruction have been undertaken and Moor Park House now serves as a college for Adult Christian Education.

RUNWICK HOUSE

A substantial square brick built and slated house on three floors, of later 18th and earlier 19th century character.

The house is not on a map of 1729 which marks Willey Mill, but Rocque, in 1768, shows Lower House — by which name it was still known in 1812 when occupied by George Coldham Knight (*qv*). Bryant's map of 1823 marked Rudgwick House, but the name Lower House had not gone out of general use in 1855. After Charles Knight, James Knight and Charles Roumieu (*qqv*) Runwick estate was occupied by various members of the Trimmer (*qv*) family, who offered it for sale in lots in 1920, at which time the house was William Trimmer's.

A manuscript which probably dates from the late 18th century states, when noting places around Farnham, 'Dippenhall or Runwick a good house belonging to Mr. Mill and built by his father'. See Dippen Hall and Ivy House.

WAVERLEY ABBEY

A large brick built mansion in the grounds of the Cistercian House. After its dissolution the Abbey estate was held first by the Fitzwilliam family. In 1609 it was conveyed to John Coldham for £2,800. The Coldhams, Knights and Vernons were connected by marriage. In 1756 Mary Coldham married John Knight. Richard Coldham was taxed on nine hearths in 1664, and in the 1720s the same family sold Waverley to John Aislabie for £10,000. He is said to have built the house to the designs of none less than Campbell, who died in 1729. This was probably Farnham's only first-hand experience of Renaissance building by a master. A memorial in Ripon Cathedral commemorates William Aislabie's (d 1752) marriage to a Vernon (qv) and in Yorkshire the Aislabies were friends of Campbell's as well as patrons. Hence, presumably, Campbell at Farnham.

There is an engraving of the Abbey ruins dated 1737 showing this house in the background. It is very different from the one there now, and even from the one Hassell drew in 1822. It was of Palladian character. The house we see today is possibly that built first by Thomas Orby Hunter between 1747 and 1770, to which Sir Robert Rich had added wings by 1786. A manuscript probably of late 18th century origin says though that they were added by Mr. Hunter. The house was largely rebuilt again in 1833 after fire. The main front at least did not change greatly from what had been there immediately before.

William Cobbett (qv) knew the estate. His observations and opinions on its upkeep and owner are recorded in 'The English Gardener'. Elmer (qv) painted murals in the house. See illustration on page 103.

WEYBOURNE HOUSE

Brick built, parapeted and tiled, the house is said to have been built in 1729 by Peter Coldham (d 1732), until shortly before that date owner of Waverley Abbey (qv). Some of the fabric of the latter is said to have gone into Weybourne House. It is enriched with cut brickwork, and is one of that early group which set the architectural pace for Georgian building for the next hundred years in the Farnham district.

In 1836 George Knight of Sloane Street, Chelsea, held a copyhold house and land at Weybourne Place. John Henry Knight (qv), famous for his mechanical inventiveness, was born at Weybourne House in 1847. He moved to Barfield in 1888. A hundred years after his birth, Farnham Council bought Weybourne House from Sir Henry Knight, after which date alterations and additions were made.

BADSHOT HOUSE

This was a large and parapeted house on three full floors and of nine symmetrically disposed bays.

Hassell's drawing of 1822 shows us the mansion. It is inscribed '. . . Badshott Manor House, Jno. Williams Esq.' This is the only known visual record of the building which was demolished *c* 1825 to 1830. The U-shaped moat on modern OS maps is said to mark its site.

It was probably the biggest local house of the day and its date of building should have made it most interesting to compare with Weybourne, Willmer and Sandford Houses (*qqv*).

The existence of a moat implies the presence of a pre-18th century house. 'The capital messuage called Badshott' was included with estates of the Woodroffes of Poyle House nearby, in 1652. Their property was extensive and included The Swan (*qv*) in West Street. When King Charles was at Vernon House (*qv*) it was planned that he should visit his loyal friends, Lord and Lady Newburgh at Bagshot House. He went, under armed escort, but his escape was frustrated. So it is recorded.

In 1664 Mr. Lampard of Badshott paid tax on eleven hearths. This was a substantial number, but need not have been the hearths of buildings on the same site, although 'John Lampard built Bagshot Place' in 1734, having bought the property from John Stevens. Lampard bequeathed Bagshot House to Peckham Williams, and 'Batchett Place' is marked on Rocque's map of 1768.

Peckham Williams (*qv*) of Badshot Place is said to have introduced the white bine hop to Farnham. Boswell's daughter lived at the house for some time and Boswell's Journals include details of the visits to Williams and tells of their tea party with the Rycrofts at Firgrove House (*qv*). Williams' daughter, Elizabeth, married Miles Poole Penfold. They owned, amongst other property, Guildford House and Cedar Court (*qqv*), both in Castle Street. See Plate.

DIPPEN HALL

This was a large house of asymmetrical plan and façade, with gables, stone mullioned and transomed windows and on two principal floors. Hassell's drawing of 1824 suggests that it was a Tudor building altered, and perhaps partly demolished later.

The name is of considerable antiquity; 1224, Depehal; 1294, Depenhale; 1485, Debnall. In 1680 it is marked on Sellar's map as Ditton Hall, and the year before Hassell's drawing, Bryant named it Dipnell Great House.

The hall was probably used as a private school in the 18th century. It was demolished *c* 1835. Some of its fabric and woodwork were rebuilt in other houses locally. In 1909 J. H. Knight (*qv*) wrote that the house could still be traced by depressions in the ground where cellars had been. See Runwick House and Plate.

INDEX

Coxbridge Farm 64.
Cranley 91, 142.
Cricket 158.
Cricketer's Arms, The. *See* Inns.
Cricket Ground 108.
Crondall 17, 35, 141, 160, 180.
Crondall Lane 180, 183.
Crookham Church, 184.
Crooksbury House 106.
Crystal Palace 179.
Culver Hall. *See* 28 West Street.
Culvers 155.
Cumberland Friendly Society 10.
Cupgate (Cobgate?) 154.
Currier. *See* Trades.
Curtis Museum 108.
Cutler. *See* Trades.
Dairyman. *See* Trades.
Dean's Farm 181.
Defence Line 183.
Dell, The 228.
Dentist. *See* Trades, etc.
Dipnell Great House 233.
Dippen Hall 233.
Dippenhall 57, 80, 203, 230, 232.
Dippenhall Farm 79.
Ditton Hall 233.
Dockenfield (Docking Field) 80.
Dockenford 154.
Doctor. *See* Trades, etc.
Dog Breaker. *See* Trades.
Dugflud Street 13, 130.
Dogmersfield 61.
Dorking 172, 181, 217.
Dorset 182.

DOWNING STREET 32, 63, 69-85, 91,
 97, 99, 106, 111, 126, 131, 133, 134,
 160, 179, 180, 184, 193, 196, 223.
 1 : 69-70, 73.
 2 : 49, 71, 115, 119, 120.
 3 : Longbridge House : 44, 45, 70,
 71-73, 78.
 4 : 22, 38, 74-75; *74.*
 5A : 76; *76.*
 5-7 : 76, 115; *76.*
 14 : 64.
 17 : 77.
 18 : 77.
 22 : 77.
 23 : 26.
 35-36 · 78.
 37-38 : 81-82; *69.*
 42 : 82.
 43 : 82-83; *82.*
 44 : 179, 180.
 45 : 126
 46-47 : 83-84, 121, 208.
 48, 49, 50 : 84-85.
 63-64 : Hop Bag. *See* Inns.
 Ivy House : 37, 72, 78-81.

Draper. *See* Trades.
Draughtsman. *See* Trades.

Dressmaker. *See* Trades.
Druggist. *See* Trades.
Dudman's Seminary. *See* Schools.
Duke of Cambridge, The. *See* Inns.
Dutch House. *See* 46A West Street.
Dye House 90.
Eagle, The. *See* Inns.
East Mill 156.

EAST STREET 32, 55, 63, 77, 79, 87,
 109-126, 131, 142, 143, 149, 160, 179,
 180, 208, 212, 217, 220, 227; *212.*
 4 : Royal Deer. *See* Inns.
 8 : 112.
 13 : 137.
 14 : Marlborough Head. *See* Inns.
 18 : 116.
 26, 27, 28 : 114, 117, 119, 124; *117.*
 28 : 36. *See also* 26-28.
 29 : Still House : 49, 71, 114-116, 117,
 118; *117.*
 35-42 : 116-118; *124.*
 55 : 118.
 62 : Surrey Arms. *See* Inns.
 73 : Eagle. *See* Inns.
 75 : 121.
 80 : 122.
 83 : 123.
 84 (and 84 & 85) : 116, 123-124; *124.*
 88 : Seven Stars. *See* Inns.
 89-90 : 122, 125-126; *126.*
 93 : 126-127, 128.
 94-95 : 127.
 99-100 : 128.
 109 : 115.
 110 : 127.
 111 : 128.
 114-115 : 219.
 117 : 218.
 118 : 128-129.
 119 : 129.
 120 : 129-130.
 124-125 : 125, 130-131.
 Bath Terrace : 120-121, 185, 197.
 Brightwell House : 113, 127.
 National Schools. *See* Schools.
 Park School. *See* Schools.
 Red Cross House : 120.
 St. Mary's Place : 118.
 Tanfield Cottage : 174.
 Tanfield House : 174.
 West Meon House : *See* Bath
 Terrace.
 Zingari Terrace : 44, 45, 71, 118-120.

East Street School. *See* Schools : Park.
East Worldam 154.
Ecclesiastics. *See* Trades, etc.
Electric Theatre 112.
Elliott's Brewery 180.
Elm Grove. *See* Old Roof.
Elmer House. *See* 41 West Street.
Elstead 221, 226.
Engineer. *See* Trades.

Epsom 196.
Estate Agent. *See* Trades.
Excise Officer. *See* Trades, etc.
Ewart Bequest 193.
Exeter 67, 152.

FACTORY YARD 33, 55, 144-145, 207-208, 209.
   Arundell Place : 207, 208, 209.

Fanshawe Street (London) 90.
Farnborough 110, 227.
Farmer. *See* Trades.
Farnham Brewery 52, 85, 93, 127, 131, 143, 179.
Farnham Castle 63.
Farnham Conservative Club 81.
Farnham Female School of Industry 158.
Farnham Friendly Society 53, 96.
Farnham Gas Company 32, 117.
Farnham Girls' Grammar School.
   See Schools.
Farnham Grammar School.
   See Schools.
Farnham Herald 224.
Farnham Rectory 189.
Farnham High School. *See* Schools.
Farnham Market and Town Hall Co. 11, 12, 14, 15.
Farnham Mill 156.
Farnham Museum 163, 170. *See also* 38 West Street.
Farnham Park 13, 61, 158, 227, 229.
Farnham School of Art. *See* Schools.
Farnham United Breweries 18, 20, 83, 95, 118, 129, 165, 197, 198.
Farnham Water Co. 14.
Farnham Working Men's Conservative Club 79.
Farrier. *See* Trades.
Feathers, The. *See* Inns.
Felmonger. *See* Trades.
Fermans 216.
Figg's Yard 119.
Fire Acts 50-51, 220.
Fire Chief. *See* Trades.
Fire Engines 17.
Fire Station 10, 11, 13, 107.
Firgrove 93, 100-102.
Firgrove Cottage. *See* 11 Bridge Square.
Firgrove House 100-102, 232; *102.*
Firgrove Lodge 183.
First Church of Christ, Scientist 176.
Fish Cross 13, 70.
Fishmonger. *See* Trades.
Fleur-de-Lys, The. *See* Inns.
Florist. *See* Trades.
Folly, The 127.
Folly Hill 127.
Forge 16.
Fourteen-Penny House, The. *See* Inns.
Fox, The. *See* Inns.

Fox & Hounds, The. *See* Inns.
Fox Yard 133, 196, 197.
Frensham 57, 71, 138, 146.
Frensham Church 184.
Fribourg & Treyer 28.
Friendly Societies 10, 53, 222.
Frimley 38.
Froyle 79, 116.
Froyle Church 184.
Furniture Dealer. *See* Trades.
Gamekeeper. *See* Trades.
Gardener. *See* Trades.
Gas Works. *See* Farnham Gas Co.
George, The. *See* Inns.
Gerard Street (London) 163.
Glass Dealer. *See* Trades.
Glazier. *See* Trades.
Gloucester 5, 56, 92.
Glover. *See* Trades.
Goat's Head, The. *See* Inns.
Godalming 96, 149, 192.
Golden Section 168.
Gosport 10, 227.
Gosport Diligence 10.
Gostreeds 18.
Gostrey Meadow 18, 105.
Governess. *See* Teachers.
Granary 146, 194.
Grange. *See* Castle Hill.
Greengrocer. *See* Trades.
Green Man, The. *See* Inns.
Grocer. *See* Trades.
Groom. *See* Trades.
Grove Cottages 186.
Guildford 5, 38, 84, 105, 125, 130, 195, 216, 227.
Guildford House. *See* Castle Street.

GUILDFORD ROAD
   Grove Cottages : 186.
   Stanley Villas : 115, 119, 184, 185.

Gunsmith. *See* Trades.
Haberdasher. *See* Trades.
Haberdashers' Company 144.
Hackney 6.
Haircloth Factors. *See* Trades.
Hairdresser. *See* Trades.
Hale 73, 185, 228.
Halimote Manor 205.
Hammersmith 9, 134.
Hampshire Hunt, The 226.
Hampstead 37.
Handsworth 5.
Hangars Mill 156.
Harleston (Staffs.) 157.
Harness Maker. *See* Trades.
Hart, The (Place) 183, 190, 219, 221.
   See also Inns.
Hart (Road) 204, 205.
Hart Kiln *178.*
Hart's Yard 133.
Hartley Wintney 170.
Haslemere 27, 47, 112, 124, 127, 227.

Wheelwright.   *See* Trades.
White Hart, The.   *See* Inns.
White Horse, The.   *See* Inns.
Whiteley Papers, The 162.
White Swan, The.   *See* Inns.
Whitmore 146.
Wicke 216.
Wickham 215.
Wickham House.   *See* 40 West Street.
Wigrams 158.
Willey Mill 230.
Willmer's School.   *See* Schools.
Willmer House.   *See* 38 West Street.
Winchester 53, 141, 146, 155, 226.
Windsor Almshouses.   *See* Castle Street.
Windlesham 91.
Wine Merchant.   *See* Trades.

Winnowing Machine 28.
Woodbridge House 53.
Wool (Dorset) 84.
Woolcomber.   *See* Trades.
Woollen Draper.   *See* Trades.
Wool Merchant.   *See* Trades.
Workhouse 102.
Working Men's Club 81.
Working Men's Institute 59, 108.
Wrecclesham 7, 79, 90, 123, 194, 208, 223.
Wrecclesham Church 184.
Woolstapler.   *See* Trades.
Yeoman.   *See* Trades.
Yeoman, The 227.
Zingari Terrace.   *See* East Street.

BIRCH & CO 210.
BISHOP (family) 198; Richard 156.
BLAKE, William 83.
BLANDFORD, Cyrus (Sirus) 22, 188, 189.
BOLEN, Sarah 99; Stanley 94, 99, 173; William 99.
BOLTON, Frederick 149; Jane 170.
BONE, Sarah 6.
BOOKER, Edward 117.
BOOKHAM, John 8.
BORELLI (family) 217; Angelina 21; C. 131; Charles 5, 8, 21, 24, 28, 98, 106; Charlotte 21; Clement 21, 218; Donato 21, 218; Madelena 21.
BOSWELL, James 101, 232.
BOTTING, George 127; Henry 127.
BOULT, John 139.
BOULTON, Frederick 149.
BOURNE, George. *See* STURT, George.
BOWEN, Charlotte 158; Frederick 158; Julia 158; William 158.
BOXALL, Thomas 17.
BRABANT, Petronel 208.
BRABORNE, Henry 8; John 173.
BRADFORD, John 152.
BRADLEY (family) 225; Bristow 40, 41, 134, 193, 223; George 155, 223; Henry 223, 226; John 40, 117; Margaret 223; Mary 223.
BRANSDEN, William 6.
BREWSTER, Henry 122.
BRICE, Edwin 59.
BRIDLE, John 90.
BRIGGS, Abraham 55.
BRISTOW, Andrew 57, 129, 180, 226; Collyer 226; Daniel 25, 28, 49, 57, 58, 202, 203, 204; Elizabeth 57, 58, 203, 226; John 8, 57; Julia 58; Katherine 57; Margaret 57; Martha 226; Mary 58; Richard 8, 57; Samuel 57; Thomas 57, 58; William 226.
BRISTOW & STEVENS 3.
BRISTOWE, Thomas 165.
BROCKHURST, James 223.
BROMLEY (family) 19, 125; Ann 125; Caroline 125; Celia 125; Edward 14, 125, 131; George 125; Henrietta 125; Mary 125; William 125.
BROOKE, John 147.
BROOKS, Henry 228.
BROWN (family) 9; Diana (*née* Freeharry) 129; J. 143; Joseph 186; William 165.
BROWNE 7.
BRYANT 230, 233.
BRYMER (Ring and) 210.
BRYSTOW. *See* BRISTOW.
BUCK, W. 97.
BUCKNELL, Joseph 2.
BUDD, Thomas 223.
BUDDLE, Thomas 204, 205.
BULBECK, G. 131.

BUNCH (family) 8, 47; Elizabeth 8; Francis 8, 130; John 8; Mary 8; Thomas 8, 19, 21, 130.
BURCHETT, James 178.
BURGESS, William 56.
BURNINGHAM, James 46, 186; Thomas 186, 209.
BURROWS (family) 161; John 177; Sarah 177.
BURY, Amelia 201; Caroline 201; George 201; Clarke and 40.
BUTLER, Ann(e) 155, 157; Elizabeth 138; George 223; John 155, 157.
BYWORTH, Alice 90; Ann 90; Daniel 90; John 49, 89, 90, 91; Martha 90; Petronel 90.

CAESAR, Stephen 140.
CAMPBELL, Colin 231.
CANUTE 137.
CARTWRIGHT, John 92.
CHAFFER 90.
CHAMPION, Arnold 8.
CHAPE, Thomas 165.
CHAPER, Thomas 8.
CHARLSEY 196.
CHASE, Edmund 138; George 138; Mary 138; Thomas 138.
CHASIN, George 125, 150.
CHENNELLS, A. W. 131.
CHESTON 23.
CHILCOTT, 219.
CHILD (family) 189; Anna 38; John 38; Mary 80; Thomas 80.
CHILTON, Richard 140.
CHILTON & SCAMMELL 139.
CHINNOCK 141.
CHITTY (family) 73; Bartholomew 73; C. 73; Charles 73; Christopher 73; Chrusophilus 73; Emma 73; Henry 73; Jane 73; Joan 73; John 72; Manwaring 73; Martha 73; Mary 222; Philip 73; Richard 73; Sarah 73; William 73.
CHURCH 2.
CHUTER, John 7.
CLAPHAM, Christopher 152; Thomas 152.
CLARK, John 17; Thomas 228.
CLARK & CLINCH 226.
CLARKE, Alfred 40; Charles 40; John 15; Robert 40; Robert Oke 40, 152.
CLARKE & BURY 40.
CLARKE, Oak and 40.
CLERK, William 100.
CLIFTON, William 225.
CLINCH, Robert 226.
CLINCH, Clark and 226.
COAD 33.
COBBETT, Ann(e) 97, 188; George 97, 188; John 188; Mary 189; Thomas 188, 189; William 3, 25, 26, 96, 188, 231; William Thomas 96, 97, 188.

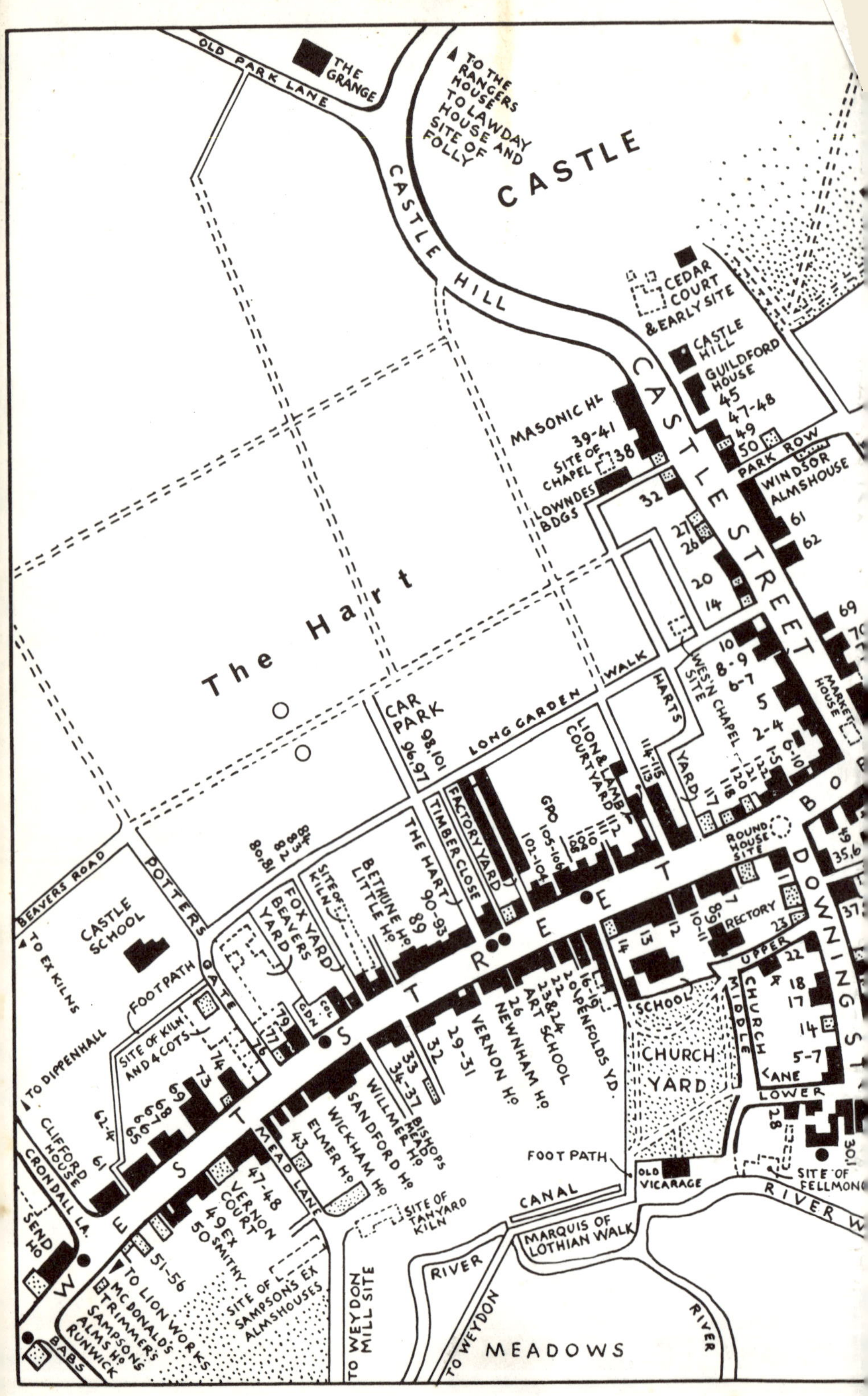

THE GRANGE
OLD PARK LANE
TO THE RANGERS HOUSE
TO LAWDAY HOUSE AND SITE OF FOLLY
CASTLE
CASTLE HILL
CEDAR COURT & EARLY SITE
CASTLE HILL
GUILDFORD HOUSE
45
47-48
49
50
PARK ROW
WINDSOR ALMSHOUSE
61
62
MASONIC H.
39-41
SITE OF CHAPEL
LOWNDES BDGS
38
32
27
26
20
14
CASTLE STREET
69
70
The Hart
LONG GARDEN WALK
CAR PARK
98,101
96,97
HARTS YARD
WES'N CHAPEL SITE
LION & LAMB COURTYARD
114-115
113
112
10
8-9
6-7
5
2-4
1-5
121
122
120
117
118
6-10
MARKET HOUSE
BEAVERS ROAD
POTTERS GATE
CASTLE SCHOOL
TO EX KILNS
TO DIPPENHALL
FOOTPATH
84
83
82
80,81
SITE OF KILN
BETHUNE H.
LITTLE H.
THE HART
90-93
89
TIMBER CLOSE
FACTORY YARD
GPO
105-106
102-104
108
110
109
ROUND HOUSE SITE
DOWNING
49,6
35,6
37
RECTORY
23
E
R
T
E
E
S
T
R
FOX YARD
BEAVERS YARD
GDN.
COL.
79
SITE OF KILN AND 4 COTS
74
76
77
73
68
66
67
69
65
61
62,4
CLIFFORD HOUSE
CRONDALL LA.
SEND HO.
W
E
S
T
MEAD LANE
43
WICKHAM HO.
ELMER HO.
SANDFORD HO.
WILLMER HO.
BISHOPS MEAD
34-37
33
32
29-31
VERNON HO.
26
NEWNHAM HO.
ART SCHOOL
23&24
20
16-19
OLPENFOLDS YD.
SCHOOL
12
13
14
10-11
8,9
7
UPPER
MIDDLE
LOWER
CHURCH LANE
22
18
17
14
5-7
4
CHURCH YARD
OLD VICARAGE
FOOT PATH
CANAL
MARQUIS OF LOTHIAN WALK
SITE OF FELLMONG
RIVER W
47-48
VERNON COURT
49 EX
50 SMITHY
51-56
TO LION WORKS
MC DONALD'S
TRIMMER'S
SAMPSONS ALMS HO.
RUNWICK
BABS
SITE OF SAMPSONS EX ALMSHOUSES
SITE OF TANYARD KILN
SITE OF TANYARD
TO WEYDON MILL SITE
RIVER WEYDON
TO WEYDON
RIVER
MEADOWS
VERNON HO.